# The Deceptive Text

# The Deceptive Text

## An Introduction to Covert Plots

### Cedric Watts

*Professor of English*
*University of Sussex*

'And then my eyes became opened to the inwardness
of things and speeches the triviality of which
had been so baffling and so tiresome.'

(Conrad: *The Shadow-Line*.)

THE HARVESTER PRESS · SUSSEX

BARNES & NOBLE BOOKS · NEW JERSEY

First published in Great Britain in 1984 by
THE HARVESTER PRESS LIMITED
*Publisher: John Spiers*
16 Ship Street, Brighton, Sussex
and in the USA by
BARNES & NOBLE BOOKS
81 Adams Drive, Totowa, New Jersey 07512

*British Library Cataloguing in Publication Data*
Watts, Cedric
    The deceptive text.
    1. English literature—History and criticism
    I. Title
    820.9 PR401

    ISBN 0–7108-0608-6

*Library of Congress Cataloging in Publication Data*

Watts, Cedric Thomas.
    The deceptive text.

    1. Conrad, Joseph, 1857–1924—Criticism and interpreta-
tion. 2. Plots (Drama, novel, etc.) I. Title.
PR6005.04Z9235    1984      823'.912      83–27512
ISBN 0–389-20459–5

Typeset in 11 point Baskerville by Radial Data Ltd.,
Bordon, Hampshire
Printed in Great Britain by
Butler & Tanner Ltd, Frome and London

To Norman and Sylvia Sherry

# Contents

# Acknowledgements

Parts of this book have previously appeared in periodicals, though I have re-considered all such material in the light of subsequent reading and reflection. The essay 'Janiform Novels' was originally published in *English* XXIV (Summer 1975); other items on which I have drawn are as follows. 'The Unseen Catastrophe of Ibsen's *Vildanden*', *Scandinavica* XII (November 1973). 'The Protean Dionysus in Euripides' *The Bacchae* and Mann's *Death in Venice*', *Studi dell'Istituto Linguistico* II (Florence, 1981). 'Conrad's Covert Plots and Transtextual Narratives', *Critical Quarterly* XXIV (Autumn 1981). '*Heart of Darkness*: The Covert Murder-Plot and the Darwinian Theme', *Conradiana* VII (May 1975). 'Reflections on *Victory*', *Conradiana* XV (January 1983). 'The covert Plot of *Almayer's Folly*', *Conradiana* XV (May 1983). 'The Narrative Enigma of Conrad's "A Smile of Fortune" ', *Conradiana* XVI (May 1984). The discussions of 'The Secret Sharer' and *The Shadow-Line* adapt part of my account of the tales in *A Preface to Conrad* (Longman, 1982). I am grateful to the editors and publishers of these volumes for permission to incorporate in my book much of this material.

Conversations with friends and colleagues have been variously instructive. I am particularly grateful to Lewis Nkosi (whose perceptive enthusiasm for 'A Smile of Fortune' proved healthily infectious), Tony Nuttall (for constructive critical comments on the MS) and to Alan Sinfield (for particular discussions and general benevolence). Farther afield, Norman Sherry and Hans van Marle have offered encouragement and guidance. I apologise to them and to the reader for the errors and eccentricities which time will naturally reveal in this book.

# Editorial Notes

All quotations from Joseph Conrad's novels, tales, essays and autobiographical works are taken from the Collected Edition of J.M. Dent and Sons (London: 1946-55).

In any quotation, a row of five dots (.....) indicates an elision that I have made, whereas a row of three dots indicates an elision already present in the original text. I have corrected Conrad's accentuation of foreign words; otherwise, apart from a few clarifications which are set in square brackets, I have endeavoured to preserve the original text exactly.

# Abbreviations

*AF*  Joseph Conrad: *Almayer's Folly* (London: Dent, 1947).
ASA  The manuscript collection of the late Admiral Sir Angus Cunninghame Graham.
*BBL*  *Joseph Conrad: Letters to William Blackwood and David S. Meldrum*, edited by William Blackburn (Durham, N.C.: Duke University Press, 1958).
*C*  Joseph Conrad: *Chance* (London: Dent, 1949).
*EG*  *Letters from Conrad 1895 to 1924,* edited by Edward Garnett (London: Nonesuch Press, 1928).
he  he or she (where appropriate).
*LCG*  *Joseph Conrad's Letters to R.B. Cunninghame Graham*, edited by C.T. Watts (London: Cambridge University Press, 1969).
MS  Manuscript.
*N*  Joseph Conrad: *Nostromo* (London: Dent, 1947).
*NLL*  Joseph Conrad: *Notes on Life and Letters* (London: Dent, 1949).
*NN*  Joseph Conrad: *The Nigger of the 'Narcissus'* (London: Dent, 1950).
*OI*  Joseph Conrad: *An Outcast of the Islands* (London: Dent, 1949).
*PR*  Joseph Conrad: *A Personal Record* (London: Dent, 1946).
*SA*  Joseph Conrad: *The Secret Agent* (London: Dent, 1947).
*SL*  Joseph Conrad: *The Shadow-Line* (London: Dent, 1950).
*T*  Joseph Conrad: *Typhoon and Other Stories* (London: Dent, 1950).

*TLAS*  Joseph Conrad: *'Twixt Land and Sea: Three Tales* (London: Dent, 1947).
*V*       Joseph Conrad: *Victory* (London: Dent, 1948).
*Y*       Joseph Conrad: *'Youth', 'Heart of Darkness', 'The End of the Tether'* (London: Dent, 1946).

# General Introduction

If intelligence is the art of seeing or creating connections between apparently unconnected things, then literary texts manifest and teach this art, for they solicit and reward their searchers.

Every narrative has an overt plot; but some narratives contain, in addition to the overt plot, at least one covert plot: a concealed plot-sequence. Some of its elements are conspicuous, but the connections between them are not, either because of authorial strategies of reticence and elision or because they are occluded by the conspicuous linkages of the overt plot. (This factor of concealment also differentiates it from a sub-plot.) When the covert is perceived, the text as a whole is seen to be more complex and more highly ordered. It is usually the case that the text then appears better than before; but this is not always the case. Quality of embodiment is decisive, and sometimes perception of the covert merely clarifies the logic of passages whose presence may actually mar the work. There is, at least, a gain in comprehension; and generally, as I have noted, the effect is to increase not only comprehension but also recognition of merit.

The sceptical reader may well say, however: 'If the covert plot matters, what is the point of making it covert? If something counts, why does the author hide it? And what is the point of hiding it if it is still doomed to be eventually found? The stuff's either seen or it isn't. If it isn't, why include it? And if it is seen, surely it isn't covert?' In the subsequent chapters, I give a variety of specific answers, but one obvious answer can be given now. Good literary texts are usually complex and intelligent; they seldom yield their riches at a first reading but solicit and reward further readings. The text searches reality and offers us a training in the searching of reality by encouraging us to search itself. Modes of concealment, as well as modes of revelation, are characteristic of all literary texts, even those which seem innocently transparent.[1] To discover is to uncover; the covering is required by the uncovering. The formal restrictions of art are liberating restrictions, precisely because they generate liberating activities by the participant; they generate not comprehension alone but the act of comprehension; they offer not perceptions alone but the training in perception. A hurdle-racer could run a hundred metres in faster time if there were no hurdles to clear; but the restrictions provided by the hurdles liberate the achievement of hurdle-racing: its particular tests of the muscles, its particular recognition of human powers of energy and co-ordination; a particular truth of human physical possibility. And the various concealment-strategies in literary texts, of which the covert plots offer interesting examples, liberate achievements in the perception of human reality.

I give many instances of covert plots. Some are more covert than others. In some cases my claims are very mild: I offer an account of what certain readers will have seen, though others will not. In a large number of cases my endeavour is to elucidate the concealed connections between various parts which themselves are conspicuous enough; and sometimes I merely postulate additions to a recognised sequence. In other cases, my claims are more egregious: I suggest, for example, that for a century there may have been a general failure to perceive in Ibsen's *The Wild Duck* a covert plot which culminates, dramatically and with supreme irony, in a suicide (that of Old Ekdal) which is unnoticed within the world of the play, just as it has gone unnoticed outside that fictional world. I imply that here and in some other texts, various commentators have possibly failed to see the wood for the trees; inspecting the small, they have overlooked the big; and occasionally they have hastened to judge before pausing to comprehend. So sometimes the reader's response to my claims may be on these lines: 'This example isn't really a *covert* plot; I've always seen this'; and sometimes on these lines: 'This isn't a covert *plot* at all: it isn't in the text: it's a figment of your imagination.' In the former case, I say, 'Well and good; but my discussions with readers and my consultation of commentators suggest that what is obvious to you isn't always obvious to others.' In the second case, my answer is: 'I've given my evidence: I've cited the parts of the text which are there and which seem to be explicable only by postulating the linkages I have specified. Can you suggest an alternative explanation, or are you content with the inexplicable? My approach implies respect for the author's co-ordinating imagination: does yours?' And more often, I hope, the reader's response will lie between these two extremes: he will feel that what he has sensed has been clarified, and that parts of a text that seemed anomalous or digressive have had their function explained, though he may well be challenged to offer alternative explanations. This book tries to be straightforwardly introductory; and the aim of my accounts is pleasure: the pleasure of learning more about literature and therefore about life.

Life, too, has its overt and covert plots, some inherent in nature and some generated by man's pattern-making abilities. From infancy onwards, we infer patterns from experience and make predictions on the basis of those patterns; when predictions are not fulfilled we revise the patterns so as to take account of the new data. The scientist seeks to make overt the covert plots of nature, and is constantly revising his sense of the covert plots to take account of new evidence; the historian, too, seeks to reconcile his sense of possible 'stories' in history with the mixture of stories and anomalies that historical data supply: the French term *histoire* is appropriately ambiguous. Nature offers its patternings on a small and large scale, from the near-symmetry of line and colour on a butterfly's wings to the great cycle of the seasons, while it offers anomalies and oddities to challenge the sense of pattern; and the challenges offered by complex narratives are not unlike these. To see nature as analogous to an author is not necessarily to be sentimentally anthropomorphic and metaphysical: to talk of purposeful design can be a reasonable and concise way of referring to the innumerable modes in which living things strive for survival and furtherance; like man, wolves and rats and worms all seek to modify their environment so as to extend its patterning in congenial ways; and if nature sometimes seems to work 'without a conscience or an aim', the same may occasionally be said of authors.

Even those authors who hold an 'existentialist' or 'absurdist' faith, those intermediaries between Nietzsche and post-structuralism who purport to believe that all is radically absurd and that there are basically no meanings or patterns in life, merely commend their own alternative patternings, their own preferred allocation of the ontologically overt and covert. Overt: the familiar world of meanings; and covert: the alleged chaotic and senseless mass of contingencies, which is presented by the author as the truth. As soon as such a view is communicated, it contradicts itself; for to communicate is to enter the world of public significances. To convey in words the claim that all is meaningless entails contradicting that claim. In *La Nausée*, Sartre's Roquentin holds that a loaf of bread, truly perceived, is without meaning or function; but he denies his thesis as soon as he sits down to eat, and he does not starve. The overt plot of that novel is the story of a hero of modern thought, courageously venturing into the true world of the senseless; but the covert plot is the story of a lonely man striving by a variety of stratagems — his journal, his recourse to music, his projected novel — to ward off the madness his mystical faith in absurdity would logically entail. The dramatist Samuel Beckett has conceded that if he himself were fully consistent in his apparent nihilism, he would be in 'an unenviable situation, familiar to psychiatrists';[2] and within *Waiting for Godot* there lurks a covert plot which Thomas Hardy might have recognised. And, furtively, such works solicit the rejoinder of much-maligned 'common sense'. Just as communication between individuals is never perfect (for perfection would require the absolute identity of people and therefore the absence of any individuals), so the symmetry of a butterfly's wings is never perfect (for such symmetry would be the product of a nature so regular and uniform as to be unnatural), and so there is an actual or potential exception to every empirical rule or generalisation or pattern (otherwise the rule would cease to be empirical and therefore useful). Within existentialism and absurdism, within solipsism and the recent claims that the world is merely a construct of 'arbitrary' linguistic conventions,[3] may be concealed a story of frustrated yearning for the certitude of a world so utterly efficient and predictable that in the end neither man nor nature could have a place in it.

Man has been called *homo significans* — man the meaning-maker.[4] There is a characteristic quality of anthropocentric vanity about the phrase. My cat has her plans and stratagems, her predictions, errors and successes, her modes of communication (linguistic and bodily) with other cats, with dogs and with humans. All living things, whether people, worms, amoebae or trees, employ values — whether consciously, unconsciously, or inherently through their biochemistry. Leaves seek light, roots seek moisture; my apple tree dislikes the salty wind from the sea, and extends its branches in the opposite direction. All living things thus interrogate the world; and in literary texts human beings have found one of the subtlest (and most subtly pleasurable) modes of interrogating both the world and the process of interrogation itself. To seek, find and explain covert plots, a critical activity which at first may seem rather peripheral or even perverse, is not greatly different from the process of recognising that this rather flat pebble in the pool is the shell of a lurking crab, that the cat which tripped me up twice in the last half-hour did so to remind me to feed it, or that oddities in a given curriculum may reveal to a student the hidden curriculum. The incidents may be trivial; the quest for fuller intelligibility is not.

*

The plan of this book is as follows.

In Part One I discuss what, with mild irony, I call Literary Janiformity: a term which generously embraces a wide variety of states of division within texts. The introductory survey then draws attention to the various ways in which some texts may be divided in their narrative structures by the presence of covert plots.

In Part Two I concentrate on works by Joseph Conrad. He is my main author because, of all writers, he is arguably the master of 'delayed decoding' and therefore of the covert plot;

and I offer examples chosen from his major and minor texts. Whereas some of these plot-sequences are confined to single works, others are 'covert' because they extend over two or more works, so that the reader who knows or remembers only one of the texts (or is inclined to regard it as an autonomous entity) will be unaware of the extent and co-ordination of the plotting: these I call the 'transtextual' narratives of Conrad. Plot and characterisation flow together: one kind of plot is the story of a character's life, so the consideration of transtextual plots is linked to the consideration of transtextual biographies; and Conrad's work is interlaced with such overlapping biographies. These can raise some intricate critical problems, as when we find that the same character appears in both the fictional and the ostensibly non-fictional writings of Conrad, and particularly when we find that a fictional characterisation corresponds closely to biographical fact while the 'non-fictional' characterisation departs from such fact.

Part Three briefly postulates covert plots in the work of a wide range of other authors, extending from Sterne to Robbe-Grillet. Although my main concern in this book is with prose narratives (novels and tales), all fictional literary works, whether poems, tales, novels or plays, have narrative structures, and therefore possess the potentiality for covert plotting. So one of my main examples, and probably the most controversial in the series, is provided by an Ibsen play. I then offer a reminder that fiction (perhaps in the form of a mythoid sub-structure) besets various ostensibly non-fictional texts.

Finally, an Appendix suggests that the reader's interest in any narrative depends on his sense of latent and conterpoised plots.

# Part One:

## Janiformity and the Covert Plot

# CHAPTER 1

# Introduction to 'Janiform Novels'

Chapter 2 was originally given as a lecture in 1973 and published as an article in the magazine *English* in Summer 1975. I provide here some personal observations on its background, for they are relevant to the discussion of covert plots.

Like many teachers of literature, I value texts which are not only meritorious but also engagingly problematic. Some texts are excellent but relatively unproblematic (e.g. *Macbeth* and *A Midsummer Night's Dream*) while others may, by traditional standards, seem less good but are still meritorious and are very problematic (e.g. *Troilus and Cressida* and *Measure for Measure*). As a teacher, my preference is for the second kind rather than the first. This is partly because the teaching of literature is (or should be) largely a matter of discussion, and the relatively problematic texts are more likely to involve the students in discussion and therefore in the process of comprehension and evaluation than are the relatively unproblematic. Such an approach has its perils but may sometimes give vitality to teaching, learning and the text.

In the 1950s and 1960s, as a student at school and university, I was often told that a good literary text should be 'an organic whole', a rich unity (an idea at least as old as Aristotle but rejuvenated by the Romantic tradition); and therefore I became increasingly interested in texts which seemed to be distinct exceptions to that rule: in works which seemed to be divided against themselves and to resemble, for example, big paradoxes or even self-contradictions. Many other people were thinking on similar lines, and there had been numerous celebrated precedents for this now-widespread critical preoccupation. As early as 1924, D.H. Lawrence's *Studies in Classic American Literature* had brilliantly postulated radical divisions in numerous American novels and offered the famous pronouncement:

> The artist usually sets out — or used to — to point a moral and adorn a tale. The tale, however, points the other way, as a rule. Two blankly opposing morals, the artist's and the tale's. Never trust the artist. Trust the tale. The proper function of a critic is to save the tale from the artist who created it.[1]

Again, William Empson's *Seven Types of Ambiguity* (1930), a work of joyously effervescent intelligence, emphasised tension after tension within poems, its 'seventh type' being 'that of full contradiction, marking a division in the author's mind'.[2] (For that matter, Darwin, Marx and Freud had all stressed states of conflict or contradiction, whether within the evolutionary process, the progress of history, or in human psychology.)

Given this background, and given a multitude of social and cultural forces which made the concept of 'organic unity' seem increasingly suspect, the opening of 'Janiform Novels' was safely predictive, a tiny part of a substantial shift in critical interest towards forms of division, whether the critic were considering the novel, drama, poetry or cultural phenomena generally. This shift took many forms in the critical movements which became particularly influential in Great Britain and elsewhere during the subsequent years. Whether the critic purported to be stucturalist, poststructuralist, 'deconstructionist', semiotician, Marxist, or traditionalist, or a combination of some of these, the common feature was repeatedly the central emphasis on the value of discovering states of radical paradox or contradiction in the works under examination. Claude Lévi-Strauss taught his structuralist followers that at the heart of a given body of myth lay a contradiction: thus, within the Oedipus myth lay, it was claimed, man's sense that he was born of the earth yet also born of woman.[3] Poststructuralists and deconstructionists were inclined to value texts only insofar as they seemed schizophrenic ('foregrounding contradiction'), particularly when the text allegedly emulated

St Paul's paradox of the Cretan by saying, in effect, 'Do not believe me: I am lies, believe me!' Semioticians claimed that the structure of a poem resembled an enacted paradox: beneath the overt 'story' of the poem (established by the heuristic reading) lay a contrasting covert story or nexus (established by the hermeneutic reading).[4] Marxists were quick to perceive that if they found contradictions in, say, Matthew Arnold's 'The Scholar-Gipsy', this might be used as evidence of large cultural contradictions and thus as support for Marx's claim that bourgeois society (like all other known societies, only more so) was divided against itself and digging its own grave with the aid of historical necessity and judicious prodding from hostile spectators.[5] Even among critics whose approach and vocabulary seemed traditional, it became a familiar procedure for the writer of a new critical study to begin by saying that the claims to unity of the works under consideration had been exaggerated and that the novelty of the new book would lie in its illustrations of states of division. Examples range from John Bayley's *The Uses of Division* (1976) to David Pirie's *William Wordsworth: The Poetry of Grandeur and of Tenderness* (1982).

My brief discussion of supposedly Janiform novels offered some misgivings and warnings. The term 'Janiform' is conveniently capacious but, like most jargon, may claim more precision than it possesses. The marshalling of divided texts may resemble a kind of critical imperialism (the critic dividing the literary territory to subject it to his rule).[6] And there was a warning against binary simplification of the works. As Jonathan Culler (in *Structuralist Poetics*) has observed:

The advantage of binarism, but also its principal danger, lies in the fact that it permits one to classify anything. Given two items one can always find some respect in which they differ and hence place them in a relation of binary opposition.[7]

This 'binarist fallacy' is widespread and hard to avoid. Frequently, critics reduce complexities to binary oppositions; tension is dramatised as conflict; a qualified meaning is melodramatised as a subverted meaning; and texts are even treated as mysteriously self-cancelling, as though the presence of a saint and a sinner in the same room were tantamount to emptying that room. The reason why a critical book which portrays Janus on its front cover should portray Proteus on its rear cover is that any 'divided' text can be reconstituted as 'complex'. Even Janus, with his two heads, has only one body.

The idea of the divided novel and the related idea of the hidden narrative may be fruitful or pernicious, depending on their use and context. Some good novels, whether complex or 'Janiform', arguably contain covert plots; some do not. The postulated contrast between covert and overt plots will repeatedly tempt the postulator into the binarist fallacy; on the other hand, the postulation of a covert plot may beckon the reader who has seen only the overt plot towards a recognition of the complexity of the given work. In the following chapter, I emphasise moral and thematic division; but since a covert plot may be a means to such division, it is not coincidental that three of the best examples of the Janiform text (*Heart of Darkness*, *Brighton Rock* and *Pincher Martin*) also, in my view, contain covert plots. Whether the reader agrees with me about the presence and extent of a particular covert plot will depend on a variety of factors, among them the author's cunning, the definitions of 'plot' and 'covert', and the reader's prior impressions; but even where there is disagreement, there may eventually still accrue a renewed experience of the text.

Part of that experience is our assessment of the relative claims of the whole and the hole. To reduce the apparent holes in a text by magnifying its elements of thematic or narrative continuity need be no more conservative or 'recuperative' than to enlarge the apparent holes by magnifying its elements of tension or contradiction. Much depends on the prevailing assumptions of the reader. The value of a given critical notion may depend largely on its challenge to previous notions; but the more cogent its challenge, the more fully it may become assimilated into the familiar. As Crazy Jane remarked to the Bishop, 'Nothing can be sole or whole/That has not been rent.'

# CHAPTER 2

# *'Janiform Novels'*

*Janiform Novels* is the title of a critical book which, as far as I know, hasn't been written yet; but so many shorter studies deal variously with the problems and examples it would put together that its coming is as inevitable as a heavy cold after many sneezes. I can imagine what this unwritten book would look like, and I will attempt to describe it.

The cover would bear a bold picture of the god Janus. He might be holding an axe and standing close to some object symbolic of organic unity: for example, an oak tree. Since Janus looks both ways at once, the fate of the tree would be in considerable doubt.

The text would open with a definition on these lines: 'As Janus is the two-headed god, a Janiform novel is a two-faced novel: morally it seems to be centrally or importantly para-doxical or self-contradictory.' Not merely ambiguous or complex, but paradoxical or self-contradictory. An admirably stark example is, of course, Golding's *Pincher Martin*, which, by offering the conceptual paradox that at one and the same time Pincher was apparently alive and dead, forces the reader into a conceptual and moral double-take. Another familiar example is Greene's *Brighton Rock*, which is alarmingly two-faced through its presentation of the theological paradox that in the eyes of God, evil may have greater worth than secular decency. A third example is a short novel which is so fully and variously Janiform that, not surprisingly, the central character comes to resemble Janus himself. In *Heart of Darkness*, Conrad's Mr

Kurtz seems to split under thematic pressure, so that to some commentators he presents the face of a contemptibly hollow man, while to others he offers the face of an impressively full man. These three very diverse texts have in common several features which are integral with the matter of their Janiformity. All three offer us, after the ostensible climax of the narrative, a conclusion for which the word 'coda' proves grossly inadequate because of the force with which the final section accentuates the problems and turns us back, searching more anxiously into the novel's meaning. In all three cases, readers are obliged to cope with alternative, though simultaneous, narratives; and all three works present an ancient literary-critical problem, the problem of the moral paradoxicality created by the reader's imaginative complicity with a corrupt character. So in the later stages of his book, our anonymous critic would give close attention to these works; but in the earlier stages he would consider some of the problems arising from his definitions and would arrange sequences of examples.

First problem. Given that his definition of Janiformity was quite elastic and capacious, what critical value could the concept have? At first it seems that Janiformity is a toothless concept, critically neutral; for a Janiform novel could be good, bad, or indifferent. I recall a particularly wretched specimen — a product of the Hank Janson syndicate — which I chanced to find beneath a barrack-room mattress at R.A.F. Wythall. The narrator seized numerous opportunities to commend racial tolerance; yet his narrative seized numerous opportunities to subject the white heroine to bizarre and energetic indignities at the hands of black men.

Nevertheless, although a Janiform novel could be good, bad, or indifferent, our imaginary book about the *genre* could have a broad, if not sharp, cutting edge. Its writer could suggest that criticism of the novel has been dominated too long by the Aristotelian idea that a good literary work has an evident beginning, middle and end; by the idea that in a novel the narrative should be linear, consecutive and obviously climactic; and by the idea that in a good novel, as in a well-organised seminar under a firmly controlling and eloquent chairman, the author's moral recommendations, though richly, subtly and variously manifest, are nevertheless clearly, coherently and eloquently manifest. Yet in the last seventy-five years, obviously enough, an increasing number of works has challenged extensively all these presuppositions. So, in some modern novels, as in some modern plays and poems, we have become familiar with structures which challenge or counter-point the consecutive, linear and climactic: sometimes the form is cyclical; sometimes the work has strange gaps, ellipses and opacities; and sometimes, in a kind of epistemological and moral schizophrenia, the work seems wretchedly or heroically trapped between an honest silence, given the alleged disorder of actual experience, and hypocritical or noble or cowardly lies of eloquence, given the fact that to describe experience is to order and judge it. Instead of the paradigm of the well-organised seminar, which is perhaps an appropriate one for a George Eliot novel, the newer paradigm is that of the very quarrelsome seminar in which the chairman seems to have polarised a conflict, with half the speakers contradicting the other half, while the chairman himself seems strangely reticent; and instead of giving a concluding speech of reconciliation, the chairman prefers to brandish a mirror at the disputants, or to thrust on the spectator the task of reconciliation.

Clearly, our imaginary critic would be obliged to devote a chapter to the problem of defining intentionality. I don't envy him the task. However, he could point out that it is critically sterile to attempt to distinguish between conscious and unconscious intentions, but critically fruitful to distinguish between imaginative intention and the want of it. His rule could be this: an apparently anomalous part of a text is imaginatively intentional if predictions made by the reader on the assumption of its intentionality are fulfilled. He could then proceed to give his examples of intentional and unintentional Janiformity. For familiar reasons (related to the historical conflict between secular liberalism and illiberal alternatives) his examples of the intentional kind will be mainly of the late nineteenth and twentieth centuries: not only works by Conrad, Greene and Golding, but Camus's *L'Etranger* and, particularly, *La Chute*, in which the narrator says that his sign is 'a double face, a charming Janus, and above it the motto of the house, "Don't rely on it".' Before this period, examples may be few;

but one of them might well be *Wuthering Heights*, because of the vigorously maintained tension between two kinds of romanticism: on the one side, sociable romanticism, commending relatively domestic and constructive feelings, expressed in Nelly as well as in young Cathy and Hareton, and on the other side, lonely, aspiring and anti-social romanticism, expressed in Heathcliff and the elder Cathy. The difficulty with this example is that, as so often, the presence of an intensely energetic destructive character tends to breed contradictions which over-complicate the intended structure. Heathcliff is open to quite contradictory readings: one being a secular Godwinian reading (here was a potentially admirable being who, through intolerance and oppression, became an intolerant oppressor), and the other being a supernatural reading, according to which Heathcliff is preterhumanly fiendish.

In the second category, novels of *un*intentional Janiformity, our critic could find plenty of examples in the eighteenth century. When Janus hovers over the works of Defoe, one face looks piously up to God and the other looks with crafty complicity towards Mammon. One test of unintentional Janiformity is this: the novel bulges with ironic pregnancy, but the irony is stillborn; there's a pressure of latent, not manifest, irony; predictions based on the assumption of ironic intent by the author are thwarted by the novel's ending. The reader of *Moll Flanders* senses well that if they were taken out of the present frustrating context, many of the passages would be superbly ironic. (We recall, for instance, the way in which, after stealing the watch and purse of a drunken gentleman, Moll cites the Bible in a vehement condemnation not of theft but of drunkenness.) The pressure to resolve the unresolved then forces the reader to postulate a knowing author who is deploying an unwittingly hypocritical narrator; but this postulate is defeated when the author fails to make evident any critical distance between himself and the fictional narrator, so that the reader is finally obliged to postulate an unwittingly hypocritical author — one whose religion has become so secularised that his very loyalty to God is celebrated in terms which make it look like treachery. Even in *Robinson Crusoe* this Janiformity is evident. Crusoe's religion is far more than what several critics have assessed as mere 'Sunday religion',[1] for the novel can be read as the story of a man who constantly, and at length successfully, strives to discover, understand and deserve the patronage of Divine Providence. It can also, of course, be read as the story of a resilient and resourceful egotist who succeeds in becoming a ruthlessly efficient colonialist, whose island finally becomes a profitable colony with a population of Spaniards and natives working for the benefit of their paternalistic landlord. For Defoe, both stories are completely congruent and harmonic; for the reader, their tension breeds the strange experience of ironic pregnancy. Here's a characteristic passage. Robinson watches as the as-yet-unnamed Man Friday flees from his cannibal captors:

> [W]hen the Savage escaping came thither [i.e., to the creek], he made nothing of it, tho' the Tide was then up, but plunging in, swam thro' in about Thirty Strokes or thereabouts, landed and ran on with exceeding Strength and Swiftness.....
> I observ'd, that the two [pursuers] who swam, were yet more than twice as long swimming over the Creek, as the Fellow was, that fled from them: It came now very warmly upon my Thoughts, and indeed irresistibly, that now was my Time to get me a Servant, and perhaps a Companion, or Assistant; and that I was call'd plainly by Providence to save this poor Creature's Life.....[2]

The pressure of latent irony is here proportionate to the coincidence of the voice of Providence not with Christian charity or mercy but with economic expediency; but latent it remains, since Defoe's Providence continues to use the criterion of utility to the end.

Another novel of the eighteenth century which is, unintentionally, morally Janiform, and in which the consequent moral tensions breed latent ironies is — notoriously — Richardson's *Pamela.* Here one face of Janus bears a puritanically demure expression, and the other face a calculatingly covetous expression. Another rule follows: the unintentionally Janiform work begs parody as a wife in labour begs a midwife. Richardson's *Pamela* found its midwife in Fielding's *Shamela,* just as *Robinson Crusoe* found its midwife in Adrian Mitchell's television-play of 1972. In both cases the parody delivered the ironic burden with which the original bulged; and in both cases the mechanism of the parody was to resolve, by presenting as hypocrisy, the unwitting moral duplicity of the original characters.

This duplicity is partly a technical consequence of the

pseudo-autobiographical mode, for a first-person narrator, unable to allocate self-description to an omniscient author, may seem hypocritically self-regarding. So the Janiformity of Defoe and Richardson can be related to the puritanical tendency of eighteenth-century writers to feel dubious and guilty about the status of the novel and to feel, accordingly, a need to disguise the novel as some other kind of work: as autobiography or an allegoric version of the non-fictional. Fielding mocked this bad faith of novelists, this quest for respectability, and the general unease about the status of the novel, when, in his preface to *Joseph Andrews*, he allocated *Joseph Andrews* and other comic novels to the *genre* of 'the comic Epic-Poem in Prose': a phrase which continues to gull commentators unappreciative of Professor Stanley Unwin;[3] a phrase so perfectly two-faced that it might almost serve as an epigraph to *Janiform Novels*. Above the words 'comic Epic-Poem in Prose' hover two faces: one is the owlish face of the pedant who feels that a novel isn't respectable unless it can shelter under the aegis of some ancient *genre* like epic; and the other face offers a broad grin and a wink to those who note that the precedent cited, Homer's *Margites*, long ago vanished without trace, and who know that Fielding, his tongue still in his cheek, will proceed to allocate *Joseph Andrews*, like Richardson's *Pamela*, to the *genre* of biography.

When our imaginary critic looks for examples of unintentional Janiformity in novels of the subsequent century, an excellent example would be provided by *Oliver Twist*: here both Arnold Kettle and Graham Greene have, from different standpoints but for largely congruent reasons, discovered an extreme tension between 'plot' and 'pattern'.[4] The moral implication of the plot, which requires characteristically awkward contrivance and coincidence, is one of benevolent optimism: the social world, for all its class oppression and personal injustices, may be redeemed by the examples of the charitably benevolent Brownlows and Maylies. Against this, the moral implication of the pattern, a pattern which elicits far more potent creative energies from the writer, is that the dark, corrupt, brutal nightmare of the social world is unconquerably enduring. Our critic's main problem might well be to find some freshly economical way of presenting what is basically a very familiar case, the case that in Dickens's works the decent, respectable, well-meaning middle-class characters are often presented in a relatively naturalistic and less persuasive convention, whereas the lower-class characters, particularly the corrupt, bullying and predatory, are often presented in relatively surrealistic terms as memorably vivid grotesques. The most economical approach might well be to concentrate on the 'bridging' or 'intermediary' characters, those beings who, while moving knowledgeably in the world of corruption or violence and callousness, yet have sufficient virtue in them to be able to inform and help the decent characters of the upper world. In this respect, there is a clear connection between Nancy of *Oliver Twist*, Louisa in *Hard Times* and Edith in *Dombey and Son*; and a gauge of Janiformity might be the implausibility of these hybrid linking-characters whose knowledge of true goodness is strangely evident in their very lamentations that they have been conditioned to be ignorant of true goodness.[5]

The example of *Oliver Twist* might suggest in the boldest possible way that an intense selectivity of vision which liberates a writer's most distinctive innovatory imaginative powers may often be subversive of the moral implications of the narrative structure. Our critic's discussion of unintentional Janiformity could therefore extend, though with increasing difficulty, to some works of Jane Austen, Henry James and Virginia Woolf. With Woolf's *To the Lighthouse*, for example, he could suggest that characters float, become waterlogged, and almost drown in the stream of consciousness. He could argue that the near-solipsistic and passivity-inducing characteristics of that technique, coupled with the hypnotic brightness of a world bathed in the shimmering waters of that stream of consciousness, imply a recommendation of aesthetic sensitivity which conflicts with the paraphrasable narrative's recommendation of mutual affection and co-operation. With Henry James, our critic might have an easier but still controversial task. James has said that the moral value of a work of literature depends on the amount of 'felt life' that has gone into the creation of that work;[6] and it has become a hallowed tradition, almost a ritual, for James's critics to use his own criterion as a basis for hostile comments on his later novels, by arguing that though the feel may be of elaborate sensitivity, the amount of life thus felt is all too small. Our imaginary critic could give some originality to this kind of claim by applying it to a relatively *early* novel, *The Portrait of a Lady*, and by suggesting that there the recommendation of emotional warmth and altruism, and the scepticism about the value of aesthetic connoisseurship, implicit in the hostile presentation of Osmond and Madame Merle, are largely subverted by the fastidious connoisseurship of the novel's techniques. The suspicion is created that Madame Merle, who helps to ensnare Isobel, would be more likely to read to the end a novel of this kind than would Caspar Goodwood, Lord Warburton, Henrietta Stackpole, or even Isobel herself.

It's with Jane Austen, I think, that our critic might have some of his best opportunities. He might suggest that a commonplace and apparently philistine objection to her work may actually come from those who are most responsive to the direction of her ironies. In *Emma*, the ironies stem largely from the premises that egoistic people tend to be short-sighted in judgement: being self-centred, they mis-read the natures of other people; consequently, they make inaccurate predictions about them; and therefore they may come to grief or disaster. As a corollary, altruistic people tend to be long-sighted: they read accurately the natures of others, make accurate predictions about them, and often come to happiness. Mr Knightley belongs to the second group; and ironies radiate around Emma because for much of the time she belongs to the first group, and her egotism entails myopia. However, through her capacity to learn, albeit slowly, from experience, the value of altruism and long sight, she comes to happiness. Intimately related to the exploration of Emma's character is Jane Austen's general attack on the evils of social snobbery: the characterisation of Mrs Elton shows, blatantly enough, that wealth doesn't entail moral worth; and the social fate which nearly befalls Jane Fairfax — the fate of becoming a governess — proves as clearly that a common social tragedy may be the poverty of those whose kindness, gentleness and sensitivity make them morally superior to those who have power and wealth. Nevertheless, in the novel *Emma*, as students are often prompt to observe, the poor cottagers aren't seen by us, and the food is placed on the tables by invisible servants. It may not always be the case that such students are damning Jane Austen for failing to write a socialist tract or *Saturday Night and Sunday Morning*. It may be that when they offer the familiar objection that her social range is very narrow, it is not sufficient to make the standard reply that through the subtlety and acuteness of her ironic treatment of a limited social area, her works gain general relevance. It may be that those who complain of limited social range have in fact sensed a radical inconsistency between the humane longsightedness commended by her most probing ironies and the social shortsightedness implicit in the selectivity of her social descriptions. The charge may really be one of moral self-contradiction, or of what our critic's jargon calls unintentional Janiformity.

When Janiformity is unintentional, the text seems to ambush the author; but when it is intentional, the text seems to ambush the reader. Among the more recent works, Conrad's *Heart of Darkness,* with its doubly oblique narrative procedures, sets the reader an inescapable ambush. We're tempted to identify with the anonymous narrator; but then we find that his assertions are subverted when Marlow enters the tale. In turn, we identify with Marlow, and thus, because of Marlow's fascination by Kurtz, we are led into a kind of complicity with the tale's central figure of corruption.

For our imaginary critic, the crux of the tale would come at the point where the endeavour to control the narrative's paradoxes threatens to become too difficult for Conrad, so that Kurtz, as a characterisation, seems to split under conflicting thematic pressures. Like Janus, Kurtz presents two contrasting faces to Marlow and to commentators. One face has a vacuous expression: he's a hollow man. The other face has a ferociously intense expression: he's a remarkably full man. The evidence of Kurtz's hollowness is quite explicit: he's called by Marlow a hollow sham; we're told that the wilderness echoed loudly within him because he was hollow at the core; and the emphasis on his peculiar eloquence suggests that he has the proverbial noisiness of an empty vessel. It's true that in Europe he showed immense promise as a musician or as a popular political leader, and it's true that he came out to Africa as an idealist; but the purpose of this information may be to indicate that even the seeming exception proves the rule: the rule that the mass of civilised men lack inner moral resources. Thus, in becoming corrupted by the jungle, Kurtz takes his place in the long line of hollow men that we have met during the narrative.

But against this, the text quite as firmly suggests that in the extremity of his ambitions, of his corruption and of his depraved appetites, Kurtz in ontological fulness offers a challenging *contrast* to the long line of hollow men. This Kurtz commands awe rather then dismissive contempt; and Marlow feels that if he had a choice of nightmares, a choice of evils, his loyalty would be to the Faustian Kurtz rather than to the flabby devils. Here the emphasis on his many talents suggests that Kurtz has maintained a spectacular, exceptional genius even in Africa; and an important question raised is this: Does Kurtz's conduct as tribal deity offer a grotesque parody of the civilised leader he might have been, or does that presentation of Kurtz in the jungle suggest that apparently civilised conduct is merely a hypocritical sophistication of basically savage impulses? Some readers gain from *Heart of Darkness* the impression that civilisation is a precious, perilously vulnerable achievement to be guarded vigilantly against perils from within and without; while other readers put down the tale with the impression that civilisation generally is a matter of automatised savagery.

So the main Janiformity of Kurtz's character is expressive of the extreme moral paradoxicality of the whole work. When liberal moral values are uppermost in Marlow's imagination, Kurtz is seen as contemptibly hollow. When the sceptical, subversive side of his imagination is at work, Kurtz exerts a peculiar fascination. Now one can reconcile the full Kurtz with the hollow Kurtz by saying that a man may be morally hollow yet full of anarchic appetites and ambitions. However, when Kurtz is at death's door and makes his final exclamation, 'The horror! The horror!', the prevailing mode of intentional Janiformity seems to be disrupted by the unintentional: paradox becomes self-contradiction. Even the remarkable Mr Kurtz cannot simultaneously affirm and deny a moral judgement; yet, according to Marlow, that's what he does in that last cry. Marlow offers contradictory interpretations of it, while seeming strangely unaware of contradiction. He explains that the cry is a moral victory, a condemnation by Kurtz of his past conduct. Yet Marlow also explains that the same exclamation is a judgement of the whole universe, the whole scheme of things. So if Kurtz is finally offering an indictment of a universe which is so horrifying (perhaps in its sheer meaning-lessness), this would be a statement of self-justification rather than self-condemnation: for in so horrifying a universe, any code of conduct, however destructive and violent, may be justified, so long as it enables a man to stamp his individuality on the senseless environment.

Although Conrad may thus seem to be confused at this point in the work, a defender of Conrad could argue that the author is deliberately deploying a confused narrator, Marlow, as a way of indicating the near-impossibility of conveying in words the most profound experiences or the innermost nature of another personality. Then our imaginary critic, to answer this objection, would have to cite not only the insistent stridency of Marlow's tone when seeking to define the meaning of Kurtz's words, but also Conrad's failure to distance himself from Marlow by means of the device previously used in the narrative, a sceptical interruption by Marlow's captive audience. In any case, by concentrating on the Janiform qualities of *Heart of Darkness*, it's likely that our critic could at last explain the very strange conflicts among previous commentators on the work. Some, like Douglas Brown, have argued that Kurtz is a hollow sham to be regarded with contempt; while others, like Robert Haugh, have argued that Kurtz is an awe-inspiring moral adventurer who calls in question liberal morality.[7] Our critic could show that such a dispute is indicative of the text's Janiformity, and he would be led to analyse a perennial source of Janiformity in literature, in poetry and drama as well as in the novel, in *Paradise Lost* and *Volpone* as well as *Heart of Darkness*: the paradox of the virtue of evil.

He would have to offer reasons for the fact that in literature, as in life, an energetically corrupt character so often seems to exert a judgement-subverting power over the observer or recorder. A platitudinous reason is that the corrupt characters often do what we would like to do and might well do if we weren't so responsible, foresighted, or fearful of being caught.

A second and more interesting reason is that we become ethically confused when such a character is not simply corrupt, but positively perverse, through his ability to recognise virtue and corruption in others. Another reason is that we're often inclined to forgive what we understand, and the author may put us in the position of being privileged spectators at, or imaginative accomplices in, extreme corruption: we may have far greater knowledge of the methods and intentions of that character than have those assailed by him. Furthermore, the corrupt character often has greater freedom of action than the virtuous one: a devil may for his purpose pretend to be an angel, but an angel might have scruples about impersonating a devil: so our approval of narrative excitement clouds our disapproval of a character's nature. In addition, a primitive justice is often enlisted to win our sympathy for the villains: the ones we find hard to condemn are those who were victims of some real or supposed injustice, and who, but for this, might not have embarked on their destructive courses. Kurtz was one such victim, being highly gifted but poor, being idealistic but resented by his fellow-imperialists. And another reason for our imaginative lenience with intensely corrupt characters is that even their apparently successful progress may so much resemble a journey through purgatory that to deny them lenience would be to punish them twice.

Several of these factors influence our judgement not only of Conrad's Kurtz but also of Greene's Pinkie in *Brighton Rock*. And with *Brighton Rock* our critic runs the risk of being too solemn, because although this novel asks most taxing moral questions, it does so by presenting a world which is in many ways as bizarrely and grotesquely stylised as the world of some Jacobean revenge drama. The initial effect of the stylisation is to give starkness and incisiveness to the moral questions; but the after-effect may be to make us suspect a speciousness about both the questions emphasised and the answers suggested by means of such a stylised mode. Nevertheless, the narrative seems evidently and designedly Janiform: we are offered two contrasted but simultaneous cliff-hangers. On one narrative level, the central question is this: Will Ida succeed in hounding down Pinkie and delivering him to justice before he can destroy Rose? On another narrative level, the central question is this: Will the Holy Ghost succeed in penetrating Pinkie and delivering him, through repentance, to divine mercy, before he destroys himself? Morally, the central paradox is that in the intensity of his corruption, in his sense of the reality of evil, and in his recognition that his own course is hell-bound, a vicious thug seems to acquire greater moral status than a kindly well-meaning secular person like Ida. The case for Pinkie entails some very ingenious special pleading by the author, the ingenuity lying largely in the simultaneous appeal to opposed temperamental extremes. On the one hand, there is the religious argument: that Pinkie consciously manifests the sinfulness which others deny, but which is always present in human nature like the lettering down the middle of a stick of rock; and on the other, there is the socialist argument, which invites us to see Pinkie as someone taking revenge for social injustice, as someone whose life might have been different and better had he not experienced the squalid horrors of childhood in an overcrowded slum. And much of the special pleading is implicit in the scenic descriptions by the omniscient narrator, whose jaundiced eye, by lingering with fascinated disgust on seaside vulgarities, refuse in the gutter, rusting prams in gardens, and 'the open door where the jerry stood', tends to endorse Pinkie's loathing of life.

As with part of Conrad's characterisation of Kurtz, so with much of the presentation of Pinkie: there is some dependence on the ancient theological paradox that in the eyes of God, those who are evil may have greater moral worth than those who are morally nondescript, or even than those who are good but in wholly secular terms. When Dante had made his imaginary journey to hell, he had found that whereas full-blown sinners had at least the dignity of particular torments in hell proper, those who had lived without praise or blame were an undifferentiated wailing mass of dismal souls consigned to the eternal indignity of the dreary vestibule. 'The deep Hell receives them not, for the wicked would have some glory over them.'[8] Now, in *Brighton Rock* the possibility is raised that in the 'appalling strangeness' of His mercy, God may even save a person who dies in mortal sin; and even if it's still a virtual certainty that Pinkie is consigned to hell, his identity will endure, whereas secular Fred Hale, Pinkie's victim, merely becomes, it seems, no more than 'part of the smoke nuisance over London'. The same paradox of the virtue of evil had been exploited, of course, in *The Waste Land*, particularly with its suggestion that what's wrong with the copulation of the typist and the house agent's clerk is not that it's sinful, but that the two people involved fail to regard it as sin, and merely accept the act as a mechanical routine. And one of the best commentaries on *The Waste Land* and on the Janiformity of *Brighton Rock* remains that notorious passage in T.S. Eliot's essay on Baudelaire, in which Eliot says: 'The possibility of damnation is so immense a relief in a world of electoral reform, plebiscites, sex reform and dress reform, that damnation itself is an immediate form of salvation — of salvation from the ennui of modern life, because it at last gives some significance to living.'[9]

The engagingly blasphemous quality of Eliot's comment lies in the suggestion that the prospect of damnation may be justified as a means to a very worldly end: the living of a vivid life. We may speculate that God might appropriately repay the man who acts on such principles, by consigning that man to a hell which exactly resembles modern life with its alleged ennui. A sceptic who wished to oppose Eliot's melodramatic view with an equally melodramatic one of his own could perhaps assert that the life of a secular man has greater moral fulness than that of a believer, precisely because the secular man works in a more limited time-span and may feel a greater weight of responsibility for his actions, being less able to refer for guidance to a traditional and hallowed body of moral precepts. Nevertheless, not only Eliot and Greene but also the thoroughly sceptical Conrad concur in suggesting that secular man, in his pride of selfhood, may, ironically, have dwarfed himself; no longer casting a shadow through all eternity, and no longer projecting an enduring identity even through the flames of hell.

And this simple paradox, that in the pride of individualistic selfhood, secular man betrays and diminishes, rather than asserts and aggrandises himself, is the basis of the intentional Janiformity of our critic's last example, Golding's *Pincher Martin*. With this, as with the previous examples of intentional Janiformity, the text conducts a peculiarly active campaign against the reader, tempting him into imaginative sanctuary that turns out to be a baited trap, or impaling him on the horns of a dilemma. Imaginative security dissolves, like the rock beneath Pincher.

Most readers, as they proceed through the book for the first time, are seduced into imagining that Pincher survived for several days on his rock before succumbing to madness and death; and they are shocked by the final information that Pincher drowned before reaching any rock; drowned, indeed, before he could tug off his boots. And the readers have to resolve the paradox not only by reconsidering the account of Pincher on the rock but also by reappraising the moral basis of their empathy with him. It's helpful, but inadequate, to consider that the island-experience was an after-life, a purgatory which was utterly appropriate, in its stark isolation, to the thoroughly self-centred life of the sufferer. It's also helpful, but not quite adequate, to think that in his dying moments as a drowning man, Pincher — like the hanged man in Ambrose Bierce's 'Occurrence at Owl Creek Bridge' — attempted to defy or elude death by means of a willed dream of survival, with every atom of his imaginative energy going into the creation of a dream which projects into the future, with actual moments being expanded by will into ostensible days. Most of us have had dreams that seemed to last for hours although they took place in a few moments; most of us have had the experience of responding to impending crisis by imagining that we're somewhere else doing something different. And in masturbation, the novel reminds us, the body can be seduced into physical endorsement of a willed dream. Pincher, in an act of ontological masturbation which is true to his self-centred and grasping character, attempts to evade death by a willed dream of survival: a project to expand time. The ironic image of the manipulated glass man in the bottle prompts the act. But the dream crumbles; the fabric dissolves, for all his efforts of will. He's trapped by inconsistencies: soluble guano, a red lobster in the sea; and one of his greatest moments of horror comes as he tries to fight off imaginative recognition that the topography of the craggy island has been suggested by the feel of his own teeth against his tongue.

The notion of a postmortal purgatorial island is reconcilable with the concept of the willed pre-mortal island if we imagine that God may have permitted an act in which the endeavour to survive would create a state identical to the purgatory that God deems appropriate to such a selfhood. (The irony in the image of the glass diver in the jar is that it is as appropriate to the idea of God's control of Pincher as it is to the idea of Pincher's mental control of his drowning state.) But as the island dissolves about Pincher, the narrator's language almost collapses into insoluble enigma in the effort to contain the paradox. We're told that the black lightning pried at the claws that had been hands, 'prying for a weakness, wearing them away in a compassion that was timeless and without mercy'.[10] Compassion without mercy? Perhaps this timeless force is without mercy because it brings total destruction, without any kind of afterlife, to Pincher; but is compassionate in that it understands his scepticism and fulfils it by annihilation, while erasing the willed purgatory that had been the attempt to evade the annihilation the scepticism had foreseen.

Perhaps. What is certain is that this novel's conceptual paradox is also a moral one. When the reader first shares Pincher's experiences on the rock, he may see various connections between Pincher's corrupt past and his present situation, but nevertheless he is likely to be seduced into pity and admiration for, and above all into complicity with, the struggles of the defiant solitary. When the conceptual paradox strikes, and the reader is forced to reappraise the struggles on the rock, to see the days as stolen time, and to see this Prometheus as a parody-Prometheus whose theft is for himself, the reader is also forced to reappraise critically his own complicity and to consider the extent to which his imaginative sympathy may have been the narcissism of the arrogantly sceptical. Pincher did not create his island alone; we created it with him.

The English novel began in guilt towards its readers, and as a form it tried to pass itself off as something else. And eventually the novel takes its revenge: it lays traps to induce guilt in readers. *Heart of Darkness* and *Pincher Martin* make their readers the guilty accomplices of men whose exuberant imaginations create alternative and perilous worlds.

So our imaginary critic claims; and in his final chapter he

reasserts that for an interesting minority of novels, and particularly for those in which the reader experiences something resembling a moral ambush, the notion of Janiformity may be a useful alternative to the traditional notion of the organic whole. It may serve to suggest that in general the moral value of literary works lies in their dialectical rather than in their exemplary force: in other words, in the effectiveness of their challenges to moral presuppositions rather than in their commendation of any readily-definable moral positions.

Our critic then concludes his discussion by showing that his book is itself appropriately Janiform: for he claims, finally, that although the notion of Janiformity may have some value in provoking discussion about how novels work, it is clearly pernicious as a critical tool: irredeemably schematic. And therefore this imaginary book, whose front cover bore a picture of Janus, bears on its rear cover a picture of Proteus, the god who defies wrestlers by assuming an infinite number of shapes while yet preserving his living identity.

# CHAPTER 3

# The Nature and Consequences of the Covert Plot

Defining a covert plot is a matter which may present few difficulties to people of common sense but considerable difficulties to those of a more philosophical or pedantic outlook. Hence this chapter.

If we take the term 'a narrative' to mean 'a story told in some way', it follows, tautologically, that all narratives (novels or tales or plays or narrative poems, or works approaching these in structure) have an overt main plot: a purposeful and, in varying degrees, conclusive sequence of incidents involving characters; and they may also have overt subsidiary plots. (Certain 'anti-novels', 'cut-ups' and similarly experimental works may lack an overt main plot; to that extent they cease to deserve the term 'narrative'.) In addition, some narratives have a covert plot: another purposeful sequence, but one which is partly hidden, so that it may elude readers (including some 'professional' readers, the literary critics and commentators) at a first reading, or at the first and second readings, or even at the first and second and subsequent readings, and may even elude them for decades. When it is eventually seen, the covert plot proves to organise and explain those elements of the text which at first may have seemed odd or anomalous, obscure or redundant; and the whole text is in various ways transformed.

The extent to which the covert plot remains covert or emerges into recognition depends on many factors, including the imaginative resourcefulness of the writer and the analytic intelligence of the reader. What commonly happens is that the reader notes as odd or puzzling some conspicuous elements of the covert plot but does not proceed to infer their linkages; and what the initiated reader, critic or commentator may helpfully do (perhaps because he or she has the advantage of multiple hindsight after several readings of the text) is to show how these elements cohere logically as a sequence. The elements themselves may be very conspicuous; it is usually the connections that are elusive. In other cases, the gist of the covert plot may emerge at a first reading but some of its ramifications may elude recognition at that stage. It is important to distinguish between, on the one hand, 'plots' or intrigues by characters, which may be largely concealed from another character but yet quite evident to the reader, and, on the other hand, plotting by an author which may be largely concealed from the reader; the latter rather than the former kind is my concern. A sophisticated author may, however, effect a large measure of convergence between the two, perhaps by making the reader strongly dependent on the perceptions of a character who is deceived by appearances.

The process of recognising a covert plot is usually as follows. The reader notices an anomaly: some detail which seems discordant with the overt plot. It may be discordant through apparent implausibility or oddity (the oddity perhaps being due to the fact that it seems to have a potential significance not elucidated by the immediate context). The reader then searches the text for similar anomalies. The search may be retrospective, if he retraces the narrative in memory or actually thumbs back through the pages; or prospective, if he looks out for similar occurrences as he reads on; or both. Having found two or more such anomalies, he formulates (perhaps 'instinctively', without any deliberate effort) their common feature or features. He then mentally postulates a possible narrative sequence (or sequences) which would explain, co-ordinate and conclude such occurrences; and he confirms or revises this postulate as the reading proceeds and new evidence comes to light. If both stages of the predictive process are fulfilled, so that there is not only further co-ordination but also an appropriate conclusion to the sequence, the covert plot is complete and may be deemed imaginatively intentional. If the earlier stage is fulfilled but the later is not, so that there is further co-ordination but no appropriate conclusion, the covert plot is incomplete and may be deemed imaginatively unintentional: a preoccupation has recurred but has not been resolved. Final harmonistion or union with the overt plot may take the form of assimilation of the covert by the overt (as when the former is subsumed in the greater comprehensiveness of the latter — perhaps when the covert matter becomes conspicuous to and is recognised by particular characters) or the subjugation of the overt by the covert (when the latter, by virtue of its greater comprehensiveness, exposes ironically the inadequacy of the former).

The basic process can be illustrated by further reference to Golding's *Pincher Martin*. This example will be relatively uncontroversial, because the text belongs to that category (listed above) in which the gist of the covert plot eventually emerges at a first reading but some of its ramifications elude recognition. The main overt plot concerns Pincher's struggles to survive on his rocky islet in the Atlantic. At some stage, perhaps at the point when Pincher recoils violently from perception of the fragile preservation of the water in the pool,[1] the reader senses an anomaly. Pincher's terror seems less the predictable terror at the perilousness of his survival on the rock than an ontological terror about the status of his very being and perceptions. The reader then searches the text, retrospectively and subsequently, for similar anomalies. Various other examples of this anomalous terror occur; the reader seeks their connecting logic, and sees that they occur when Pincher seems to fighting off the recognition that the island may be a fantasy maintained by act of will, and the recurrent association of the rock with a tooth hints at its origin. Various implausibilities (e.g. Pincher's use of limpets as transferable handholds) now make sense. The reader can then predict that the act of will must prove too great and that Pincher must relapse into the death he seeks to deny. The prediction is fulfilled as Pincher recognises implausibilities in the fantasy (a red lobster in the sea, reptilian gulls, soluble guano) and senses the dental shape of the island; as he strains to generate a madness that would accommodate the implausibilities; as the island dissolves; and as the final chapter, with its shift to an external viewpoint, confirms that Pincher drowned in the sea. The overt plot is thus finally vanquished by the covert, which exposes ironically the inadequacy of the former. In retrospect or at a subsequent reading, the reader may elucidate the ramifications — the details and significance — of the covert and its relationship to the overt. He will notice that the barriers to early identification of the island as fantasy include not only the sensuous vividness of evocation (apt support for a thesis that literary vividness may be a compensation for solipsistic fears)[2] but also the fact that Golding occasionally has apparently 'cheated' by adopting a viewpoint which, though seemingly external to Pincher, implies the objectivity of his rock and sense of survival: 'The man lay, huddled in his crevice, left cheek pillowed on black oilskin and his hands were glimmering patches on either side. Every now and then there came a faint scratching sound of oilskin as the body shivered.'[3] A theological justification would be that God chooses for a while to validate Pincher's fantasy as a sufficient Purgatory.

When we consider this and other texts, we see that although the covert plot may contrast in implication with the overt plot, it usually tends to blend (as a sequence of incidents) with the overt, since both inhabit the same imaginative territory. The blending-area, in which the unseen emerges into the light of the seen, will again vary according to the reader's abilities. Thus, in Conrad's *The Secret Agent*, whether the sequence of Lombrosian ironies is seen as part of the overt plot or lurks largely unseen as a subsidiary covert plot will depend on the reader's knowledge or ignorance of the theories of Cesare Lombroso. To the extent that he is ignorant of them, an important area of the narrative will be concealed in the darkness of that ignorance (to be mocked by the text: for Conrad explicitly refers to Lombroso, but does not do the reader's thinking for him by pointing out that Comrade Ossipon, Lombroso's fictional disciple, is in his physical appearance a living instance of his master's theories of physically-identifiable criminality and degeneracy).[4] The same may apply to that plot of *The Secret Agent* which in Chapter 7 I have chosen to treat as covert, but there my grounds for regarding it as covert are not only the frequency with which, in discussion, I find that it has gone un-noted, but also that, as with many of the more interesting covert plots, its moral implications work against, and substantially contradict, the moral implications of the main plot.

The general consequences of recognition of particular covert plots can now be recapitulated. When once the covert plot is perceived (its parts resolved into a sequence), the whole work is seen to be more complex and more fully structured. As complexity and structural fulness are not always virtues, and as so much depends on the quality of embodiment of the material, the text will not necessarily appear better as a result, but this is most frequently the case.

The meaning of the work accordingly changes. Often ironies and moral and philosophical complications are perceived which otherwise had been overlooked. All irony depends on recognition of a conflict between an overt and a covert significance; and to perceive a covert plot is to perceive an extension of irony, perhaps in the form of, for example, a transforming depth of characterisation. Thus, when once the covert plot of Conrad's *Almayer's Folly* (discussed in Chapter 5) is recognised, the character Abdulla gains markedly in importance and Almayer is seen to be ironically imperceptive in this respect. When the covert plots are transtextual, extending across different texts, irony may be proleptic and analeptic on a vast scale. The triumph of Abdulla in *Almayer's Folly* lends prospective irony to his previous triumph, described in the subsequent novel, *An Outcast of the Island*: the triumph which occurred when he outwitted those who had thought they were using him as a tool to advance their interests. (Lakamba and Babalatchi had introduced Abdulla to their region in order to further their ambition of wresting the throne from Patalolo for Lakamba; and they succeed in this aim, but only to find that Abdulla has tamed their power by making the region subject to Dutch control, so as to guard his own interests in the trade rivalry with the whites who claim British protection.) The main irony lies in our consequent recognition that history — along with human psychology, ambition, treachery and myopia — repeats itself, and that few people learn its lessons.

In discussions, it is frequently suggested to me that whereas the overt plot may proceed from the author's conscious mind, the covert plot may often proceed from the unconscious or subconscious mind. Genetically, this suggestion may occasionally be valid; my main objection to it is that it is critically sterile. Sometimes the conscious mind may be intelligent and sometimes it may (even in the same person) be stupid; and, if we assume that we can infer the nature of the unconscious mind from dreams and from other acts performed without conscious volition, sometimes the unconscious mind may be intelligent and sometimes it may (even in the same person) be stupid. As critical readers, we are concerned with the results and not the genetics, just as the carpenter is concerned with the timber and not with the acorns. The imaginary author of *Janiform Novels* attempted to cut through a labyrinth of critical theory by affirming that what matters critically is not whether the source of the material is conscious or unconscious but whether the material exhibits imaginative intentionality or the want of such intentionality. (This affirmation eludes the main perils of the 'Intentional Fallacy'.)[5] That author suggested a simple rule for distinguishing between the two, and I repeat it here because it is crucial to the identification of covert as well as overt plots:

An apparently anomalous part of a text is imaginatively intentional if predictions made by the reader on the assumption of its intentionality are fulfilled.

The rule specifies an 'apparently anomalous' part of a text because if there is no apparently anomalous part, the problem does not arise in the first place. Normally the area of fulfilment of predictions, if they are fulfilled, comes towards the end of the narrative in question; but since some narratives are transtextual, the area of fulfilment may be located in a text other than that in which the anomalies are first detected. That part of one text may be vindicated by part of another is one of many answers to any critic who attempts the impossible by attempting to treat a particular literary text as though it were divorced from its literary context.

A covert plot presents an enigma which is subsequently resolved; so does the classic detective novel or tale. Nevertheless the covert plots which concern me seem starkly different from the plots of detective novels. In the latter, we are

customarily told of a particular crime and we then watch for
clues which may enable us to identify the criminal or agency of
that crime; often we lag behind the perceptiveness of the
seeker (a detective of some kind) who finally unmasks the
agent and resolves the enigma; and the text confirms the
adequacy of the resolution. In the covert plot, on the other
hand, there may be no 'crime', or if there is we may long be
unaware of it: recognition of the wrongdoing may dawn only
tardily with recognition of the structure of events as a whole.
Instead of consciously watching out for clues to enable us to
identify a particular wrongdoer, our process is rather that of
sensing various oddities and speculating about their possible
rationale. The text may provide someone whose rôle resembles
that of a detective (like Captain Giles in Conrad's *The Shadow-
Line*), or it may provide no 'detective' at all: the 'private eye' is
the reader's. Whereas the detective story offers a final, public
and confirmed resolution of the enigma, the covert plot may
be resolved only in the sense that we see how events confirm
our hypotheses about their structure: there is private clarification for us, but there may not be public clarification among
the characters of the fiction: thus, at the end of Ibsen's *The Wild
Duck*, we can infer that a suicide may be taking place behind the
doors at the rear of the main room, but the play's philosphers
wrangle on to the last, unaware. Frequently in Conrad's
narratives, we 'see through the eyes' or 'see over the shoulder'
of a protagonist who is at first unaware that he is the object of
manipulations or machinations by others; events strike him as
odd rather than sinister; and only tardily does realisation
come to him and to us of the scheme being woven about him.
Furthermore, our sense of the extent of the scheme will often
exceed his. In these cases, Conrad's use of the covert plot may
initially give a strong sense of absurdity and later a strong sense
that the world is a place of ambushes of various kinds. The
covert plots that this book discusses are part of the general
authorial strategy of interrogating reality; the searches in
which they involve us are generally probing, whereas the
searches of a typical detective story are relatively superficial
and tend to confirm rather than question familiar and
conventional ideas of life's ordering. The differences are so
stark that there are few 'intermediate' texts. Conrad's *The Secret*

*Agent* may at first appear to be such an intermediate text (for it has its mysterious crime and its resourceful detective), but it will soon be seen that it reverses the procedures and subverts the conventions of a detective novel: from the start, we know who the instigator and agent of the crime are; the text deliberately confuses us about the nature of the disaster in the park; and we watch the process of detection (by Chief Inspector Heat and the Assistant Commissioner) with critical fore-knowledge, realising that the story says more about urban life and the ironies of politics than does any contemporaneous detective story or crime novel. Here my argument runs the risk of circularity, because the more a text of the latter two *genres* offers a searching account of reality, the more likely it is to be called simply 'a good novel', leaving those *genres* permanently under the shadow of a tacit pejorative (and Raymond Chandler's *The Long Good-bye* is an example of a text which in critical estimation over the years has emerged from that shadow); but demonstrably there remain the conspicuous contrasts in nature, strategy and implication between the enigmas of covert plots and the lesser enigmas of detective stories.

Conan Doyle's 'The Empty House',[6] a Sherlock Holmes story set in a London roughly contemporaneous with the London of *The Secret Agent*, presents a characteristic sequence of enigmas: who shot the Honourable Ronald Adair, how and why? Holmes ingeniously resolves the enigmas, sets a trap for the killer, and dramatically captures him in a way that verifies, before police witnesses, all his deductions. The story offers a basically conventional and conservative polarity: on the one hand are the forces of law, order, justice and decency; on the other are the forces of vice and crime. Much of the interest is narrowed to matters of technical ingenuity: thus, the villain's special device, an air-rifle of amazing power and quietness, is thwarted by Holmes's special device, a remarkably life-like bust of Holmes which the villain mistakes for the detective himself. Whereas Conan Doyle's enigmas deflect attention from political questioning, Conrad's entail such questioning. Notably, Conrad questions the conventional polarity by suggesting some resemblances between the forces of law and the forces of anarchy; and the technical devices beloved of the detective story are set in an ironically reductive context: the special explosive made by the Professor is prematurely detonated by sheer accident, and the Professor's personal bomb with its ingenious detonator may give him immunity from arrest but cannot make a significant difference to London and its masses.

Plot and theme are not separate: there is no story, however trivial, which cannot be seen as expressive of a theme. Themes tend to be passive and synchronic, in that they can generally be specified without reference to intention or causality (e.g., 'the theme of the disparity between ideal and actuality in *Heart of Darkness*'), whereas plots are active and diachronic, and are generally specified by reference to intention and the sequence of cause and effect. Recognition of a covert plot always entails recognition of a change in the thematic nature of the work: sometimes a previously-perceived theme gains greater emphasis; sometimes new and contrasting thematic material may be introduced.

Politically, the implications of the covert plot vary greatly from text to text. It may, compared with the overt plot, be relatively conservative; or it may be relatively subversive. The author of *Janiform Novels* suggested that the moral value of literary works lies in their dialectical rather than their exemplary force: in the effectiveness of their challenges to moral presuppositions rather than in their commendation of any readily-definable moral positions. The truth is more of a muddle, though, than this suggests. We value some works for their challenges, some for their support, and many for their mixture of both; vitality of embodiment is what counts in the works of merit. The originality of mind that makes an admirable literary work may often be linked to a subversive attitude towards cultural prejudices and assumptions; but we should beware of sentimentalising such subversiveness by deeming it to be necessarily 'liberal' or 'progressive'. As the available mishmash of cultural prejudices and presuppositions includes both the democratically liberal and the illiberal, so the work may as readily subvert the former by its illiberality of outlook as the latter by its liberality. In such cases we are usually thinking of the relatively paraphrasable aspects of the work. Whatever its doctrinal direction, however, the work of merit still celebrates humanity obliquely through its apparently non-doctrinal characteristics of intelligence and imaginativeness of presentation of experience.[7] This is what the history of literary criticism itself teaches. An admirable critic may be Christian or atheist, Tory or socialist; and his merit depends not on his doctrinal assumptions (though they may well influence all that he writes) but on the intelligence of his responsiveness to the works he discusses. Similarly, a creative writer's merits depend not on his doctrinal assumptions (though, again, they may well permeate all that he writes) but on his acumen as creative writer. The latter is inseparable from the former, but the former do not entail the latter. Some attention to covert plots may help us to define that acumen.

## Part Two:

## Conrad's Covert Plots and Transtextual Narratives

# CHAPTER 4

# Conrad and Delayed Decoding

In this book, most of my main examples are taken from the works of Joseph Conrad. The obvious reason is that Conrad was the master of the covert plot. Very few other writers seem to offer a comparable number, range and variety of covert plots; and I am encouraged to use the term by numerous discussions of his work with fellow-students, for such experience suggests that these plots have often eluded full recognition by various readers and commentators. Conrad has received much acclaim, but in some areas of his writing his intelligence has not yet received its due appreciation.

Furthermore, in the case of Conrad we are discovering a creative nexus: an imaginative preoccupation which largely gives identity to his work and which inter-relates small, medium and big matters. The elision or delay of logical connections preoccupies Conrad the descriptive artist as it preoccupies Conrad the story-teller. If we pursue the secret of the vividness and resonance of his most effective descriptive passages, we repeatedly find that the secret lies in the procedure which I once clumsily called 'the cart-before-horse method' and which Ian Watt, more elegantly and much more fruitfully, has called 'delayed decoding'.[1] For reasons temperamental, aesthestic, moral and philosophical, Conrad developed to sophisticated extremes this art of delayed decoding. In descriptive passages its consequence is that a given experience seems to bombard the senses and to elude rationality for a while. Conrad presents the *effect*, in terms of immediate sense-data, while withholding or delaying an understanding of its *cause*; and the result is that the event gains a vividness of impact while initially seeming strange, random or absurd. This quality of strangeness (perhaps of the dreamlike or nightmarish) is diminished but seldom fully erased by our subsequent perception of the rational explanation. In the terminology of Conrad's contemporary, Viktor Shklovsky, this is a 'defamiliarisation device',[2] and many writers have employed it for a variety of serious, comic and philosophical purposes, but few more repeatedly and variously than has Conrad.

In his works there are hundreds of possible examples, including the presentation of the death of Marlow's helmsman in *Heart of Darkness*, the explosion of the coal-gas in 'Youth', and the onset of rain in *The Shadow-Line*. I cite the last example here because of its convenient brevity.

> By an effort which absorbed all my faculties I managed to keep my jaw still. It required much attention, and while thus engaged I became bothered by curious, irregular sounds of faint tapping on the deck. They could be heard single, in pairs, in groups. While I wondered at this mysterious devilry, I received a slight blow under the left eye and felt an enormous tear run down my cheek. Raindrops.
>
> (*SL*, 113.)

This instance shows that there may be not two but three stages in the process of delayed decoding. First stage: the impinging sense-data, undeciphered ('curious, irregular sounds of faint tapping on the deck'); second stage: the first, incomplete or inaccurate decoding (here, a Poltergeist or alien spirit at work — 'mysterious devilry'); third stage: eventual full or accurate decoding — 'Raindrops'. The same three stages are found in the case of the other two examples I have mentioned. In *Heart of Darkness*, Marlow sees his helmsman quickly fall and stretch on the deck; he first infers that the man has seized a cane and over-balanced at a most inappropriate time, and secondly (the third stage) recognises tardily that the man has been slain by a thrown spear. In the other example, the captain of 'Youth' becomes 'aware of a queer sensation, of an absurd delusion, — I seemed somehow to be in the air'; he feels that it is 'as if a thousand giants simultaneously had said Phoo!'; and then he, in two further guesses, reaches the true decoding: ' "What is it? — Some accident — Submarine volcano? — Coals, gas! — By Jove! we are being blown up....." ' (*Y*, 23.) Conrad likes to make ironic jokes about his own techniques, and delayed decoding is no exception. In *Heart of Darkness*, Marlow finds a book which has incomprehensible writings in the margin; he makes the first, incorrect decoding: these must be writings in code — 'They were in cipher!'; but many pages later comes the true second decoding: the 'cipher' is not code at all but notes by a Russian.

What is particularly fruitful is that the concept of delayed decoding applies not only to many of Conrad's most vivid descriptive passages but also to longer narrative sequences and ultimately to the narrative strategies of whole works: as in *Heart of Darkness*, where we have to interpret Marlow's own reported attempt to decipher and comprehend the meaning of the journey into the Congo which he is recalling, and as in *Nostromo*, where the reader is set the challenge of ordering, unifying and reconciling the multiple viewpoints and the jumbled chronology of the text. It is clear that a novelist who is interested in descriptive modes of delayed decoding may well be interested in covert narrative sequences, for the former resemble (if on a smaller scale) the latter, and entail kindred scrutinies. We see how one modulates towards the other in a central sequence in Conrad's first novel, *Almayer's Folly*.

The Balinese hero, Dain, sets out at night to cross a dangerously turbulent river; Babalatchi suggests that he may drown. The next morning a mutilated corpse is found among logs by the riverside; its face is unrecognisable, but Babalatchi identifies it as Dain's by a ring and a bangle. Almayer is distraught, believing that his partner, Dain, is dead. Subsequently, when Dutch officers arrive in pursuit of Dain, he shows them the corpse; and they go away, thinking their pursuit is at an end. Only tardily does Almayer later discover that Dain is alive and that the body was that of one of Dain's boatmen who had drowned during the nocturnal crossing of the river. (Mrs Almayer had mutilated the corpse's face and Dain had provided the ring and bangle to aid the deception, so that his pursuers would be tricked.) Thus Almayer passes through the three stages of delayed decoding: first, he has the encounter with shocking or bewildering events; secondly he makes the incorrect decoding, that this corpse is indeed Dain's; and thirdly, he eventually learns the correct decoding, that this was only a boatman. Conrad deliberately permits the reader to be deceived for a while, though not for as long as Almayer: the plotting (and literally the plot by Mrs Almayer and Dain) is covert — concealed from the reader for several pages, although we are let into the secret before Almayer; and, as is customary with a covert plot, an attentive reader will find a few clues to guide him to an early inference of the truth. One clue is the calm reticence of Nina, who, as the lover of Dain, seems remarkably stoical when confronted by the apparent fact of his death; and the text ambiguously yet (to our hindsight) pointedly observes:

> With her heart deeply moved by the sight of Almayer's misery, knowing it in her power to end it was with a word, longing to bring peace to that troubled heart, she heard with terror the voice of her overpowering love commanding her to be silent.
>
> (*AF*, 103.)

This implies that she knows of the deception, knows that Dain lives, but chooses to keep the secret. Eventually, the deception is fully clarified and explained in the dialogue between Babalatchi and Lakamba at the beginning of Chapter 9, so this part of the plot is made, retrospectively, fully overt; but Conrad has clearly been interested in the possibility of letting the reader share for some while the misleadingly incomplete vision of the central observer, here Almayer; and, as we shall see in my subsequent chapter, this novel does contain one extensive covert plot of which Almayer dies unaware — an unawareness shared by numerous readers during the many years since the novel first appeared.

# CHAPTER 5

# The Covert Plot of Almayer's Folly: Abdulla's Stratagem

Recently, while reading *Almayer's Folly* for perhaps the fourth time, I realised that this novel has an important covert plot which so far, to the best of my knowledge, has eluded the recognition of the work's critics and commentators. Discussion with fellow-Conradians has confirmed my sense that my tardiness in perceiving this plot was a consequence of Conrad's cunning rather than my obtuseness; and a significant confirmation is that Ian Watt's impressive *Conrad in the Nineteenth Century* (1980), which devotes thirty-three pages to the analysis of *Almayer's Folly* and gives particular attention to its narrative techniques, offers no suggestion of Abdulla's central rôle as strategist — indeed, Watt's chapter on this novel does not even mention the name of Abdulla. My analysis will necessarily be intricate.

The covert plot of *Almayer's Folly* is largely Syed Abdulla's plot, and therefore it is the crowning irony of this first novel that the narrative ends with Abdulla breathing an apparently pious prayer to 'Allah! The Merciful! The Compassionate!' over the body of Almayer, whom Abdulla has so ruthlessly and successfully schemed to vanquish. As in the later *Outcast of the Islands* and *Heart of Darkness*, at the centre of the hidden machinations is a scheme by a trader to eliminate a rival and secure for himself the control of a commercial territory. *Almayer's Folly*, which is proleptic in its richness of political, racial, sexual and philosophical themes, is thus seen to be structurally proleptic too.

47

If we first consider the *overt* plot of the novel, we see that much of the story is presented retrospectively, in the form of ruminations by Almayer and reportage by the narrator. The crucial starting-point of the 'present' and 'future' action is the ambush of Dain Maroola by the Dutch authorities. All else stems from this — Dain's flight, pursued by the Dutch officers (for in escaping from their ambush he had been responsible for the deaths of two Dutchmen); his feigned death; and his precipitated elopement with Nina, leading to Almayer's appalled realisation that he, Almayer, had been deceived both by Dain and by his beloved daughter and that his quest for gold must be abandoned and the daughter relinquished for ever. Almayer's death results from this utterly demoralising realisation.

The *covert* plot is revealed if we ask the following questions: How did Dain come to be ambushed? Was he betrayed? if so, by whom, and for what purpose? If, with these questions in mind, we re-examine the text minutely, we find just a few clues: but these prove to be consistent, and quite sufficient to show that it was through the treachery of the Arab trader, Syed Abdulla, that the ambush of Dain's brig had taken place. The background is this. Abdulla had long wished to dominate trade on the River Pantai and to overcome his rival, Almayer, in one way or another. One method that he had considered was a scheme of marriage: he had thought that his loyal nephew, Reshid, might marry Nina, so that the rival would thus become a relative and partner. An apparently friendly meeting of a Dutch commission with Almayer had strengthened this resolve. Abdulla and Reshid had then visited Almayer; Abdulla 'made a polite allusion to the great consideration shown him (Almayer) by the Dutch "Commissie," and drew thence the flattering inference of Almayer's great importance amongst his own people' (44-5); and he had offered three thousand dollars as dowry if Nina would marry Reshid. Almayer had been appalled (mainly for racial reasons) by the idea and had coldly declined the offer. After this, Reshid had made a long trading voyage in quest of gunpowder, at a time when the trade was banned by the Dutch; he had brought some powder almost all the way back to Rajah Lakamba, but had been stopped by the authorities and his cargo confiscated.

'Reshid's wrath was principally directed against Almayer, whom he suspected of having notified the Dutch authorities of the desultory warfare carried on by the Arabs and the Rajah with the up-river Dyak tribes' (48). To Reshid's surprise, 'the Rajah received his complaints very coldly' (49), because the Rajah knew that Almayer was innocent in this respect and had in any case been reconciled to Almayer by Dain, the latter having become (with Almayer's unlawful help) a new source of supply of gunpowder. Abdulla and Reshid then planned to turn the tables on Dain, we infer; and it is from the Dutchmen who visit Almayer in their subsequent pursuit of the betrayed Dain that we learn how the tables were turned.

The Dutch lieutenant accuses Almayer of having sold to Dain the gunpowder that was carried in Dain's brig.

'How did you hear about the brig?' asked Almayer.....
'An Arab trader of this place has sent the information about your goings on here to Batavia, a couple of months ago,' said the officer. 'We were waiting for the brig outside, but he slipped past us at the mouth of the river, and we had to chase the fellow to the southward. When he sighted us he ran inside the reefs and put the brig ashore. The crew escaped in boats before we could take possession. As our boats neared the craft it blew up with a tremendous explosion; one of the boats being too near got swamped. Two men drowned — that is the result of your speculation, Mr. Almayer. Now we want this Dain. We have good grounds to suppose he is hiding in Sambir.'
                                                                                                      (123.)

The crucial statement here is 'An Arab trader of this place has sent the information'. In this sentence lies the explicit linkage of the overt and the covert plots. Abdulla and Reshid have aptly turned the tables on Dain and Almayer: evidently Abdulla, the senior and wilier of the two Arabs, sent via his nephew Reshid the message to the authorities which resulted in the ambush, the deaths, the pursuit and the dénouement. The fugitive Dain quite rightly suspected treachery:

'Believe me, Rajah,' he [Dain] went on, with sudden energy, 'the Orang Blanda [Dutchmen] have good friends in Sambir, or else how did they know I was coming thence?'
Lakamba gave Dain a short and hostile glance. Babalatchi rose quietly, and, going to the arm-rack, struck the gong violently.
Outside the door there was a shuffle of bare feet; inside, the guard woke up and sat staring in sleepy surprise.

'Yes, you faithful friend of the white Rajah,' went on Dain, scornfully, turning to Babalatchi, who had returned to his place, 'I have escaped, and I am here to gladden your heart.'

(79.)

Dain has reason to be distrustful of Lakamba and Babalatchi, who are inveterate schemers; but, as the Dutch lieutenant's subsequent words prove, Dain's imputations are here misdirected: Abdulla and Reshid, rather than Lakamba and Babalatchi, were the agents of his disaster. Though Lakamba and Babalatchi would be happy to see Almayer arrested by the Dutch and taken away, they wish to preserve Dain, believing that he shares Almayer's knowledge of the location of the inland gold. 'After the Dutch went away Lakamba and Dain would get the treasure without any trouble, and there would be one person less to share it.' (84.)

Furthermore, another small detail of the text proves that the Arabs' act of treachery is repeated. At first the Dutchmen, like Almayer, are persuaded that the boatman's corpse is Dain's, and they go away. Soon, however, they receive a message that they have been cheated and that Dain lives; so they renew their pursuit, and the fugitive is forced to flee to his homeland across the sea. If we ask who despatched this warning to the Dutch, a crucial detail of text supplies the answer. It provides the delayed decoding of the second pursuit and also confirmation of the covert plot of treachery. Babalatchi tells Dain and Almayer:

'She [Taminah] yelled at Abdulla's gate till she woke up all Sambir. Now the white officers are coming guided by her and Reshid. If you want to live, do not look at me, but go!'
'How do you know this?' asked Almayer.
'Oh, Tuan! what matters how I know! I have only one eye, but I saw lights in Abdulla's house and in his campong as we were paddling past. I have ears, and while we lay under the bank I have heard the messengers sent out to the white men's house.'

(182.)

Thus, Taminah had warned Abdulla that Dain was still alive; Abdulla had sent messengers to tell the Dutch, and in addition he had directed Taminah and Reshid to guide the pursuers upstream to Dain's hiding-place.

As Conrad's critics have usually failed to perceive that the fulcrum of the plot is provided by the Arab traders' betrayal of Dain, they have proportionately failed to perceive the intensely ironic complex of racial, national and sexual revenge which this novel offers. Arab betrays Balinese and European, as once European had prevented marriage of half-caste to Arab, and as once European had been thought to have betrayed Arab (Reshid) into ambush. The 'Christian' is outwitted by the devout Muslim who regards Christians as infidels. Arabs who trade under the Dutch flag and are protected by the Dutchmen successfully scheme against a European of Dutch parentage who trades under the British flag. (Furthermore, according to the subsequent novel, the Arab, Abdulla, is British! [*OI*, 179.]) Dain's life is threatened by the combination of Arab, Dutch and Siamese (for Taminah is a Siamese girl); his life is preserved by a combination of Sulu (Mrs Almayer and Babalatchi), Malay (Lakamba and his men) and Dutchman (for Almayer, though jealous and despairing, abets Dain's escape). There is even sexual revenge: Mrs Almayer, scorned and detested by her husband, takes a form of sexual revenge against him by helping Nina to elope with Dain; while Taminah, who loves Dain and is jealous of Nina, seeks revenge by betraying Dain to Abdulla and thus to the Dutch.

Readers who perceive all this intricate plotting will see that Conrad, in his pessimism and scepticism about human nature, vigorously transcends the racial and cultural prejudices of his times. Whatever the race, colour, nation or creed, Conrad thus suggests in *Almayer's Folly*, we see equivalences in motive, desire, craft and need. A tiny instance of Conrad's vast strategy is supplied by the tag, 'the elder statesman of Sambir', which is repeatedly attached to Babalatchi. At first we may think that it is mockingly ironic, for this one-eyed Sulu in his bamboo hut in the Bornean jungle seems a ludicrous contrast to the image of the dignified, frock-coated statesman of Europe which the phrase brings to mind. But by the final stages of the novel, the original irony has evaporated from the phrase, which now seems reasonably appropriate to Babalatchi's experience and skill in stratagem; and a new irony has come to invest it: for we realise that European 'elder statesmen' may in principle be no different from that crafty ex-warrior in the jungles of the east. Some black critics have, in recent years, accused Conrad of racial prejudice; the covert plot of *Almayer's Folly* provides good evidence of the injustice of such accusations.

As I have mentioned, readers who decode the covert plot will recognise that the novel's ending, far from being a quiet coda featuring a minor character, is the resonantly conclusive irony, given that the prayer to Allah at Almayer's death is uttered by the arch-rival, Abdulla, whose cunning had brought about the reversal, loss and disillusionment which led to that death. Almayer is indeed the man whom Abdulla 'had fought so long and had bested so many times' (208). The linkage with the theme of treachery in the subsequent novel, *An Outcast of the Islands*, at once becomes apparent, as indeed does the linkage between *Almayer's Folly* and the numerous subsequent works (e.g. 'An Outpost of Progress', *Heart of Darkness* and *Nostromo*) in which a dominant theme is the treachery — of man to man, class to class and race to race — entailed by the pursuit of 'material interests'. In addition, the initiate who is aware of the covert plot will also see that *Almayer's Folly*, though in some respects a cumbrous and laboured first novel, is in this respect a subtle and worthy forerunner of those later Conradian texts, particularly *Lord Jim*, *Nostromo* and *The Secret Agent,* whose obliquities and ellipses have long been a topic of critical discussion.

A rather neglected aspect of *Almayer's Folly* (and one which, again, provides a clear answer to critics who unjustly accuse Conrad of 'racism') is that the tragedy of Almayer is one generated largely by his own racial prejudice. He regards his beloved daughter's elopement with the olive-skinned prince as both a personal and a racial betrayal. Yet his intense, if possessive, love for Nina makes his attitude ambivalent. When he accompanies the two fugitives downstream during their escape to the sea, his ostensible motive is to avert the racial disgrace that he feels their capture would entail:

'I am a white man, and of good family..... It would be a disgrace... all over the island,... the only white man on the east coast. No, it cannot be... white men finding my daughter with a Malay. My daughter!'

(184.)

Nevertheless, his rôle in accompanying them to the coast is as much that of paternal accomplice as of a man seeking to avert disgrace (for the capture of Dain would have prevented what he regards as a racially shameful marriage). And when the three reach the coast, and Dain and Nina prepare to sail to their new life across the sea, there comes a moment when his own tragedy could be averted and a new life could begin for Almayer too.

What if he should suddenly take her to his heart, forget his shame, and pain, and anger, and — follow her! What if he changed his heart if not his skin and made her life easier between the two loves that would guard her from any mischance! His heart yearned for her. What if he should say that his love for her was greater than...

'I will never forgive you, Nina!' he shouted, leaping up madly in the sudden fear of his dream.

(192.)

'What if he should say that his love for her was greater than...'. If we ask which suppressed phrase lurks behind the three dots of the textual elision, the answer must surely be 'racial prejudice'. But it is that which triumphs, and the consequence is that Almayer dies a lonely and wretched death. In the quoted passage, the quality of the prose is poor: stereotyped in phrase and melodramatic in tone; for hopes of mutuality never quickened Conrad's imagination as much as did revelations of isolation. The possibility of a victory of harmony over prejudice is at least raised, however wanly, as an important moment in the novel's racial and psychological discussion. One corollary of Conrad's interest in covert narratives is his interest in *latent* if unrealisable narratives: the stories of what might have been.

# CHAPTER 6

# 'Metaphysical' Plots: Supernatural Elements in The Nigger of the 'Narcissus', Heart of Darkness, 'The Secret Sharer', The Shadow-Line and Victory

In religious matters, Conrad's outlook was predominantly and often eloquently sceptical. At Christmas 1920 he wrote to Edward Garnett:

It's strange how I always, from the age of fourteen, disliked the Christian religion, its doctrines, ceremonies and festivals..... And the most galling feature is that nobody — not a single Bishop of them — believes in it. The business in the stable isn't convincing.....

(EG, 188-9.)

And in 1898 he had told Cunninghame Graham:

The mysteries of a universe made of drops of fire and clods of mud do not concern us in the least. The fate of a humanity condemned ultimately to perish from cold is not worth troubling about..... Faith is a myth and beliefs shift like mists on the shore.....

(*LCG*, 65.)

These two friends of Conrad were themselves sceptics. Garnett once wrote to Graham:

Come, don't you think the earth is *mad,* to go on producing these eternal birth pangs, these shameless swarms of stupid life mechanically, like an automatic mother in parturition, after one single impregnation by the Almighty?

(31.1.1899. MS: ASA.)

And Cunninghame Graham once declared on a public platform that 'God was a man of the very best intentions who died young' (*LCG*, 67) — a declaration which in its premises is impeccably Christian but in its implications is patently profane. Nevertheless, as in the cases of Garnett and Graham (and of Graham's acquaintance, Thomas Hardy), Conrad's attitudes to religion extended over a very wide range: there was piety of a kind, agnosticism, Pyrrhonism, atheism, antitheism, and a sense of radical absurdity or meaninglessness. In his fiction he could draw on any or all of these.

The 'piety of a kind' stemmed partly from his early upbringing as a Roman Catholic in Poland — that beleaguered land in which Catholicism has for centuries been so bound up with nationalism that nobody as patriotic as Conrad could fail to respect some aspects of the traditional faith. In turn, Conrad claimed to have arranged a Catholic baptism for his firstborn son, Borys (who, in old age, told me that he had always remained a Roman Catholic), and was himself eventually interred amid Catholic funeral rites at Canterbury. If an agnostic is one who professes not to know whether there is a God and to be certain only of uncertainty in such matters, then Conrad was, from time to time, an agnostic: 'As our peasants say: "Pray, brother, forgive me for the love of God". And we don't know what forgiveness is, nor what love is, nor where God is.' 'As to the soul You and I cher ami, are too honest to talk of what we know nothing about.' (*LCG*, 65, 190.) This attitude may modulate towards Pyrrhonism: the outlook of those who are so radically sceptical as to be sceptical even of scepticism. Again, if an antitheist is one who believes that if there be a God, He must be cruel, hostile or uncaring, then there were times when Conrad could sound like an antitheist: 'I don't know that the ben [evolent] Crea[tor] is serene; — but if he is (as they say) then he *must* be idiotic..... looking at the precious mess he has made of his only job.' (*LCG*, 50.) As we have seen, the last lines of *Almayer's Folly* have multiple ironies. Uttering the Koranic formula, Abdulla invokes 'Allah! The Merciful! The Compassionate!', while contemplating the corpse of his rival; and one irony lies in the obvious implication that events in this world, so often cruel and harsh, appear to contradict the belief that the Maker is 'merciful' and 'compassionate'.

In accordance with his predominantly sceptical outlook, Conrad's narratives offer actions which are largely explicable in secular, realistic terms. Indeed, by the standards of his times, Conrad was distinguished as a novelist by his readiness to offer so searchingly sceptical a vision: the pessimism of his novels stems partly from his energetic undercutting of orthodox conceptions of Divine Providence and cosmic justice. Interpretations of his fiction which proceed from secular and sceptical premises are therefore, up to a point, appropriate and sound. But only up to a point. Against the sceptical narratives work plot-elements which depend on a metaphysical understanding; and it is these more covert plot-elements which often transmit the symbolic glow and resonance of his novels and tales. A writer who employs symbolism invokes metaphysical habits of imagination; and the more his symbols are dynamic (i.e. by permitting and fulfilling narrative predictions) the more such habits are validated during the reading-experience.[1]

In the 'Author's Note' to *The Shadow-Line*, however, Conrad explicitly repudiated a 'supernatural' interpretation:

> This story, which I admit to be in its brevity a fairly complex piece of work, was not intended to touch on the supernatural. Yet more than one critic has been inclined to take it in that way, seeing in it an attempt on my part to give the fullest scope to my imagination by taking it beyond the confines of the world of the living, suffering humanity. But as a matter of fact my imagination is not made of stuff so elastic as all that..... No, I am too firm in my consciousness of the marvellous to be ever fascinated by the mere supernatural, which (take it any way you like) is but a manufactured article.....
>
> (*SL*, v.)

By the 'mere' supernatural he may mean something more credulous and unsophisticated than he actually offers, so that he thus differentiates his work from the *genre* of 'ghost stories'. In any case, as is well known, his 'Author's Notes' are sometimes (whether by accident or design) misleading, providing accounts which simplify some of the effects of the works they introduce. He says that the supernatural material of *The Shadow-Line* is confined to the 'superstitious fancy' of a single character; but this is not the case. *The Shadow-Line* is one of numerous Conradian narratives which rely for much of their force on supernatural or metaphysical elements which combine to make a plot-sequence that is partly harmonic with, and partly contrapuntal to, the predominant secular plot-sequence.

If we consider why a markedly sceptical writer should offer supernatural plot-sequences, there are various answers. One is obvious: a writer of fiction, seeking to create rich and resonant works, is at liberty to draw on religious and super-natural material if he wishes to do so. Secondly, a writer draws on his own experience; and Conrad had diverse experience of the significance, for others and sometimes for himself (as cultural fact if not as personal conviction), of the metaphysical. We have noted his Catholic upbringing and the fact that no patriotic Pole can divorce himself from some respect for Catholic Christiantity. This point was well made during the rise of Solidarność in 1980-81, when the Polish free trade-union deployed a Christian iconography (the crucifix, photo-graphs of the Pope and images of the Madonna) in deliberate contrast to the heathen iconography of the oppressive régime (the hammer-and-sickle banner, and posters of Marx, Engels and Lenin). Conrad's father Apollo had been as mystically devout in his nationalism as in his Catholicism.

Again, like many of his contemporaries, Conrad was so well versed in the Bible that biblical motifs, symbols, stories and phrases came readily to him during composition. One prom-inent example is the most important recurrent phrase in *Lord Jim*, 'one of us', which is a quotation (with varying degrees of irony) of God's words to the angels at the time of Adam's fall: 'Behold, the man is become as one of us, to know good and evil' (Genesis 3, verse 22). In *Nostromo,* when the owl seems to cry 'It is finished; it is finished' to Nostromo himself (*N*, 418), those words are the last words of Christ on the cross (John 19, verse 30). The community of cultural reference on which Conrad could rely in his day has, for better and worse, gradually dissolved during this century; a dissolution resulting not only from general secularisation but also from the modernising 'translations' of liturgy and of the Bible itself. Today's reader of the Oxford and Cambridge *New English Bible* will encounter there not 'It is finished' but 'It is accomplished', so the Conradian echo may fade from earshot. The Christian myth of the Fall provided a recurrent pattern in Conrad's fiction: in *Lord Jim*, *Nostromo* and *Victory*. The story of the fall of Lucifer lies behind the characterisation of Gentleman Jones in *Victory*, and that very word 'gentleman' carries a theological irony. By such allusions, Conrad was establishing common ground with his readers, while undermining it in various ways. Conrad could be sceptical, cynical and nihilistic, but he was also strongly idealistic; and when an idealist seeks to express his ideals and affirmations, the religious tradition provides a ready terminology. Noticeably, when speaking most positively about both his chosen careers, that of seaman and that of writer, Conrad sometimes refers to each as a kind of priestcraft requiring 'fidelity', 'dedication' and 'a spirit of piety'.[2]

As a writer, Conrad was both Romantic and anti-Romantic: intelligently critical of Romantic stereotypes and preoccupations, but thoroughly familiar with them, and often inclined to use them as the bases of his fictional structures. And the Romantic tradition draws strongly on the Christian tradition, even when the writer purports to be anti-Christian or strongly heterodox. For example, the story of the Faustian pact with the Devil, as treated by Christopher Marlowe, can be seen as inaugurating the Romantic tradition of the brilliant rebel who is destroyed by his rebellion; and, as even that adjective 'brilliant' suggests, it blends with the classical Promethean myth as well as with the story of Lucifer. So many Romantic protagonists have Promethean and Faustian resemblances: the Byronic hero (of *Childe Harold* and *Manfred*, and even Byron himself); Blake's Milton; Emily Brontë's Heathcliff. Shelley dramatised Prometheus in his *Prometheus Unbound*, and even Mary Shelley's *Frankenstein* has the sub-title *The New Prometheus*. Whether we look at Kurtz in *Heart of Darkness* or Gould in *Nostromo,* we see continuity, albeit partly parodic, with the Romantic Promethean and the Faustian traditions.[3]

Again, being a former seaman as well as a widely-read European familiar with Christian, classical and Romantic traditions, Conrad knew the wealth of stories and legends which invest the sea with supernatural significance. From Noah sailing across the deluge, to Jonah and the whale, and to Christ stilling the raging waves, Christian imagery blends with marine imagery; and, in turn, some of the most famous legends of the sea have strong Christian elements. Conrad knew well the legend of the Flying Dutchman (to which he refers explicitly in *A Personal Record*, 'Falk' and *The Shadow-Line*), one version of which suggests that the captain doomed to sail endlessly is being punished for blasphemy. Conrad may have known the adaptations by Sir Walter Scott and by Wagner. A partial counterpart to the Flying Dutchman is Coleridge's wandering seaman in 'The Rime of the Ancyent Marinere'; and Conrad was familiar with Coleridge's poem, echoing it in *The Shadow-Line*. For Conrad, an important nexus of 'aquatic', classical, Christian, Romantic and superstitious material was provided by his memories of journeys into an underworld: he could associate the classical account of the underworld (its rivers Styx, Acheron and Lethe, its boatman Charon, its shades of the dead — he cites Virgil's *Aeneid* occasionally[4]) with the Christianised account in Dante's *Inferno* (Acheron, Charon, the wailing souls), with Romantic voyages by sea and river into the unknown, and with the idea (variously Christian and classical, Romantic and occult) of the living dead — those who are physically dead but whose souls still wander until, after propitiatory or exorcistic rites, they may lie in peace. This nexus is strong in *Heart of Darkness*, *Nostromo*, *The Shadow-Line* and 'The Secret Sharer'. When referring to the dead or the living, Conrad often shows a predilection for a terminology ('shades',[5] 'wraith', 'spectre', 'shadow') which equivocates between the metaphorical and literal, secular and supernatural, and thus helps to generate covert narratives.

## (i) THE NIGGER OF THE 'NARCISSUS'

The covert plot of *The Nigger of the 'Narcissus'* has two interlinked aspects: the first is that of 'seaman's superstition', the second that of symbolic patterning. The two blend with each other.

The former, 'superstitious' aspect of the plot is easily summarised. Singleton, the old patriarchal seaman, taciturn yet a repository of maritime wisdom, remains aloof from the crew's corrupting involvement with James Wait. Wait is confusingly ambiguous, a living lie. Throughout the voyage,

as the text makes clear, he suffers from tuberculosis (on the
first night his 'roaring, rattling cough..... shook him like a
hurricane'); but when his illness is relatively mild, he exagger-
ates it in order to malinger, while when the illness becomes
mortal, he lies to others and to himself that he is fit. To the
extent that the crew are sentimentally involved with him
(because of 'the latent egoism of tenderness to suffering'[6]) they
become unreliable, mutinous, forgetful of duty. Singleton,
however, is uncontaminated; he does his duty consistently.
His judgement of Donkin, 'Damn you', puts curtly in two
syllables the condemnation that the narrator, in his repeatedly
pejorative descriptions of Donkin, requires many eloquent
sentences to convey; and his judgement of Wait is trenchant
and borne out by the text.

Whereas the crew generally tries to support and console
Jimmy, participating in his lies, uncertain of whether he is
dying or shamming, Singleton says curtly: 'You can't help him;
die he must'; and indeed Jimmy dies on the voyage. More
verifiably, Singleton offers a detailed superstitious explanation
of Jimmy's case, although, like traditional oracles of classical
literature and folk-tale, he speaks brokenly and enigmatically,
in a form of trance:

> He chewed words, mumbled behind tangled white hairs; incomprehensible
> and exciting, like an oracle behind a veil... — 'Stop ashore—sick—Instead—
> bringing all this head wind. Afraid. The sea will have her own. — Die in sight
> of land. Always so. They know it — long passage — more days, more dollars.
> — You keep quiet. — What do you want? Can't help him.' He seemed to
> wake up from a dream. 'You can't help yourselves', he said, austerely.
>
> (*NN*, 130.)

Thus, Singleton's claims are these. James Wait belongs to a
particular class of malingerers. He should have stayed ashore
to die, for his kind is inimical to the sea and ships, and likes
retarded passages, knowing that pay is by the day. He brings
bad luck to the ship, for he brings adverse headwinds and is in
various ways an impediment, a burden. Yet, although he has
power to delay the voyage, he cannot stop it, any more than he
can prevent the arrival of the death he fears. The superstition
further claims that when at last land is sighted, then he will die,
and the ship will no longer be retarded.

The superstitious analysis and predictions are fulfilled in specific detail by the narrative. James Wait proves indeed burdensome to the ship; and the voyage is repeatedly beset by difficulties and perils: a storm which turns the vessel on her side and threatens to sink her; a near-mutiny, occasioned by Jimmy's malingering, by Donkin's subversive rhetoric and the crew's sentimentality (and by a brief flaw in the captain, who for a while is himself moved by sentimental pity for Jimmy's plight); and a long calm spell in which the ship seems, for weeks on end, to be doomed to make no progress. Eventually, land is sighted — the island of Flores, first seen at evening; and within a few hours, during the subsequent night, Jimmy dies, as the superstition had foretold. Even after death, Jimmy, true to his character as one who had feared to face death and particularly feared burial in the inimical sea, seems to cling to the ship: his enshrouded body apparently refuses to slide into the waters but lingers on the plank, waiting even there, until the most affectionate and sentimental of his friends, Belfast, cries: 'Jimmy, be a man!...... Go, Jimmy! — Jimmy, go! Go!', and touches the corpse's head, whereupon, as if responsive to his exorcistic appeal, the body 'reluctantly' but rapidly slides off into the depths. Again, as if this had indeed been a supernatural burden, the ship then rolls and her sails flap.

Furthermore, as though Wait had indeed wielded supernatural power over the ship's progress and the very elements, immediately after his corpse has gone overboard, the wind rises: the sails start 'fluttering', the master cries 'Breeze coming', and from then onward the ship makes rapid progress — 'she skimmed low over the blue sea like a great tired bird speeding to its nest' — until she reaches harbour in London.

Thus, the supernatural theme of the haunted ship is no mere fantasy in the imagination of a senile character. It becomes a plot-sequence: for narrative predictions based on the assumption of its validity are fulfilled. Whenever the events of the voyage may either refute or fulfil the superstitious prognostications, they fulfil them with complete consistency. Furthermore, it is not Singleton alone who voices the theme of haunting. His beliefs resonate and are amplified in the minds of the crew and, by a process of narratorial osmosis, in the mind of the ostensible narrator, whose views sometimes approximate in authority to those of an omniscient author. For example (and I quote at length here, bearing in mind critics' understandable bias towards the overt secular plot rather than this covert supernatural plot):

We all knew the old man's [i.e. Singleton's] ideas about Jimmy. They were unsettling, they caused pain; and, what was worse, they might have been true for all we knew. Only once did he condescend to explain them fully, but the impression was lasting. He said that Jimmy was the cause of head winds. Mortally sick men — he maintained — linger till the first sight of land, and then die; and Jimmy knew that the very first land would draw his life from him. It is so in every ship. Didn't we know it?..... We could not deny that it was strange. We felt uneasy..... [The ship] seemed to have forgotten the way home; she rushed to and fro, heading northwest, heading east; she ran backwards and forwards, distracted like a timid creature at the foot of a wall. Sometimes, as if tired to death, she would wallow languidly for a day in the smooth swell of an unruffled sea. All up the swinging masts the sails trashed furiously through the hot stillness of the calm. We were weary, hungry, thirsty; we commenced to believe Singleton, but with unshaken fidelity dissembled to Jimmy. We spoke to him with jocose allusiveness, like cheerful accomplices in a clever plot; but we looked to the westward over the rail with longing eyes for a sign of hope, for a sign of fair wind; even if its first breath should bring death to our reluctant Jimmy. In vain! The universe conspired with James Wait.

(142-3.)

Again, the covert plot is emphasised most explicitly at the time of Jimmy's death:

Singleton only was not surprised. 'Dead — is he? Of course,' he said, pointing at the island right abeam: for the calm still held the ship spell-bound within sight of Flores. Dead — of course. *He* wasn't surprised. Here was the land, and there, on the fore-hatch and waiting for the sailmaker — there was that corpse. Cause and effect.

(156.)

The text even confirms that the pressure in the barometer had begun to fall (a sign of imminent winds) during the night of Jimmy's death, and that the first breezes reach the ship precisely as Jimmy's body vanishes for ever beneath the waves:

Mr. Baker, perspiring abundantly, read out the last prayer in a deep rumour of excited men and fluttering sails. 'Amen!' he said in an unsteady growl, and closed the book.
'Square the yards!' thundered a voice above his head. All hands gave a

jump; one or two dropped their caps; Mr. Baker looked up surprised. The master, standing on the break of the poop, pointed to the westward. 'Breeze coming,' he said, 'Man the weather braces.'

(160.)

Another aspect of the supernatural theme which is fully endorsed by the text is that Jimmy has an uncanny ability to stir up trouble. He does so at the moment of his arrival, when he causes consternation and bewilderment merely by uttering his name, which is mistaken for an insubordinate command ('Wait!') and thus confuses the mate taking the roll-call. His ambiguous illness causes far more confusion and disorder than we may at first recognise: Belfast steals on his behalf; the crew constantly wrangles; he is the basis of the near-mutiny; and the very master weakens, in a way which accentuates dissension, when he pityingly confines Wait to his cabin: 'The notion came to me all at once, before I could think. Sorry for him..... Stand to it now, of course' (127). Even after death and before burial, Jimmy causes dissension:

Was it [i.e. the moment of his death] before or after 'that 'ere glass started down'? It was impossible to know, and it caused much contemptuous growling at one another. All of a sudden there was a great tumult forward. Pacific Knowles and good-tempered Davies had come to blows over it. The watch below interfered with spirit, and for ten minutes there was a noisy scrimmage round the hatch, where, in the balancing shade of the sails, Jimmy's body [was] wrapped up in a white blanket.....

(157.)

The details here, with the exception of the gallicism 'balancing' (for 'wavering'), are highly deliberate: even 'pacific' Knowles and 'good-tempered' Davies are reduced to fighting by Jimmy's death (so that their attempted verification of the lesser superstition unwittingly verifies the larger), and the ensuing 'noisy scrimmage' involving 'the whole watch below' takes place around the body, as though it were a supernatural source of disorder and strife.

Even the corpse's delay on the planks before sliding into the ocean is the cause of further dissension. The crew are variously angered, alarmed and distraught at the delay; subsequently the mate abuses the bosun for it, claiming that the bosun had forgotten to grease the planks, while the bosun in turn blames the others for having thrown all his tools overboard in their earlier successful quest to rescue Jimmy from his cabin — so again the blame for the trouble circles back to Wait's effect on the crew.

The supernatural theme blends with, and is largely supported by, the strong symbolic suggestions of the novel. I formulate the rule for covert plots generated by dynamic symbolism: to the extent that a work is symbolic, to the extent that the symbols interlink, and above all to the extent that narrative predictions based by the reader on the symbolic suggestions are fulfilled and not refuted within the text, the work is charged with a sense that metaphysical or supernatural forces influence the secular action.

Though written predominantly in a realistic mode, *The Nigger* is a strongly symbolic novel, and for most of the time the symbols consistently cohere in narrative patternings, although there are (notably towards the end of the work) some elements of tension or contradiction. Critics and commentators have often under-estimated the ways in which the text quite clearly and explicitly develops not one but two symbolic connotations of Jimmy's surname.[7] The one that is relatively conspicuous is, as we have seen, implicit in the fact that 'Wait' is homophonous with the imperative form of the verb meaning 'delay' or 'tarry' and with the noun meaning 'delay'. The opening scene, of the interrupted roll-call, makes this meaning quite explicit, and, as my paraphrase emphasised, it is predictive: for Wait is invested with power to delay the ship by thwarting its progress — he bears even the attributed power to interfere with meteorology by preventing favourable winds. With super-natural fidelity to his name, even after death he tarries on the planks before sliding from the ship; and that there is a secular explanation — a nail sticking up — does not refute the dramatisation of the supernatural: the secular and supernatural plots are maintained in parallel.

His surname, however, has a second symbolic connotation: it is homophonous also with 'weight', a burden, and the text repeatedly exploits this association, even to the point of making ironic and paradoxical jokes about it, as will happen again with the names 'Kurtz' (in *Heart of Darkness*) and 'Ransome' (in *The Shadow-Line*). Even though Wait is physically

light, being emaciated by consumption, he is symbolically like
a ton-weight or more:

> .....we started on our perilous journey over the main deck, dragging along
> with care that pitiful, that limp, that hateful burden. He was not very heavy,
> but had he weighed a ton he could not have been more awkward to handle.
> (72.)

Repeatedly the text emphasises this paradox that Jimmy is
physically remarkably light and symbolically remarkably
weighty:

> "Tain't his fault, is it?' argued Belfast, in a murmur; 'I've put him to bed...an'
> he ain't no heavier than an empty beef-cask.....'
> (131.)

> He was becoming immaterial like an apparition.....; and the fleshless head
> resembled a disinterred black skull.....He influenced the moral tone of our
> world as though he had it in his power to distribute honours, treasures, or
> pain; and he could give us nothing but his contempt. It was immense; it
> seemed to grow gradually larger, as his body day by day shrank a little more,
> while we looked.....He seemed unwilling to move, as if distrustful of his own
> solidity.
> (139-40.)

When the ship is turned over on her side during the storms
and nearly sinks, the text makes clear that the downward side
is that on which Wait is lurking in his cabin, as though he is the
weight threatening to drag the ship down. He is not only
morally but also, in symbolic terms, physically subversive,
since 'to subvert' means literally 'to turn under or below'. The
related 'coincidence' or fulfilled symbolic prediction is that
when he is rescued and dragged up from his cabin, the ship
subsequently rights herself. This supernatural relationship
between his symbolic weight and the apparently responsive
ship is again made explicit at the moment when his body at last
leaves the vessel:

> The ship rolled as if relieved of an unfair burden; the sails flapped.
> (160.)

Thus, at a symbolic level, the novel dramatises a contest
between the subversive force represented by Wait and the

virtuous force represented by the vessel. (Conrad often saw the activities of both sailing and swimming as analogous to the human quest for purposeful survival in an existence beset by isolation, death and chaos.) When the near-mutiny stemming from Wait and fomented by Donkin reaches its peak of violence, when Donkin has hurled a belaying-pin at the master, it is the ship which recalls men to their duty and dispels the atmosphere of imminent chaos; at a time when even the helmsman, attracted by the dissension, has committed the cardinal maritime sin of deserting the wheel:

> Meantime the helmsman, anxious to know what the row was about, had let go the wheel, and, bent double, ran with long, stealthy footsteps to the break of the poop. The *Narcissus,* left to herself, came up gently to the wind without anyone being aware of it. She gave a slight roll, and the sleeping sails woke suddenly, coming all together with a mighty flap against the masts.....The ship trembled from trucks to keel; the sails kept on rattling like a discharge of musketry; the chain sheets and loose shackles jingled aloft in a thin peal; the gin blocks groaned. It was as if an invisible hand had given the ship an angry shake to recall the men that peopled her decks to the sense of reality, vigilance, and duty. — 'Helm up!' cried the master, sharply.
>
> (124.)

'It was as if an invisible hand.....'. Whereas the overt plot of *The Nigger* can be described adequately in secular terms, the covert plot requires an act of the superstitious or religious imagination. Like other Modernist masterpieces of the period 1890-1930, *The Nigger* gratifies new scepticism while yet placating traditional pieties.

If the novel exploits the symbolic qualities of the name 'Wait', some symbolic quality is also, in this fictional context, gained by the name of Wait's main human antagonist, Singleton. Although 'Singleton' is a familiar surname, here contextual patterning and textual details elicit its connotations. As a common noun rather than a proper noun, its dictionary meaning is 'anything single' (e.g., 'a single card of its suit'); and Singleton is single in the sense of being the sole representative of the postulated older, less sophisticated and more reliable generation of seamen. He is singular, too, in his taciturn isolation from the more voluble crew-members and in the uncanny wisdom which he appears to possess. Thirdly, he has a 'singleness' of inner nature: against the 'doubleness' (ambiguity and duplicity) of James Wait, Singleton has a simple integrity: always reliable, always faithful to the call of duty, always truthful. The text stresses his simplicity and detachment: when he is first described, we are told that he, the oldest able seaman on the ship, 'sat apart on the deck':

> With his spectacles and a venerable white beard, he resembled a learned and savage patriarch, the incarnation of barbarian wisdom serene in the blasphemous turmoil of the world.
>
> (6.)

A detail which combines the realistic and the symbolic is that he needs spectacles when reading a book (which he holds at arm's-length); he does not need them when steering the ship. Plainly he is long-sighted; and his physical long sight (natural enough in a helmsman who, at fifty-seven, has served forty-five years at sea) is symbolic of his inner 'long sight': his ability to see into the natures of other people and to predict accurately the outcome of events.

Most of the other names in the book (Allistoun, Baker, Creichton, Donkin, Craik, Podmore, Charley, Davies, Knowles) appear to have the inconsequentiality of everyday reality. In Conrad's fiction, as in Hardy's, the general ratio of symbolic to non-symbolic proper nouns seems to be approximately 1:10. What does emerge as significant in respect of this crew, however, is that Conrad has striven to emphasise the cosmopolitan aspect. The captain, Allistoun, is a Scot. Baker and Creichton, the first and second mates, are both English, but from contrasting social backgrounds, with Creichton representing the 'gentry', the upper or upper-middle classes, while Baker represents the 'commoners' or lower-middle classes; he senses that Creichton will become a master, given his social background, while he himself will not. Donkin could be termed a representative of the guttersnipe *Lumpenproletariat*: a thieving ex-convict from the East End of London. Wait comes from St Kitt's (St Christopher's Island in the West Indies). Craik, as his nickname 'Belfast' shows, comes from Northern Ireland (or, more accurately for that time, northern Ireland). There is a Welshman, Davies; a 'Russian Finn', Wamibo; and two unnamed Scandinavians. This strong emphasis on the international composition of the crew has the obvious purpose of strengthening the symbolic import of the narrative by increasing the reader's illusion that he is looking at a 'microcosm', illustrative not of one or two nationalities but of human nature generally.

Of course, sailing ships in the late nineteenth century often did have international crews. The actual *Narcissus* on which Conrad sailed held a Canadian, several Norwegians, two Swedes, a Welshman from Cardiff, an Irishman from Belfast, at least two Scots, a Channel Islander, and numerous Englishmen, including at least one from London. What is noticeable, however, is that in *The Nigger of the 'Narcissus'* Conrad has chosen not only to present a crew markedly more cosmopolitan than those in his other sea-tales (more than the crews in *The Shadow-Line*, 'The Secret Sharer' and *Chance*, for example) but also to stress that socially microcosmic quality. The ship is likened to 'a small planet':

> She had her own future; she was alive with the lives of those beings who trod her decks; like that earth which had given her up to the sea, she had an intolerable load of regrets and hopes.....
>
> Youthful faces, bearded faces, dark faces: faces serene, or faces moody, but all akin with the brotherhood of the sea.....

As for the captain:

> He, the ruler of that minute world, seldom descended from the Olympian heights of his poop.
>
> (29-31.)

Such idealising rhetoric indicates that though the main symbolic narrative of Jimmy's (and Donkin's) threat to the ship is consistent, the endeavour on Conrad's part to give extreme symbolic force to the ship as microcosm does produce some elements of inconsistency and even contradiction, mainly because Conrad attempts to dramatise the ship's world both as *better than* the land-world and as a *microcosm of* that land-world. This is one of several respects in which *The Nigger of the 'Narcissus'* is an interestingly erratic, unstable work. The narrative viewpoint shifts inconsistently (i.e., with conspicuous rather than conventionally inconspicuous inconsistency), the narrator now being located among the officers, now apparently being identified as one of the ordinary seamen, and now being the customary mobile 'omniscient authorial observer'; there are numerous shifts between 'I' and 'we' and 'they' as the viewpoint changes. Similarly, there are some marked inconsistencies in moral and philosophical viewpoint. On the one hand, the *Narcissus* is a microcosm of the earth, presenting, as in a test-case isolated for clear examination, the faults, strengths and dangers of humanity at large: 'like the earth, she was unconscious, fair to see — and condemned by men to an ignoble fate' (30). On the other hand, as we have noted, the tale dramatises the *Narcissus* as a *contrast* to the shore-world: largely because there is no exact counterpart ashore for the elementally-tested traditional discipline and co-operative labour which such a voyage requires. We are told that the sea imposes 'a brotherhood' on all the crew, 'all with the same attentive expression of eyes, carefully watching the compass or the sails' (30); but against this is offered the claim that whereas Singleton's generation of seamen was relatively reliable, the new generation is relatively sophisticated and unreliable; and secondly, it is clear that on this voyage the 'brotherhood' is a particularly unruly one. ('Fraternity means nothing unless the Cain-Abel business', Conrad remarked in a letter to Cunninghame Graham.)[8] The ship herself is a beautiful craft, pure and redeeming, yet also a vessel in servitude to that commerce which is 'the sordid inspiration of her pilgrimage' (30). And if the presentation of the ship is mildly ambivalent, the symbolic presentation of England is markedly ambivalent; and the latter ambivalence stems partly from Conrad's double background (as a British master-mariner and as a scion of the Polish gentry with its hostility to commercialism) and partly from his sense of the immediate readership.

The symbolism of the *The Nigger of the 'Narcissus'* (particularly in its more conservative political aspects) may well have been influenced by the fact that while Conrad was writing this novel it was offered to W.E. Henley, who promptly published it as a serial in his *New Review*. Henley was a friend of Kipling, and a staunch jingoist; and Conrad's heavily emotive description of England as the 'ship mother of fleets and nations' seems largely calculated to flatter the patriotism of Henley and his circle (which was known as the 'Henley Regatta'); indeed, the description approaches the rhetoric of one of Henley's own poems, 'What have I done for you, / England, my England?'. That poem's final verse reads:

> Mother of Ships whose might,
>     England, my England,
> Is the fierce old Sea's delight,
>     England, my own,
> Chosen daughter of the Lord,
> Spouse-in-Chief of the ancient sword,
> There's the menace of the Word
>     In the Song on your bugles blown,
>         England—
> Out of heaven on your bugles blown![9]

Conrad echoes not only the idea but also the now-embarrassing tone of incantatory and exclamatory fervour when he describes England, near the close of the novel:

A great ship! For ages had the ocean battered in vain her enduring sides; she was there when the world was vaster and darker, when the sea was great and mysterious, and ready to surrender the prize of fame to audacious men. A ship mother of fleets and nations! The great flagship of the race; stronger than the storms! and anchored in the open sea.

(163.)

It is not surprising that Henley was enthusiastic about publishing *The Nigger*.[10] In spite of this fervent tribute to the 'ship mother', however, the subsequent pages describing the landfall emphasise that the urban England of the dockside is squalid and oppressive. The very breeze is 'impure', the river is 'murky'; 'A mad jumble of begrimed walls loomed up vaguely in the smoke'; the walls are, unsurprisingly, 'soulless'; and as the ship enters their shadow, 'a swarm of strange men..... took possession of her in the name of the sordid earth. She had ceased to live' (164-5). Though the sunshine eventually falls 'like a gift of grace on the mud of the earth', it shines particularly on 'the stained front of the Mint', a 'palace' of finance. Here, in a sordid London, Donkin is at home, while most of the seamen seem 'lost, alone, forgetful, and doomed'. Thus, the ship is not only a fine emanation of a great nation but also a pure creature sullied and made moribund by the commercial urbanism of the industrial world which England signally represents.

Any survey of the covert and symbolic aspects of this novel should take note of the very name of that ship. Conrad had sailed on a vessel actually called *Narcissus*; but his reason for retaining the name (instead of modifying it or inventing a new one, as generally happens with other vessels described in his fiction) is evidently that its symbolic suggestions were thematically valuable. At the centre of the tale's moral and political allegory is the distinction between, on the one hand, sentimental pseudo-solidarity, which resembles altruism but is really vicarious self-pity ('the latent egoism of tenderness to suffering'), and which therefore can be divisive and destructive; and, on the other hand, true solidarity, entailing respect for discipline, duty and tradition: such true solidarity may seem ruthless to individual cases, but it is, in the long run, altruistic, for it ensures the survival of the community. In the ancient Greek legend, Narcissus was a beautiful youth who fell in love with his own reflection in a pool, thinking it to be a beautiful nymph; he pined and died. By reminding us of the legend, the ship's name reminds us of the danger of mistaking for altruism what is really a reflected narcissism. This theme is illustrated in the novel in a variety of ways: Wait is self-centred and evasive of truth, a moral narcissist; Donkin, who purports to be concerned for the men and their rights, is seeking his own ends: he even (in a private 'covert plot') robs the dying Jimmy of his savings; and, when ashore, his contempt for the crew breaks out: ' "I 'ave friends well off..... Ye're the scum of the world. Work and starve!" ' Repeatedly those who conspire to help Jimmy are shown to be deluded sentimentalists who imperil the general welfare, cause dissension and endanger the ship. In pitying Jimmy, they are pitying a reflection of their own mortality. Generally, therefore, the moral and political tone of *The Nigger* is markedly more ruthless and conservative than is that of Conrad's superior works, notably *Heart of Darkness* and *Nostromo*; and, in *The Nigger*, even moderate reformers, like the followers of Samuel Plimsoll who saved seamen's lives, are derided.[11]

We have seen that the covert 'supernatural' plot of *The Nigger of the 'Narcissus'* is given resonance by the symbolic terms which in turn blend with the 'realistic' action. There are numerous ironic and 'scaling-down' effects, but they do not demolish or dispel the metaphysical dimension. For example, Singleton, the oracular and patriarchal, is also seen as a scruffy old man who on shore leads an alcoholic existence in which he is unable to distinguish day from night, and who is regarded by the pay-office clerk as a 'disgusting old brute'; but though this anchors the characterisation to the familiar mundane particularity of the everyday world, it does not impugn but makes more credible the Singleton who is possessor of a kind of wisdom which the sea-voyage liberates.

The supernatural plot derives some strength from the Christian tradition, with its concepts of grace, the tempter, the Fall, and the nobility of unappreciated self-sacrifice for others; but it is differentiated from Christianity by being less specifically doctrinal and by drawing on myth, folk-tale and marine legend. Against Singleton's oracular and accurate superstitions is set as contrast the grotesque Christianity (Calvinistic, offering hell-fires for the many and salvation for the Elect) offered by Podmore, who is seen as a half-crazed and partly-disruptive figure. And in its narratorial references to religion, the text varies between apparent endorsement and scepticism.

> The true peace of God begins at any spot a thousand miles from the nearest land; and when He sends there the messengers of His might it is not in terrible wrath against crime, presumption, and folly, but paternally, to chasten simple hearts — ignorant hearts that know nothing of life, and beat undisturbed by envy or greed.
>
> (31.)

That the 'simple hearts' on the ship actually prove to be disturbed by both envy and greed exposes the hollowness of this passage, whose apparent piety appears in retrospect as rhetorical scene-setting by means of metaphorical clichés. Podmore's faith is described as 'the infernal fog of his supreme conceit' (116), and the following passage seems to imply that religious sages who talk of heaven are in fact talking of vacuity:

> the weary succession of days and nights tainted by the obstinate clamour of sages, demanding bliss and an empty heaven, is redeemed at last by the vast silence of pain and labour.....
>
> (90.)

When the same paragraph also invokes 'the eternal pity that

commands toil to be hard and unceasing', the terminology is religious but the import is secular: hard work prevents reflection on life's woes and on death; perhaps ignorance is bliss, and it is folly to be wise.

In a literary text, the criterion of the value of any narrative or thematic patterning should be its quality of embodiment as fiction: its richness, vividness, intelligence and persuasiveness as a searching rendition of life. If we apply this test to the relationship of the supernatural plot and the secular plot, we see that generally the novel is most effective where both are in balance, both working together. The most memorably rich passages include the opening, when Wait first emerges from the night to disrupt the roll-call; the storm at sea; and the 're-birth' of Wait from his half-submerged cabin. On all these occasions the particularities of realistic detail are numerous and persuasive, while the symbolic dimension lends evocative and suggestive power, magnifying potential significances. The novel's weaknesses occur when rhetorical insistence on signifi-cance is too strident and patent, whether this be in that passage celebrating England as 'ship mother' or in the emotive insistence that Donkin is corrupt and unsavoury: in such cases complexity is being sacrificed for the sake of specious force which entails simplification.

It has recently been argued by a black critic that the most obnoxious aspect of The Nigger of the 'Narcissus' is the presence of a form of covert plot which is invisible to white readers (because it matches their prejudices) but highly conspicuous to black readers: a plot which, by making Wait the mysterious source of strife and disorder, demonstrates white racial superiority. 'Through him', says Eugene B. Redmond, 'Conrad and the critical establishment practice racism under the banner of realism and symbolism.'[12] In the case of The Nigger of the 'Narcissus', I think there is some truth in this accusation. The contrast offered by the more radical, sceptical and humane Heart of Darkness and Nostromo does emphasise the sometimes recalcitrant combination of conservatism, mystification and severity in the earlier novel. As the text shows (' "You wouldn't call me nigger if I wasn't half dead, you Irish beggar!" ' [79-80]), Conrad knew that the term 'nigger' was pejorative,[13] and though the novel's title can be defended as, say, reportage of

the kind of phrase that a white seaman would naturally use
when telling the story, elaborate feats of ingenuity are required
to defend the notorious statement about

a head powerful and misshapen with a tormented and flattened face — a
face pathetic and brutal: the tragic, the mysterious, the repulsive mask of a
nigger's soul.

(18.)

I do not intend to offer such feats of ingenuity, for I think that
even the racist aspects of this ambiguous statement may
represent what Conrad occasionally felt. What matters is that it
was not what he felt when he was writing more intelligently.
And the case for prejudice in *The Nigger of the 'Narcissus'* fails in
one obvious respect. The worst character in the book is not
Jimmy but the white Londoner, Donkin, who is treacherous,
malicious and vicious: a predator, compared with whom
Jimmy is sympathetic.[14] Furthermore Jimmy is subversive not
because of his blackness but because of a singular and non-
racial characteristic: he is ambiguous, in being a consumptive
who lies about the extent of his illness; and thus he belongs to a
large family of subversively ambiguous figures in Conrad's
fiction, most of whom happen to be white.[15] Colour and 'race'
are never reliable guides to the vices or virtues of Conradian
characters.

## (ii) HEART OF DARKNESS

### (a) The Faustian Narrative
*Heart of Darkness* was based on Conrad's own journey through
the Belgian Congo in 1890, and it is partly autobiographical
and historical: locations, characters encountered, itinerary,
and the moral and psychological observations often accord
quite closely with what we know of the Congo from Conrad's
Journal and letters, his essays, and from contemporary
reports. Naturally, when writing the story he also changed
events so as to add excitement and suspense to the narrative
and to extend its significance: for example, there is no
evidence that Mr Kurtz's real-life counterpart, Georges Antoine
Klein,[16] was guilty of the dramatic forms of corruption

attributed to Kurtz. The story was further enriched and modified by Conrad's incorporation of a variety of motifs from religion, folk-tale, legend and literary tradition generally: such allusions give symbolic strength, and help to make the work a discussion not simply of Belgian imperialism or of European imperialism at large but of civilisation and the very nature of what it is to be a civilised being.

As so often in Conrad's work, the terminology is sometimes equivocally metaphorical: when he, or his Marlow, talks of wraiths, phantoms, shades or a pact with darkness, this vocabulary may appear a metaphoric (and often ironic) way of referring to the secular by invoking the apparently non-secular; but the effect of so many such references, in the contexts he provides, is occasionally to generate a literal element: we sense that there is validity in considering Kurtz as one who has literally made a pact with forces of evil. The most important 'supernatural' covert plot is certainly the Faustian.

Conrad read very widely among the classics of European literature; almost certainly, he knew Christopher Marlowe's works (and just possibly the dramatist's name suggested the name of Conrad's narrator and recurrent character, Charles Marlow),[17] and the internal evidence of *Heart of Darkness* indicates that he knew Marlowe's play *Doctor Faustus*. In any case, Conrad was certainly familiar with the legend of Faust, which has had so many literary and musical manifestations since its early appearance as the German *Faustbuch*. Famous nineteenth-century versions included Goethe's *Faust*, Gounod's opera *Faust* and Berlioz' opera *The Damnation of Faust*. (Since Conrad, the literary tradition has been maintained by such diverse novels as Thomas Mann's *Doctor Faustus,* Klaus Mann's *Mephisto* and Robert Nye's *Faust*.) Conrad once commended to his readers what he termed 'the magnificent Invocation' by the French occultist, Sar Péladan. This is interesting in its linkage (which anticipates Jung's)[18] of the Faustian and Oedipal legends; for Kurtz resembles both Faust and Oedipus to the extent of being a person of some brilliance who, by challenging the unknown, seeks to bring great benefits but instead brings disaster to himself. Here is Conrad's translation of Péladan's 'Invocation':

'O Nature, indulgent Mother, forgive! Open your arms to the son, prodigal and weary.

I have attempted to tear asunder the veil you have hung to conceal from us the pain of life, and I have been wounded by the mystery... Œdipus, half way to finding the word of the enigma, young Faust, regretting already the simple life, the life of the heart, I come back to you repentant, reconciled, O gentle deceiver!'[19]

(NLL, 70.)

The supernatural covert plot of *Heart of Darkness* seems to me to derive most strongly from Marlowe's *Doctor Faustus*, though it also draws on the traditional motif of the Infernal Journey (which has its fullest presentations in Virgil's *Aeneid*, Book VI, and in Dante's *Inferno*); and it acquires other elements from the vast Christian and Romantic paradox of 'the virtue of evil' and from racial ideas current in Conrad's day.

It will be recalled that in Marlowe's play, Faustus is reputedly a man of immense talents in a wide variety of fields, held in awe and reverence by his colleagues and students. He seeks ambitiously to extend his power by magical means, resorts to black magic, summons Lucifer's agent, Mephistopheles ('Mephostophilis' in early texts), and makes a pact. According to the pact's terms, Faustus for twenty-four years gains Mephistopheles as his servant to effect all his wishes; in return, Faustus surrenders his body and soul to Satan, and thus pledges his own damnation. One of the apparent inconsistencies in Marlowe's text is the discrepancy between what the pact affirms and what the subsequent dramatic interest suggests. Dramatic interest depends on suspense, which in this case is generated largely by our hopes that Faustus may repent and be saved; and these hopes are kept alive throughout the main action (by, for example, the intervention of the Good Angel and the virtuous Old Man, who both assure Faustus that his salvation is still possible); yet the terms of the pact strongly imply that Faustus is damned from the moment of signing it: for its first condition is that henceforth 'Faustus may be a spirit in form and substance' — 'spirit' here meaning 'devil'. Another possible inconsistency for the legally-minded is that in the action Faustus appears to seal his fate not when he signs the pact but when he subsequently commits the sin of demoniality—

fornication with a devil. At his behest, Mephistopheles summons up a devil in the shape of Helen of Troy; Faustus, delighted, embraces her, taking her as his paramour.

> Sweet Helen, make me immortal with a kiss.
> Her lips suck forth my soul: see where it flies.[20]

This amatory conceit has appalling irony for the theological reader or hearer: in committing the sin of demoniality, Faustus is gaining vile mortality rather than blissful immortality: her lips indeed suck forth his soul — to damnation. Appropriately, it is immediately after this embrace that the Old Man says it is now too late for Faustus to be saved, and in the following scene even the Good Angel ceases to plead. Faustus's achievements by magic, which he and others, like the Duke and Duchess of Vanholt, deem to be so splendid (but which Benvolio enviously begrudges), often in the play seem specious or tawdry. And eventually, in an ecstasy of terror and horror, recognising too late the folly of his pact, Faustus is carried down to hell-fires. The Chorus then pronounces the moral of the tale:

> Cut is the branch that might have grown full straight,
> And burnèd is Apollo's laurel bough,
> That sometime grew within this learned man.
> Faustus is gone. Regard his hellish fall,
> Whose fiendful fortune may exhort the wise
> Only to wonder at unlawful things,
> Whose deepness doth entice such forward wits
> To practise more than heavenly power permits.

As my paraphrase has been calculated to suggest (even by the references to envious Benvolio and the theme of specious achievement), the analogies between Marlowe's Faustus and Marlow's Kurtz are numerous, and some appear to be clearly pointed in Conrad's narrative. The reader will notice that behind both protagonists, like an archetype engendering later ectypes, stands the Christian legend of Lucifer. (In Marlowe's play, 'Lucifer' is consistently used as the Devil's cast-name.) Lucifer, whose name means 'The Light-bearer', was once the brightest of the heavenly angels; but, moved by jealousy of God's power, he conspired against God; in the war in heaven, he was defeated, and was cast down to Hell, where he rules in titular irony as the Prince of Darkness. Conrad's tale has a strong and heavily ironic theme of 'light-bearers heading into darkness': from the opening description of sunset on the Thames to the glimpse of Marlow's face briefly illuminated in the flare of a match, images of the engulfment of light by obscurity are repeatedly offered. Explorers and colonisers are termed men 'bearing the sword, and often the torch, messengers of the might within the land, bearers of a spark from the sacred fire' ($Y$ 47). Kurtz's painting depicts a blindfolded figure carrying a torch into the dark. Recurrently appears the imagery of white against blackness, fire against night, light turning to darkness. And Kurtz himself is ostensibly a Lucifer, a light-bearer: his report expresses his belief that white men come to Africans 'in the nature of supernatural beings — we approach them with the might as of a deity' and should 'exert a power of good practically unbounded'; and his eloquence is 'the pulsating stream of light, or the deceitful flow from the heart of an impenetrable darkness'. Like Lucifer, this bright adventurer driven by pride has his downfall, though one in which he indeed becomes a Prince of Darkness — a despotic ruler over a savage tribe in the heart of darkest Africa, in what is described as an 'infernal' setting of death and torment. If the name 'Lucifer' proved ironic, so did the name 'Faustus', which means 'fortunate, happy, blessed', and so does the name 'Kurtz', which means 'short' but applies to a tall man ('He looked at least seven feet long')[21] with immense ambitions and a very long reach.

Like Marlowe's Faustus, Kurtz is a 'universal genius', immensely talented and promising, according to various friends and acquaintances (the Intended, the journalist, the organist, the company's official in Belgium, and the Russian 'harlequin'). Like Faustus, he thirsts impatiently for power; and like Faustus, he has made, the text suggests, a pact with Satanic powers, gaining gratification at the expense of his soul. 'He had taken a high seat among the devils of the land — I mean literally', says Marlow. 'I take it, no fool ever made a bargain for his soul with the devil'. Kurtz is an 'initiated wraith'; the wilderness has 'beguiled his unlawful soul beyond the bounds of permitted aspirations'. (116, 117, 144.) When

Kurtz seeks to return to his tribe, he crawls towards 'a black figure..... It had horns..... it looked fiend-like enough' (143). 'But both the diabolic love and the unearthly hate of the mysteries it had penetrated fought for the possession of that soul' (147).

Thus the metaphoric rhetoric not only expresses a Faustian theme but also generates a covert Faustian plot which plays against the secular plot of corruption and madness in modern Africa. Kurtz, like Faust, has been tempted to make a diabolic pact, sacrificing his soul for worldly gratification. If Faustus's fate was sealed when he embraced a devil who appeared in the guise of the seductive Helen, Kurtz has embraced the spirit of the wilderness in the form of his black mistress: the wilderness has 'loved him, embraced him, got into his veins, and sealed his soul to his own', and the black mistress is presented (in similarly inferior 'Conradese') as an incarnation of that wilderness:

.....the immense wilderness, the colossal body of the fecund and mysterious life seemed to look at her, pensive, as though it had been looking at the image of its own tenebrous and passionate soul.....

She stood looking at us without a stir, and like the wilderness itself, with an air of brooding over an inscrutable purpose.

(136.)

The phrasing deliberately echoes that of the now-notorious sentence describing the jungle's stillness: 'It was the stillness of an implacable force brooding over an inscrutable intention' (93). Although such polysyllabic privative adjectives ('inscrutable', 'implacable') have their clear function in a tale about men's encounter with various kinds of darkness, including whatever may be opaque to language and intelligence, they lose force through repetition. Conrad's imaginative energy is strongly sceptical, particularly in *Heart of Darkness*, and it is a relatively superficial imagination that here emphasises the metaphysical plot; but the Faustian parallels seem to be worked out in considerable detail.

Like Faustus, the declining Kurtz oscillates in attitude between pride in his achievements and disgust at the plight into which his ambitions have led him; and Faustus's last speech of horror, as hell gapes, has its counterpart in that crucially enigmatic pronouncement by Kurtz, 'The horror! The horror!', which apparently refers, among other things, both to the horror of the corruption into which he has fallen and to horrors looming before him in the grave — 'he had looked over the brink'. In the 'B Text' of *Doctor Faustus*, the Epilogue's epitome is preceded by a final scene in which Faustus's former colleagues emphasise his earlier brilliance and great potential; and after Kurtz's death, *Heart of Darkness* provides the sequence set in his homeland in which former colleagues emphasise Kurtz's promising qualities.

Thus, as we have seen, *Heart of Darkness* preserves certain salient features of the Faust drama: the principle of the evil pact, the cutting of 'the branch that might have grown full straight', the sense that the bargain has been deceptive and brings largely illusory triumphs, the sense of psychomachia (the struggle for a soul — most explicit in the tale when Marlow persuades Kurtz to abandon his return to the horned shapes in the jungle), and the linkage of an irredeemable fall with the succumbing to sexual temptation. Both works dramatise the challenge that the criterion of ontological fulness makes to the criterion of orthodox morality. Conrad makes at least one explicit reference to the legend, when the manager's assistant is described as a 'papier-maché Mephistopheles' (81), which implies (with ironic humour) that the manager himself is the counterpart to the Devil; and since, as the covert murder-plot shows, the manager is largely responsible for Kurtz's long isolation in the region of temptation and thus for Kurtz's final decline into death, this too is partly appropriate.

Marlowe's *Doctor Faustus* is greater in potential than in actuality, greater in promise than in what it presents. All the surviving early texts are unsatisfactory: the 'A' series (1604-11) offers a play of jerky brevity; the 'B' series (1616-31) is longer but contains much drossy material. In both series, the poetry varies between the admirable and the wooden; in both, the comic action threatens to debase the main action: for example, Mephistopheles, who intially speaks with sinister dignity and some theological sophistication, is debased to a farcical figure when compelled to appear at the behest of Rafe and Robin. Both 'A' and 'B' texts probably vary considerably from what Marlowe originally wrote: at least two other writers (Birde and

Rowley) were paid by Henslowe to augment the script, and there may well have been local playhouse accretions. In performance over the years, the play seems to have evolved from 'The Tragicall History of Doctor Faustus' into 'The Doctor Faustus Show', with tricks and illusions to employ all the props in the playhouse stores, from horns and wax grapes to fireworks and a false leg. Intermittently, however, the potential of the play is strongly suggested. The work is, among other things, about the conflict between the claims of intense experience in this world and the claims of morality and religion; about the new Renaissance sense of proud selfhood, balanced against traditional exhortations to humility and contempt for the world; and about the fear which the book of Genesis had long ago defined, that to eat the apple of the tree of knowledge is to eat a forbidden fruit which will taste of ashes and bring corruption and death.

To this potential, *Heart of Darkness* does magnificent justice. It is Conrad's richest and greatest work. It has its flaws, however, and among critics there is some consensus that the flaws are closely related to those elements which I have defined as the 'Faustian' plot-elements. F.R. Leavis, Terry Eagleton and other commentators have condemned the attempts by Conrad to magnify the 'metaphysical' significance of Kurtz's plight.[22] As we have seen, it is true that the texture of the descriptive prose is often least reliable and most suspiciously incantatory when the notion of the occult and of the sinister pact with diabolic forces is being suggested, and Conrad himself felt that he might have erred in making Kurtz 'too symbolic'.[23] This remains true even though it is understandably the case that those critics who themselves are sceptics in religious matters are happiest with the relatively sceptical Conrad and express resistance when Conrad modulates towards apparent endorsement of the supernatural. Nevertheless, although the Faustian theme is weakest when most melodramatically explicit, its implications extend into every part of the tale and underlie the most vivid, telling and effective of the scenes. Whether the reader recalls the French man-of-war shelling the coast, the chain-gang with its swinging bights, the wasteful havoc of the outer station or the moribund figures in the grove of death, the Faustian theme of false power achieved at the price of destruction and death, the theme of the hubris of the arrogant and soul-destroying quest to conquer the earth, is being maintained. The tale is not just an indictment of Belgian, or European, imperialism; it is a dramatisation of the ways in which civilised man generally may be in the grip of a desire to know and to conquer which in the long run inflicts destruction on the environment and self-destruction on the moral nature of that civilisation itself. At the most effective scenes of the narrative, the covert metaphysical plot blends with the overt secular plot, and the symbolic implications are grounded in close observation of the plausibly familiar.

*(b) The Double and the Haunting*
The theme of the Double (or *Doppelgänger*) is commonly encountered in Romantic and post-Romantic writing: it is an obvious way of dramatising in characters those divisions and paradoxes which may be widespread in a given cultural phase; and its effects on characterisation resemble those of Janiformity on the general nature of a text. Famous literary treatments of the theme of the Double include William Godwin's *Caleb Williams*, Mary Shelley's *Frankenstein*, Poe's 'William Wilson', Melville's *Moby Dick*, Dostoyevsky's *The Double*, Stevenson's *Dr. Jekyll and Mr. Hyde* and Wilde's *The Picture of Dorian Gray*. The conventions of the 'Double' narrative are these: Centrally, the narrative presents an uncanny symbiosis or interdependence of two ostensibly contrasting characters who may prove to be aspects of one being or entity. The relationship is one both of hostility and dependence. The two characters may interchange the rôles of pursuer and pursued, victimiser and victim. They are repeatedly drawn together despite a variety of barriers. Their perils coincide, and it is sometimes the case that death for one entails death or near-death for the other. A link with the Faustian theme is that the antagonistic division has often been engendered by the pursuit of forbidden knowledge or power.

The application of this pattern to *Heart of Darkness* is clear. Marlow feels uncanny fascination for, and a kind of complicity with, Kurtz. Both are men of ideals, intelligence and imagination; both belong, it is said, to the 'gang of virtue' in Africa, and seem to be differentiated by talents and outlook from the mass of the 'pilgrims', who are dominated by unimaginative avarice or unreflective service of the Company. Marlow seeks Kurtz and is drawn to him in spite of dangers and impediments; after Kurtz's death he feels he is being pursued and virtually haunted by him. Though Kurtz has become corrupt, Marlow is fascinated by the corruption. As we have noted, it is a convention of 'Double' literature that death for one of the pair entails death or near-death for the other: and not only is the rescue of the dying Kurtz perilous for Marlow, but after Kurtz has died and been buried, Marlow, touched with fever on the journey, undergoes a nearly-mortal illness and breakdown. Just as Kurtz haunts Marlow's reflections before their meeting, so Kurtz posthumously haunts him: when Marlow enters the Intended's house,

> The vision seemed to enter the house with me — the stretcher, the phantom-bearers, the wild crowd of obedient worshippers, the gloom of the forests, the glitter of the reach between the murky bends, the beat of the drum, regular and muffled like the beating of a heart — the heart of a conquering darkness. It was a moment of triumph for the wilderness, an invading and vengeful rush which, it seemed to me, I would have to keep back alone for the salvation of another soul..... I rang the bell before a mahogany door on the first floor, and while I waited he seemed to stare at me out of the glassy panel — stare with that wide and immense stare embracing, condeming, loathing all the universe. I seemed to hear the whispered cry, 'The horror! The horror!'
>
> (155-6.)

If I.A. Richards was correct in dividing a metaphor into a literal 'tenor' and a figurative 'vehicle',[24] the allusion here to 'the salvation of another soul' can be regarded as a metaphor whose literal tenor is quite secular (the preservation of the Intended's faith in Kurtz and thus in life) and whose figurative vehicle is merely a hyperbolic intensifier of that secular sense. But in fact the covert plot's theme of 'losing one's soul' provides a context which here lends an additional literal force to the religious phrasing; just as, in the quoted passage, 'a conquering darkness' connotes not only the wilderness, the unknown, the sinister and the corrupt, but also metaphysical evil. The 'Double' theme is interestingly maintained when Kurtz 'seemed to stare at [Marlow] out of the glassy panel': for the implication is that Marlow's own reflection resembles Kurtz's face: as in the Double tradition, the 'haunting' is symbiotic. Repeatedly during the interview with the Intended, there is a sense of Kurtz's presence — evoked not merely through Marlow's memories but also through graphic details: the Intended stretches out her arms as though to the Kurtz she loves, imitating unawares the gesture of the black woman; and the very piano in her room has dark gleams 'like a sombre and polished sarcophagus'. Marlow claims that he 'laid the ghost of [Kurtz's] gifts with a lie' — the lie to the Intended that Kurtz died faithful to her; but it is inadequate as exorcism, for it still extends Kurtz's empire of falsehood and his power over the girl; and Marlow, in the very act of telling his tale years later, is still extending the haunting power of Kurtz. The dying trader had been emaciated and hollow-faced, a gaunt spectre amid darkness; and Marlow, illuminated by the flare of a match as he tells his tale, reveals a 'lean face....., worn, hollow, with downward folds and dropped eyelids' (114). When Marlow had found Kurtz, the latter 'was very little more than a voice' (115), and now, as Marlow recalls him, he himself in the darkness is 'no more to us than a voice' (83). Kurtz was celebrated for his charismatic eloquence: and this is the quality that Marlow too possesses, as his hearers listen so spellbound that they miss the awaited turn of the tide.

## (iii) 'THE SECRET SHARER'

Against the secular plot of this tale plays a supernatural plot, and at the intermediate level where the two blend lies the motif of the uncanny Double.

The elements which evoke supernatural possibilities are these. First, the initial appearance of Leggatt as an apparently headless corpse:

I saw at once something elongated and pale floating very close to the ladder. Before I could form a guess a faint flash of phosphorescent light, which seemed to issue suddenly from the naked body of a man, flickered in the sleeping water with the elusive, silent play of summer lightning in a night sky. With a gasp I saw revealed to my stare a pair of feet, the long legs, a broad livid back immersed right up to the neck in a greenish cadaverous glow.

One hand, awash, clutched the bottom rung of the ladder. He was complete but for the head. A headless corpse!

(*TLAS*, 97.)

Of course, Leggatt appears headless only because his head is concealed by the shadow of the ship's side under the night sky (the 'headless corpse' is another instance of the second, erroneous stage of delayed decoding); but this appearance establishes, along with such details as the 'greenish cadaverous glow', a strong atmosphere of the uncanny[25] and lets the suggestion linger that Leggatt has emerged from the region of the dead. Secondly, there is the strange matter of the ladder. The ship's ladder should have been stowed away at night, but owing to the captain's presence it has been left hanging providentially over the side; hence Leggatt's lingering in the ship's shadow, and hence the captain's ability to take the fugitive quickly and quietly up on deck. Thirdly, the captain's suite — cabin and bathroom — seems by its layout providentially arranged to conceal Leggatt (even on those occasions when the suite must be cleaned by the steward): and its plan, as the text specifies, forms a capital L: it is indeed the L for Leggatt. Fourthly, the name 'Leggatt' is homophonous with 'Legate', meaning an envoy from some great power. Fifthly, Leggatt's presence is analogous to a haunting, since he is seen by the captain but is unseen by the other crewmen, his presence causes disturbance, and he is uncannily the *alter ego* of the narrator. Here some of the uncanny qualities are familiar aspects of the Double tradition. As before, we encounter a relationship between two characters who contrast markedly with each other yet are interdependent, so that peril for one entails peril for the other. (Leggatt is a murderer and fugitive from justice; the narrator is a law-abiding captain, yet he feels at once bound to shelter and aid Leggatt; they resemble each other in age, build, class-background and education; both are ex-*Conway* boys.) Like the strange visitant in Henry James's tale 'The Jolly Corner', Leggatt represents an alternative destiny that the captain might have followed; furthermore, what is entertained by Conrad, lightly and intermittently as one possibility in the various modes of his narrative, is the suggestion that Leggatt may also be a supernatural visitant: a man who perhaps drowned on his swim but whose soul still haunts a kindred living being until it has received due recognition, tribute and committal.[26]

One reason for the extreme suspense of 'The Secret Sharer' is that the tale's two main predictive sequences are in very close balance, so that quite contrasting outcomes can both be clearly foreseen, and we therefore read with eagerness to discover which will prevail.[27] One predictive sequence is the optimistic: we predict a happy outcome for the narrator and his ship. The other predictive sequence is the pessimistic: we predict a disaster for the narrator and his ship. As we read on, support for each sequence accumulates; and the supernatural pattern supports both. It helps the pessimistic sequence (by its suggestions of the sinister, unnatural and dangerous) and the optimistic (if we remember that there are precedents for laying a troubled soul to rest after some transaction with the visitant). It permits a small prediction of its own: that Leggatt's final escape may resemble a form of burial, a committal to an underworld; and this predicted analogy is indeed supplied when we are reminded thrice that the nocturnal approach to the island of Koh-ring is like the entry at 'the very gateway of Erebus', the dark cavern through which the shades of the dead passed to Hades. 'Such a hush had fallen on the ship that she might have been a bark of the dead floating in slowly under the very gate of Erebus' (140). Leggatt swims for this 'gateway'; the captain and ship are narrowly saved from disaster by the floating hat which the fugitive leaves in his wake;[28] and the captain turns, relieved and confident, to the world of everyday responsibilities.

As I have emphasised, these extreme supernatural elements appear only intermittently as a varying penumbra around the central lighting of the tale. There can be no doubt, however, that the tale dramatises the motif of the Double in such a way as to offer coincidences so remarkable that they seem 'providential' or metaphysically-ordained. From the captain's unorthodox and crucial decision to take the first night-watch himself, the presence of the ladder alongside, and the layout of his suite, to the remarkable likenesses between himself and the fugitive, with the repeated sense that he is looking at a mirror-image: the tale, while never fully endorsing the supernatural, repeatedly evokes and nowhere refutes such an inference. And it draws on both classical and Biblical recollections of the supernatural. If the references to Erebus remind us of Charon and journeys into Hades, the references to the story of Cain and Abel remind us of another precedent for part of the narrative.

'Am I my brother's keeper?', Cain had asked. In Genesis, Chapter 4, God rebukes Cain for the murder of Abel by declaring: 'A fugitive and a vagabond shalt thou be in the earth'; and he replies: 'My punishment is greater than I can bear. Behold, thou hast driven me this day from the face of the earth; and from thy face shall I be hid; and I shall be a fugitive and a vagabond in the earth.' Then God brands Cain's brow. On the ship in 'The Secret Sharer', an ironic counterpoint to the biblical theme is played. The hero is keeper to his brother-seaman Leggatt, who regards himself as a Cain-figure, the rôle of Abel being taken by the allegedly contemptible fellow-seaman he had murdered. Leggatt tells the hero:

'She [his captain's wife] would have been only too glad to have me out of the ship in any way. The "brand of Cain" business, don't you see. That's all right. I was ready enough to go off wandering on the face of the earth — and that was price enough to pay for an Abel of that sort.'

(107.)

And when explaining his determination not to face trial, Leggatt says:

'You don't suppose I am afraid of what can be done to me? Prison or gallows or whatever they may please. But you don't see me coming back to explain such things to an old fellow in a wig and twelve respectable tradesmen, do you? What can they know whether I am guilty or not — or of *what* I am guilty, either? That's my affair. What does the Bible say? "Driven off the face of the earth." Very well. I am off the face of the earth now. As I came at night so I shall go.'
'Impossible!' I murmured. 'You can't.'
'Can't?...Not naked like a soul on the Day of Judgment. I shall freeze on to this sleeping-suit. The Last Day is not yet — and...you have understood thoroughly.'

(131-2.)

Given that Leggatt is an Anglican clergyman's son, it is natural that at the time of his crisis biblical echoes should sound so readily in his speech. Structurally, the allusions to the

Cain-Abel legend further augment the Janiform symmetry of the tale. The account in Genesis, it may be noted, is ethically ambiguous. God punishes Cain for the murder by making him a wanderer on the face of the earth (a prototype of the Wandering Jew, Ahasuerus), yet God seems benevolent to Cain in giving him the mark on the brow which will guard him from the wrath of men. Thus, again, the allusions aid both the main predictive sequences. The pessimistic sequence is supported by our recognition that Leggatt has resemblances to Cain, who was punished by God; which suggests that the captain who protects him may be courting disaster. The optimistic sequence is supported by our recollection that Cain was not to be punished by men; which suggests that the captain's lenience may be right. On the whole, the paradoxical effect of these Christian references is to accentuate the tale's own rather Nietzschian implications that orthodox morality partakes of slave-morality and that certain men constitute a bold élite with the right to override customary ethical principles. For liberal and humane readers of 'The Secret Sharer', these implications may well be the most indigestible of its ingredients; and indeed it could be argued that this splendid tale embodies several rather pernicious moral recommendations. For example: trust your hunch rather than prudence; deceive your fellow-workers rather than betray a kindred spirit; and take a romantic risk rather than conform to law or practicality. However, if (as the author of *Janiform Novels* speculated) the moral value of a work of literature resides centrally in its dialectical force, i.e., in its ability to offer an imaginative challenge to our normal moral presuppositions, then the tale vigorously offers such a salutary challenge.

Finally, it may be noted that the covert plot-elements I have isolated, by suggesting a supernatural penumbra of the action, question the sense that moral systems based on a secular view of the world are fully adequate; and they therefore constitute an important part of the multiple moral paradoxes of this elegantly lucid yet enigmatic tale. One of the most interesting uncanny features of the narrative is that the hero's experience, when his ship approaches the crisis at Koh-ring, strangely recapitulates, as though in a mobile mirror-image, the former crisis on Leggatt's ship. When Leggatt's vessel seemed about to founder, the captain had shown signs of panic, whereas the first mate (Leggatt) was bold in facing the emergency. This is mirrored when the hero's ship seems about to founder, and the captain is bold in facing the emergency, whereas the first mate shows signs of panic ('She will never get out...She'll drift ashore... O my God!'). Again: on the *Sephora*, Leggatt had seized the insolent seaman by the throat 'and went on shaking him like a rat'. This is mirrored when, on the narrator's ship, the captain seizes the terrified first mate by the arm and proceeds to shake it violently and continuously:

> I caught his arm as he was raising it to batter his poor devoted head, and shook it violently.
> 'She's ashore already,' he wailed, trying to tear himself away.....
> I hadn't let go the mate's arm and went on shaking it. 'Ready about, do you hear? You go forward' — shake — 'and stop there' — shake — 'and hold your noise' — shake — 'and see these head-sheets properly overhauled' — shake, shake — shake.
>
> (141.)

Exorcism, whether by witch-doctors or psychoanalysts, customarily requires some recapitulation of the original crisis; and here the narrative emphasis on the persistence of the shaking (after which the seaman runs away 'as if fleeing for dear life') is clearly designed to evoke our sense of an uncanny yet relatively innocuous recapitulation of that earlier, lethal violence at a time of similar crisis and dispute aboard an imperilled ship at night.

The most uncanny symmetry of all is perhaps this: On the *Sephora*, Leggatt destroyed one man's life in order to save the ship and her crew; and on the other vessel, the captain risks the destruction of the ship and her crew in order to save one man — Leggatt. The reader's sympathies, if illiberal, are thus forced into alliance with liberal ones; and his sympathies, if liberal, are thus forced into alliance with illiberal ones. If he sympathises with the ruthless Leggatt, who has killed once and could easily (to judge from his temper and determination) kill again, he must be sympathetic to the humane captain who shelters him. If he sympathises with the humane captain, he finds himself an accomplice of the captain's determination to help Leggatt's evasion of justice. This elegant yet searching moral paradox is the nexus of the tale's structure; and that

'The Secret Sharer' *is* a tale, with its various forms of aesthetic distancing, further refines the paradox.


## (iv) THE SHADOW-LINE

The supernatural plot of *The Shadow-Line*, which interweaves, contrasts and blends with the secular main plot, is one of curse and exorcism which draws on Christianity (particularly the belief that Christ ransomed mankind from Satan's curse), on literary and marine legends of curse and exorcism (e.g., Coleridge's 'Rime of the Ancyent Marinere' and the saga of the Flying Dutchman), on seamen's superstitions of the kinds subsequently recorded by Arthur Mason and others, and on Baudelaire's poem 'La Musique' (which provided Conrad's epigraph, with its suggestion of a symbolic relationship between states of mind and states of the ocean).

The sequence of the supernatural plot is as follows. The superstitious mate, Burns, claims that the former captain of his ship, after a love-affair with a woman who resembled a fortune-teller, came to hate the ship and her crew, and effectively pronounced a curse upon it: ' "If I had my wish, neither the ship nor any of you would ever reach a port. And I hope you won't." ' (SL,61.) Having performed feats of ostentatiously futile navigation, he died in his cabin, and was buried at sea at the entrance to the Gulf of Siam — precisely at latitude eight degrees twenty minutes north. The hero, the new captain, is alarmed by this report about his predecessor. 'It appeared that even at sea a man could become the victim of evil spirits. I felt on my face the breath of unknown powers that shape our destinies.' (62.) Before the ship can put to sea under the new captain, the crew is stricken by cholera — all except the hero and the remarkably helpful cook-cum-steward whose name is Ransome. After several weeks' delay, the hero puts to sea, believing that there his troubles will be over; but at once, the ship is becalmed. Burns claims that this is 'the fault of the "old man" — the late captain — ambushed down there under the sea with some evil intention'; 'It was a weird story'. The ship remains becalmed and the fever returns to the crew. Burns insists that the cause of the troubles is the dead captain, who is 'right in the ship's way' (83), lying in wait at the entrance to the Gulf as though to bar the vessel's passage.

> 'Are you still thinking of your late Captain, Mr. Burns?' I said. 'I imagine the dead feel no animosity against the living. They care nothing for them.'
>
> 'You don't know that one,' he breathed out feebly.
>
> 'No. I didn't know him, and he didn't know me. And so he can't have any grievance against me, anyway.'
>
> 'Yes. But there's all the rest of us on board,' he insisted.
>
> I felt the inexpugnable strength of common sense being insidiously menaced by this gruesome, this insane delusion.
>
> (82.)

This 'insane delusion', however, becomes increasingly plausible to the young captain as ill-luck accumulates. He himself thinks of the ship as being in the grip of 'the evil spell' (83), though he also thinks that Burns's belief in the curse is a delusion maintained by his illness.

> 'It's like being bewitched, upon my word,' I said once to Mr.Burns..... He nodded.....
>
> 'Oh, yes, I know what you mean,' I said. 'But you cannot expect me to believe that a dead man has the power to put out of joint the meteorology of this part of the world. Though indeed it seems to have gone utterly wrong. The land and sea breezes have got broken up into small pieces.....'
>
> 'It won't be very long now before I can come up on deck,' muttered Mr. Burns, 'and then we shall see.'
>
> Whether he meant this for a promise to grapple with supernatural evil I couldn't tell.
>
> (84-5.)

The illness persists among the crew, and Burns claims that the dead captain will 'play us some beastly trick yet'. His prophecy is fulfilled in two ways. First, against all likelihood, there comes a head-wind blowing the ship off course. 'There was no sense in it. It fitted neither with the season of the year, nor with the secular experience of seamen as recorded in books, nor with the aspect of the sky. Only purposeful malevolence could account for it.' (87.) The second fulfilment of the prophecy comes when the captain discovers that the remaining quinine-bottles in the medicine chest contain no quinine but only a useless powder. Until then, the captain had believed that the supply of quinine had power to 'break the spell' and oppose the curse.

I believed in it. I pinned my faith to it. It would save the men, the ship, break the spell by its medicinal virtue, make time of no account, the weather but a passing worry, and, like a magic powder working against mysterious malefices, secure the first passage of my first command against the evil powers of calms and pestilence.

(88.)

When Burns hears of the missing quinine, he is prompt to define the occurrence as a 'deadly trick' played by the former captain, who must have sold the powder in Tonkin.

'He feared neither God, nor devil, nor man.....But I think he was afraid to die.....If he had had his way we would have been beating up against the North-East monsoon, as long as he lived and afterwards too, for ages and ages. Acting the Flying Dutchman in the China Sea!'

(94.)

Burns had formerly defied and cowed the old captain by laughing at him, precipitating his death but possibly saving the ship (a fulfilment of the proverbial injunctions, 'Laugh at the devil' and 'He laughs who wins'). And now Burns, though still weak from fever, stays awake at nights, determined to oppose the dead captain by force of will, believing that such opposition saves the crew from succumbing to death — 'If he gets hold of one he will get them all' (102). The hero feels guilty, demoralised, 'overcome by the evil spell' (105); he shrinks from going up on deck, and it is the ever-reliable Ransome who prompts him to do his duty; and there, on deck, 'The seaman's instinct alone survived whole in my moral dissolution', he recalls; 'I waited for some time fighting against the weight of my sins, against my sense of unworthiness' (109).

The crisis comes during a black night. Rain falls, and Burns suddenly emerges on deck, having struggled up from his cabin to defy the spirit of the former captain: ' "The old dodging Devil," he screamed piercingly, and burst into such a loud laugh as I had never heard before. It was a provoking, mocking peal, with a hair-raising, screeching over-note of defiance.' (119.) The act of exorcism (as in 'The Secret Sharer') thus recapitulates the earlier crisis. Burns then collapses, but his act of defiance appears to have succeeded, because within moments the favourable wind at last starts to blow, and blows so steadily that the ship reaches harbour about forty hours later.

By the exorcising virtue of Mr. Burns' awful laugh, the malicious spectre had been laid, the evil spell broken, the curse removed. We were now in the hands of a kind and energetic Providence. It was rushing us on...

(125.)

The reader will observe that the supernatural covert plot of *The Shadow-Line* (whose presence Conrad denied) is so extensive and at times so fully explicit that now, as I summarise it, it may seem the main and overt plot. But the main plot is bigger, different and above all secular. The supernatural plot is subordinate but elaborate. As we have seen, Conrad has arranged a pattern of curse and exorcism: the curse is that imposed by the dead captain; the exorcist is Burns. However, the dead captain is also described as 'that old Devil': and therefore, to complete the structural symmetry within the supernatural plot, Conrad provides an appropriate adversary to the 'old Devil': a Christ-figure, Ransome. Where literary Christ-figures are concerned, I am a Doubting Thomas; but this one permits me little doubt.

On the ship of *The Shadow-Line,* the cook, steward, aide and moral support to captain and crew is known only by the name of Ransome. And the source of the name is, in this context, obvious. In the Gospels of St Matthew (chapter 20, verse 28) and St Mark (chapter 10, verse 45) we are told that 'the Son of man came.....to give his life a ransom for many'; and in the First Epistle to Timothy (chapter 2, verses 5-6) St Paul says: 'Christ Jesus.....gave himself a ransom for all'. As with the name of Wait in *The Nigger of the 'Narcissus'*, Conrad plays punningly on the significance of the name Ransome: the narrator observes that 'he was a priceless man altogether' (112). Ransome is given a strongly symbolic and Christ-like quality. A crucial descriptive term is 'grace' ('The man positively had grace': 73), which connotes both physical and spiritual beauty, both poised movement and spiritual virtue — the capacity to redeem the sinful. He is 'pleasant', 'intelligent', 'serene' and 'unfailing'; altruistically co-operative; and though he diligently tends the sick, he is apparently immune to the fever himself. Originally the ship's cook, he has taken the additional task of steward, is tireless as nurse, and at the crisis nearly gives his life in helping the captain to hoist sail; he glides about silently, appearing at moments of stress and

strain with words of wise advice and acts of helpfulness. 'That
man noticed everything, attended to everything, shed comfort
around him as he moved' (121). In risking his life by helping
with the sails, 'He knew what to do. Every effort, every
movement was an act of consistent heroism. It was not for me
to look at a man thus inspired.' (126.) When the weather is
about to change dramatically, Ransome is the one who notices
this and forewarns the captain; and when the captain reaches
the point of mental breakdown, unable to go up on deck, it is
Ransome who quietly recalls him to his duty, so that the ship is
just sufficiently manned to be guided through the sudden
downpour and rising winds. Ransome's rôle as helper is made
essential through the disablement by illness of every other
member of the crew; and it is not just as a physical helper but
as a moral mentor that he is vital. When the captain is almost
overcome by the sense of sinfulness — 'I feel as if all my sins
had found me out' (106) — and reflects 'I always suspected
that I might be no good', it is Ransome who redeems him.

The metaphysical plot of *The Shadow-Line* is given resonance
by echoes of Coleridge's 'Rime of the Ancyent Marinere',
another tale of curse and exorcism, of evil and redemption by
a spirit of grace. (In a subsequent letter to John Livingston
Lowes, Conrad refers familiarly to that poem by 'Dear old
Coleridge' and praises the related short story by Edgar Allen
Poe, 'MS. Found in a Bottle'.)[29] The connections between the
poem and Conrad's novel, some relatively trivial and some
relatively important, are these. Both works use the 'oblique
narrative' convention, offering a tale within a tale. In both
cases, the teller is the survivor of an appalling voyage. In both
cases, the voyager had committed an act which gave him a
burden of guilt. In each case, the vessel seems accursed: it
becomes becalmed and seems doomed to drift the seas for
ever. In 'The Ancyent Marinere', the men of the crew die but
their ghosts man the ship. In *The Shadow-Line*, the men
undergo such severe illness that they are described as ghosts:

'We must try to haul this mainsail close up,' I said.
The shadows swayed away from me without a word. Those men were the
ghosts of themselves, and their weight on a rope could be no more than the
weight of a bunch of ghosts. Indeed, if ever a sail was hauled up by sheer
spiritual strength it must have been that sail.....

(109.)

In the poem, the curse comes from a subaqueous spirit, nine fathoms deep:

> And some in dreams assurèd were
> Of the Spirit that plagued us so:
> Nine fathom deep he had follow'd us
> From the Land of Mist and Snow.[30]

And in the novel, the curse comes from the subaqueous spirit of a captain buried at sea. Again, Coleridge memorably describes the becalmed vessel:

> Day after day, day after day,
> We struck, ne breath ne motion,
> As idle as a painted Ship
> Upon a painted Ocean.

And in *The Shadow-Line*, the captain reflects:

The ship had no steerage way. She lay with her head to the westward, the everlasting Koh-ring visible over the stern, with a few small islets, black spots in the great blaze, swimming before my troubled eyes. And but for those bits of land there was no speck on the sky, no speck on the water, no shape of vapour, no wisp of smoke, no sail, no boat, no stir of humanity, no sign of life, nothing!

(95-6.)

All sense of time is lost in the monotony of expectation, of hope, and of desire.....The effect is curiously mechanical; the sun climbs and descends, the night swings over our heads as if somebody below the horizon were turning a crank.

(97.)

The Ancient Mariner feels that the dead men are looking upon him with intolerable reproach—

> The look with which they look'd at me
> Had never passed me by.....

The captain in the novel says:

No confessed criminal had ever been so oppressed by his sense of guilt.....
    I would have held them justified in tearing me limb from limb. The silence which followed upon my words was almost harder to bear than the angriest uproar. I was crushed by the infinite depth of its reproach.

(96.)

And he has even thought of the ship as one manned by the dead:

> When I turned my eyes to the ship, I had a morbid vision of her as a floating grave. Who hasn't heard of ships found drifting, haphazard, with their crews all dead?
>
> (92; cf. 102, 103.)

In the poem, the lifting of the curse is marked by a drenching downpour, followed by the roar of the wind, and the spectral crew mans the ropes; in the novel, the exorcism of the curse comes at a time of sudden downpour, followed by the rising wind and the manning of the ropes by men supposed 'dying' (124).

Although the similarities are not merely coincidental, the main resemblances between *The Shadow-Line* and 'The Ancyent Marinere' derive, I think, less from direct recollection of the earlier work than from both authors' familiarity with the long tradition of legends of curse and exorcism and purgatorial voyages. As we have seen, *The Shadow-Line* refers explicitly to the saga of the Flying Dutchman (which can be traced back at least to the seventeenth century) and, less specifically, to legends of drifting ships with dead crews — the *Todtenschiff* tradition exemplified by Wilhelm Hauff's 'Die Geschichte von dem Gespensterschiff' and Poe's 'MS. Found in a Bottle'. (The reader may also recall the real-life mystery of the *Marie Céleste*, which in December 1872 was found drifting intact but deserted.)[31] In Conrad's day, numerous tales on these themes were being recounted by popular authors like William Clark Russell (within *A Sea Queen*, for example) and John Masefield (in 'The Devil and the Old Man'). Conrad's stories frequently offer sophisticated, intelligent blends of traditional and romantic matter with more realistic and sceptical matter: he makes adventure introspective and turns yarns into odysseys.

When isolated, the metaphysical plot of *The Shadow-Line* may seem prominent, elaborate and consistent; nevertheless (during the reading of the tale and in retrospect) it is made largely covert through its occlusion by and subordination to the dominant overt plot, which, as in related works like *The Nigger of the 'Narcissus'*, is secular and governs the tone of the conclusion. Conrad's bridges between the metaphysical and the secular plots are again provided by an ambiguously metaphorical terminology: for example, the utterance 'This accursed ship!' can mean 'This ship is labouring under a real curse' or merely 'Nothing is going right on this ship', or both. Another bridge is provided when the superstitious claims originate in abnormal states of mind. It is a literary tradition as ancient as *The Oresteia* (with Cassandra) and as modern as *Lord of the Flies* (with Simon) for the medium of unworldly insight to be a character partly detached from the world by physical or mental affliction. In *Heart of Darkness*, Marlow seemed most inclined to attribute supernatural significance to Kurtz when Marlow, as he travelled deeper into Africa, was subject to physical illness (fever) and to psychological stress (through isolation, danger and the challenge of the unknown). In *The Shadow-Line*, the young captain seems most to credit the supernatural when he is closest to breakdown through stress, while Burns is most superstitious when most subject to cholera and its debilitating aftermath. At the end of the novel, there is a characteristic 'demystification' or scaling-down of the portentously symbolic into the familiar dimensions of the everyday and of the naturalistic explanation. Burns now has 'A wonderful recovery' in regarding the former captain as merely a deranged man rather than a 'Devil' (124); and Ransome reverts to ordinary stature. At the first presentation of Ransome, we had been given a natural explanation of his strange 'grace': he was a man with a weak heart, and accordingly a person who moved carefully so as to avoid sudden strain. At the end of the novel, this mundane explanation is strongly emphasised. Ransome, who had acted with heroic courage and zeal, ever-dependable, now begs to be 'sent ashore and paid off'; the captain protests, but the steward is determined to leave the sea-life which threatens his heart. 'Life was a boon to him — this precarious hard life — and he was thoroughly alarmed about himself.' (129.)

In this text, the principal mode of reconciling the overt plot with the covert is ironic: we perceive that a belief in the supernatural constitutes a demoralising temptation that the captain has to resist: to the extent that he believes in it, he is becoming incapacitated as seaman. At the supernatural level, the ship has been saved because Burns defied and exorcised the late captain's curse, while Ransome provided the spiritual grace necessary to oppose the outer evil and redeem the young captain's sense of guilt. At the secular level, the ship has been saved because, in spite of the superstitious distractions offered by Burns, the captain narrowly preserved his seaman's instincts of duty and was aided by the friendly advice and sheer hard work of Ransome. As in *The Nigger of the 'Narcissus'*, the secular view, though accommodating more of the facts than the occult view, nowhere destroys the latter by refutation. There is no controverting the facts that the ship did indeed encounter extraordinarily bad luck, that the crisis loomed when the ship with seeming reluctance (as though striving to evade a head-on approach) neared the entrance to the gulf, the very latitude where the dead captain lay, and that the voyage prospered as soon as that location was passed and Burns had performed his supposedly exorcistic rite.

The novel's title, *The Shadow-Line*, has a range of ambiguity which enables it to inaugurate equally well both the overt and the covert plots. One kind of 'shadow-line' is the border between innocence and experience, between hopeful youth and partly-disillusioned maturity (3-4, 37, 106). Another, invoked by the dedication to Borys Conrad and his generation that entered the First World War, is the biblical valley of the shadow of death. And another is that line of latitude where lies a dead man's vengeful shade.

Again we see that, like other major novelists of the past hundred years, notably Hardy, Lawrence and Golding, Conrad offers works with a dual appeal: there is much to gratify the reader's sceptical empiricism and something to gratify a need or nostalgia for the mystical and religious. Whether for better or worse, such a dual need is a familiar cultural fact. The continuing decline of Christian belief will in some ways veil and in some ways expose the religious elements in Conrad's fiction. Biblical allusions will tend to go unnoticed; but religious assumptions which earlier readers accepted as familiar will increasingly seem conspicuous and strange. This alienation may be partly reduced or offset by scepticism about the secular outlook: by the recognition that as realism is a system of conventions, so reality is in some measure a social construct, and that all discourse, to the extent that it is ethical, crosses the shadow-line of the unverifiable into the territory of the metaphysical.[32]

## (v) VICTORY

In *Victory*, the secular plot co-exists with a plot which is strongly and even heavy-handedly allegoric. The allegory has two aspects: we are offered a story about evolution and a story about a conflict between metaphysical evil and redemptive virtue.

In the secular plot, Heyst, a reflective and inhibited gentleman, attempts to follow his father's advice to remain aloof from the world; but twice, largely through pity, he is drawn into close contact with another person, and from this double involvement, coupled with the malice of others, disaster ensues. He rescues a Christian, Morrison, from a financial difficulty and for a while becomes involved with Morrison in an unsuccessful business venture; subsequently a malicious German, Schomberg, spreads the calumny that Heyst had actually exploited and ruined his collaborator. Then Heyst gallantly carries away to his island Lena, a girl who has been leading an unhappy life with a travelling orchestra. Schomberg is jealous, and combines a desire for revenge with an endeavour to rid himself of a sinister gang by telling the gang that Heyst has treasure on the island. The sinister group invades the island, Lena is shot and killed, and though the gang perishes, Heyst then commits suicide. A central irony of the main plot (and one which had recurred in Conradian novels from *Almayer's Folly* onwards) is that the man who benevolently intervenes in the lives of others actually sees disaster follow his intervention. In the case of *Victory*, there is a marked ironic paradox. Although Heyst apparently refutes his father's pessimistic doctrines by saying (in a much-quoted pronouncement), 'Ah, Davidson, woe to the man whose heart has not learned while young to hope, to love — and to put its trust in life' (*V*, 410), and though Lena's altruism seems a living contradiction of cynicism, the plot can be seen as vindicating the father's pessimistic advice that one should 'Look on — make no sound' in one's distrust of life's snares; for Heyst's involvements with Morrison and Lena interlink to create the circumstances of disaster.

Religion versus scepticism; virtue against evil. These two obvious themes of the novel connect the overt plot with the allegoric plot. The former theme has explicit and detailed exposition. Heyst is a sceptic, like his father, with no belief in God or Providence; indeed, he is inclined to see religion as a fraud ('counterfeit wages'), and though he has a gentlemanly respect for the beliefs of others, he holds that 'Man on this earth is an unforeseen accident which does not stand close investigation' (196). As early as Chapter 2, the sustained contrast between Heyst's scepticism and other people's piety is established. Morrison, the charitable and humble Christian, prays to God when reduced to desperation by his financial crisis (normally he prefers not to trouble the Almighty with his needs, deeming prayers the recourse of women and children); and, as if in answer to his prayer, Heyst providentially appears and lends him the money. As Heyst is fully aware, it is highly ironic that a sceptic should seem to be the chosen agent of divine intervention — 'that I should have been there to step into the situation of an agent of Providence. *I*, a man of universal scorn and unbelief...' (199). This irony is repeated when Heyst subsequently saves Lena from her wretched existence in the travelling orchestra (and from the lust of Schomberg) by taking her away to his island-sanctuary. Lena, though little educated, has a basic Christian piety. She feels sinful, partly because of her previous 'fallen' life and partly because of her new life as mistress to Heyst; above all, she feels unworthy of his providential gallantry in saving her from Schomberg, and wishes to prove herself worthy of him by some self-sacrificing act of love. The occasion arises when she believes she can save Heyst from death by securing Ricardo's knife; she does secure it, though receiving a mortal bullet-wound, and dies thinking that she has proved her love to Heyst.

The allegoric qualities of her situation are emphasised by her three names: she is not only 'Lena' but also 'Alma' and 'Magdalen'. 'Lena' is the name that Heyst gives her: it is presented as an almost arbitrary choice (resulting from his 'several experimental essays in combining detached letters and loose syllables': 186); but one reason for the choice may be

that it serves as an abbreviation of 'Magdalen' and 'Helena';
and the echo of 'Helena' is appropriate because the plot of
*Victory* resembles in some respects a parodic version of the
legend of the abduction of Helen of Troy. (The abduction of
the beautiful Helen brought invasion, disaster and the burning
of Ilium; the abduction of the seductive Lena results in the
invasion of the island, disaster and the burning of Heyst's
sanctuary on Samburan. In *The Rescue*, which Conrad was
completing around the time of *Victory*, the legend of Helen of
Troy is discussed early in Part One by Lingard and Shaw, and it
makes an appropriate ironic thematic prelude for the novel.)
Lena's name may thus echo Heyst's explicit misgiving that in
rescuing her he has been ensnared or ambushed by life. And,
if the situation of Heyst and Lena, isolated on their verdant
tropical island, has remote connections with the situation of
Adam and Eve, Heyst is quick to detect those too, with some
bitterness:

> 'There must be a lot of the original Adam in me, after all.'
> He reflected, too, with the sense of making a discovery, that this primeval
> ancestor is not easily suppressed. The oldest voice in the world is just the one
> that never ceases to speak. If anybody could have silenced its imperative
> echoes, it should have been Heyst's father, with his contemptuous,
> inflexible negation of all effort; but apparently he could not. There was in
> the son a lot of that first ancestor who, as soon as he could uplift his muddy
> frame from the celestial mould, started inspecting and naming the animals
> of that paradise which he was so soon to lose.
> Action — the first thought, or perhaps the first impulse, on earth! The
> barbed hook, baited with the illusion of progress, to bring out of the lightless
> void the shoals of unnumbered generations!
> 'And I, the son of my father, have been caught too, like the silliest fish of
> them all,' Heyst said to himself.
>
> (173-4.)

Lena's former names, 'Magdalen' and 'Alma', are patently
rich in allegoric suggestion. Magdalen was the Biblical 'fallen
woman', the prostitute who became a humble, loyal and
devoted follower of Christ. The name has double relevance to
the heroine of *Victory*, for she is 'fallen' as a woman of squalid
background who is on the brink of enforced prostitution at the
hands of Zangiacomo and Schomberg: indeed, the text offers
veiled hints that she is already the mistress of Zangiacomo, for
whereas the other girls of the orchestra are accommodated

together in a pavilion, Zangiacomo accommodates both his wife *and* Lena in the hotel. 'I am not what they call a good girl', she plaintively confides; but subsequently she will serve Heyst with a self-denying devotion which recalls that of the biblical Magdalen.

The name 'Alma' is equally connotative. *Alma* is both a Spanish and an Italian noun meaning 'soul'; and, as is well known, it is a Latin adjective meaning 'kind or nourishing': hence the familiar phrase *alma mater*. In the complicated allegoric context of the novel, the character called Alma is a force of love, life and goodness whose adversary is the force of evil represented by Pedro, Ricardo and Jones. The very title of the novel, *Victory*, inaugurates the allegory. 'O death, where is thy sting? O grave, where is thy victory?', asks the Bible (1 Corinthians 15, verse 55); a question quoted in Bunyan's *Pilgrim's Progress*, in the famous hymn and in every Anglican burial service, and noted gloomily by the narrator of 'A Smile of Fortune': 'What was the use of asking Death where her sting was, before that small, dark hole in the ground?' (*TLAS*, 16). In *Victory*, the biblical pronouncement is predictably echoed, and merged with an echo of the story of the Fall in Genesis, when Lena succeeds in gaining possession of Ricardo's murderous knife:

She had done it! The very sting of death was in her hands; the venom of the viper in her paradise, extracted, safe in her possession — and the viper's head all but lying under her heel.

(399.)

The latter part of that passage refers to Genesis 3, verses 14-15:

And the Lord God said unto the serpent, Because thou has done this, thou art cursed.....:
And I will put enmity between thee and the woman, and between thy seed and her seed; it shall bruise thy head, and thou shalt bruise his heel.

The naïve piety of Lena is indicated in various ways. For example, she believes the doctrine of Matthew 10, verse 29, that even the sparrows are in the loving hands of God (359-60); and though Heyst sceptically remarks 'sparrows do fall to the gound,.....they are brought down to the ground', she attempts to vindicate St Matthew by protecting Heyst. Again, as she prepares for the fatal encounter with Ricardo, she is seen by Heyst in an attitude of penitential prayer: 'all black, down on her knees, with her head and arms flung on the foot of the bed — all black in the desolation of a mourning sinner' (373). As we have noted, she believes that she finally triumphs over her murderous adversary, Ricardo; and furthermore, the text also makes her the symbolic foe of the devilish adversary, Gentleman Jones.

Jones is repeatedly termed a 'gentleman' (by Ricardo and himself); and Conrad knew well the proverbial allegoric implication of this title. As Shakespeare's Edgar had said in *King Lear*: 'The Prince of Darkness is a gentleman.' (Sir John Suckling echoes the familiar phrase in Act III of *The Goblins*: 'The Prince of Darkness is a gentleman'; and Shelley varies it in 'Peter Bell the Third': 'Sometimes/The Devil is a gentleman'.) The villain of *Lord Jim* is called 'Gentleman Brown'; and when the hero of 'A Smile of Fortune' is told to go to the Devil, he replies: 'It would be refreshing to meet a gentleman' (*TLAS*, 27). It is this time-honoured paradoxical connotation of the term which provides salient ironies in the characterisation of the villainous 'Gentleman' Jones.[33] As we would expect, *Victory*'s text underlines the allegoric significance. Heyst reports of Jones:

'Having been ejected, he said, from his proper social sphere because he had refused to conform to certain usual conventions, he was a rebel now, and was coming and going up and down the earth.....I told him that I had heard that sort of story about somebody else before. His grin is really ghastly.....Then he said:
    "As to me, I am no blacker than the gentleman you are thinking of, and I have neither more nor less determination." '

(317-18.)

The point of this exchange clearly depends on a correlation between Jones and Lucifer, the angel who rebelled through pride, was cast out of Heaven, and resolved to roam the earth to tempt humans. The ambiguity of the phrase 'coming and going up and down the earth', repeated when Heyst refers to Jones's 'comings or goings on the earth', is designed to encourage the inference that Jones is supernatural — an extra-terrestrial visitant, like Lucifer. The passage's reference to blackness invokes the proverbial notion that black is the colour of the Devil, hell and damnation: 'The devil damn thee black!', cries Shakespeare's Macbeth; 'O, the more angel she,/And you the blacker devil!', says Emilia in *Othello*. The suggestion that Jones is the Devil incarnate is intermittently maintained in such references as these: 'he was speaking faintly, in a voice which did not seem to belong to the earth' (239); he has 'devilish eyebrows' (115); he calls himself 'a sort of fate' (379); and, as if in blasphemous mockery of God's 'I am that I am' (Exodus 3, verse 14), he declares 'I am he who is' or 'I am he that is' (317, 376). Finally, to an ex-seaman like Conrad, even the common surname 'Jones' has a sinister connotation; for, as all seamen know (and the tale 'Amy Foster' reminds us),[34] 'Davy Jones' is the familiar name of the Devil: 'Davy Jones's Locker' is the maritime idiom for the marine graveyard of those who die at sea; and it is appropriate that when Jones is vanquished, he is found mysteriously dead in the sea itself. In the allegoric scheme that such devices suggest, Jones is the force of evil and Lena is the force of grace; Jones, like Lena, feels that he is facing a supreme test as the events reach their climax, and his antipathy to womanhood has its culmination when he finds that his loyal follower with 'the sting of death' has been conquered by Lena's power.

It should already be evident that one weakness of *Victory* is that Conrad loads to excess the allegoric possibilities, as though the author were compensating too explicitly and multitudinously for the melodramatic and 'popular' nature of the main overt plot. Jones is not only allegorised as the Devil: he is also, the text suggests, 'an insolent spectre on leave from Hades' (116); he resembles a 'spectre' (106, 118, 148, 227, 387), is 'spectral' (112, 381, 385, 393), and 'Like the spectre that he was, he had noiselessly vanished' (403); he resembles 'a wicked ghost' (121), 'a daylight ghost' (121) and 'a masquerading skeleton out of a grave' (390). Accordingly, he is depicted as remarkably thin and languid, skeletal and with head like a skull; so that the voluptuously feminine Lena, fit, energetic and temptingly beautiful, is an obviously appropriate allegoric antagonist.

The other dimension of the covert plotting is more secular but just as strongly allegoric; indeed, in terms of frequency of allusion it is quite as marked as the religious dimension. This sequence forms an evolutionary fable, obviously influenced by Darwinian and post-Darwinian ideas (and probably by Emile Zola's melodramatic naturalism) and with a Schopenhauerian philosophic cast. The implications of this 'evolutionary' sequence are the following.

Man evolved from the beasts, but the bestial heritage remains strong. Brute force and the predatory urge (exemplified by Pedro and Ricardo) live on. Evolution may seem to have reached its goal in the civilised gentleman, who is reflective, self-controlled and deliberate: but this outcome may be in two ways decadent. As Dostoyevsky said, 'It is the most civilised gentlemen who have been the subtlest slaughterers';[35] ancient Rome was celebrated for its murderous vice as well as for its temples and aqueducts; and in Jones we see the civilised gentleman at his most decadently ruthless. The other gentleman, Heyst, appears decent and considerate; but he manifests the familiar decadence of the reflective: he is so adept at sceptical analysis that he is virtually incapacitated when straightforwardly physical defensive action is required. He complains to Lena that he has 'Neither force nor conviction' to deal with the emergency — 'I date too late' (350, 361) — and he fails to seize various opportunities to overcome Jones: 'His very will seemed dead of weariness' (390). As Conrad, with emergent irony, remarks in the 'Author's Note':

Heyst in his fine detachment had lost the habit of asserting himself..... Thinking is the great enemy of perfection. The habit of profound reflection, I am compelled to say, is the most pernicious of all the habits formed by the civilized man.

(x-xi.)

If Jones and Heyst represent evolution carried respectively to decadently destructive and introspective extremes, Pedro and Ricardo patently represent the bestial heritage not yet outgrown. Pedro is as much animal as man. He is repeatedly likened to a bear: he resembles in clumsiness 'a creature caught in the woods and taught to walk on its hind legs' (118); he has 'little bear's eyes' (116); is a 'growling bear' with shaggy head, and 'like a bulky animal in the dusk, balancing itself on its hind legs' (240); he has 'enormous brown paws', 'a wide mouth full of fangs', a hairy throat and chest (230); 'enormous fangs' and 'bandy legs' (331). If he fights, he does so like a bear, with 'a growl and a bite' (368). For good measure, Pedro also resembles an ape (he is called an ape on pp.148 and 285); he catches things 'better than any trained ape could have done' (327); he is 'formed like a prehistoric ape' (358); he has an 'enormous gorilla back' (363), and he walks like a gorilla: 'His enormous half-closed paws swung to and fro a little in front of his bowed trunk as he walked' (369).

As for Ricardo, he may be a relative of T.S. Eliot's Macavity, for he clearly belongs to the cat family: he resembles sometimes a domestic cat, sometimes a wild cat, and sometimes a tiger. He is 'an enormous savage cat' (126), his grin is 'cat-like' (135); he has 'oblique, coyly expectant yellow eyes, like a cat watching the preparation of a saucer of milk', and after drinking he makes a sound resembling 'purring, very soft and deep in his throat' (147). He appears to have 'the morals of a cat' (148). He closes his eyes 'with the placidity of the domestic cat dozing' (148); and those eyes are 'greenish' (152) and 'yellow' (283, 301, 302, 397). His unblinking watchfulness 'gave him a dreamy air of a cat posed on a hearth-rug contemplating the fire' (283); his moustaches stir like a cat's whiskers (287, 301); he has 'slightly pointed ears' (286); he again resembles 'a stray cat' and 'a domestic cat' (286, 370), and he is inevitably 'feline' (277, 297, 374, 398), while his facial structure resembles that of 'a jaguar' (358). Like a cat, he stoops or crouches before leaping at his prey. In a particularly ludicrous incident, he makes a 'feral' leap through a curtained doorway at Lena, with intent to 'ravish or kill':

[His] body began to sway gently back and forth. The self-restraint was at an end: his psychology must have its way. The instinct for the feral spring could no longer be denied. Ravish or kill — it was all one to him, as long as by the act he liberated the suffering soul of savagery repressed for so long. After a quick glance over his shoulder, which hunters of big game tell us no lion or tiger omits to give before charging home, Ricardo charged, head down, straight at the curtain.

(288-9.)

In the first part of this passage, Ricardo's action is that of the domestic cat about to pounce on its prey; in the latter part, he belongs to the family of big and dangerous cats — lions or tigers. Ricardo is so elaborately depicted as beast that it is hard to believe in him as man. The combination of third-rate, novelettish prose with over-insistent allegorising produces an effect of the ludicrously pretentious. The passage could, unchanged, be submitted as parody.

The allegoric pattern represented by Jones, Ricardo and Pedro is summed up by Heyst: 'Here they are, the envoys of the outer world. Here they are before you — evil intelligence, instinctive savagery, arm in arm. The brute force is at the back. A trio of fitting envoys perhaps.....' (329.) In the allegoric sequence as a whole, Lena represents the force of life and potential procreation which is opposed by Jones, who is a force of death and sterility. Accordingly, Jones has an aversion to womankind in general and Lena in particular; and it is his bullet, though aimed at Ricardo, which kills her. His aversion to women, if one regards it at a non-allegoric level, bears some resemblance to the aversion of an extreme homosexual, and there is no doubt that the text raises this possibility. Jones has a languid and at times effeminate air; his eyebrows are 'beautifully pencilled' (384); and Ricardo implies that the question of his homosexuality has been asked at least once by women intrigued by his aversion (160). Ricardo is his close companion: 'secretary', 'henchman', and perhaps, the text allows us to speculate, sexual partner. In Mexico, we are told, Jones lay all day long in a dark room 'while a ragged, bare-legged boy that he had picked up in the street sat in the *patio*, between two oleanders near the open door of his room, strumming on a guitar and singing *tristes* to him from morning to night' (151). When Jones kills Lena, it is a result of his attempted murder of Ricardo during an outburst of jealous rage on discovering that his henchman has formed a treacherous alliance with a woman.

Homosexuality is not, however, an adequate explanation of Jones's aversion. If it were adequate, Ricardo would understand the aversion, but he does not.

> At bottom, he felt a certain ambiguous respect for his governor's exaggerated dislike of women, as if that horror of feminine presence were a sort of depraved morality; but still morality, since he counted it as an advantage. It prevented many undesirable complications. He did not pretend to understand it. He did not even try to investigate this idiosyncrasy of his chief. All he knew was that he himself was differently inclined, and that it did not make him any happier or safer.
>
> (266.)

The main cause of Jones's aversion is not sexual but super-natural: not psychological but allegorical. It is the authorial need to balance a death-force against a life-force which accounts for the antipathy between Jones and womanhood. The temperament has been generated by the abstract patterning of the novel — by its covert allegoric plot. Behind this allegory probably lies Conrad's reading of Arthur Schopenhauer. John Galsworthy once noted that Conrad read Schopenhauer's works;[36] the doctrines of Heyst's father resemble Schopenhauer's more than any other philosopher's; and in *Die Welt als Wille und Vorstellung* (*The World as Will and Idea*, 1818) the German pessimist appears to provide much of the thematic basis of *Victory*. Jones's melodramatic antipathy to women and Heyst's bitter misgivings about his alliance with Lena can both be related to Schopenauer's philosophical misogyny. The phil-osopher argued that women serve the life-force of the species, the urge to procreate; for this purpose, they seek out their partners. The wise man, however, refuses to participate in the futile struggle of nature on this planet; he sees the whole process as pointless, life as 'a snare and a cheat', and seeks a stoical withdrawal from it; like Heyst's father, he prefers meditation and evades involvement.

Although Schopenhauer's ideas may help to explain *Victory*, they do not redeem it. Often the presence of a covert plot makes a text better — more complex and ironic. However, it does not always improve it; and *Victory* is an interesting test-case. Assessment of its merits has long divided Conradian critics: some rate it very highly (F.R. Leavis placed it among Conrad's great masterpieces); others see it as an inferior work. A standard defence, offered by John A. Palmer and others, is that it should be read not as realism but as allegory; yet this defence may fail if the work seems *too* allegoric.[37] My view is that it is an interestingly problematic novel, but certainly not a success. It is most convincing in the first half, but with the increasing prominence of the Jones gang and of Lena as heroine, the novel declines. This is partly because Conrad's general tendency to present villains as grotesques here becomes excessive, and partly because he seldom is particularly convincing when presenting intense sexual relationships. The dialogue, especially that of Jones and Ricardo, is highly implausible, often resembling the dialogue of villains in a *Boy's*

*Own paper* serial (and around this time, according to his son John, the mature Conrad was indeed a reader of *Boy's Own Paper*).[38] Furthermore, the plot is clumsily contrived: the more Conrad seeks to explain the manifest implausibilities, the more conspicuous they become. For example: Ricardo, who has a knife, fails in his attempt to rape Lena; she not only repulses him, but does not cry out, which would have alerted Jones to her presence and set the villains against each other; next, she promptly pretends to be conspiring with Ricardo against Heyst, telling Heyst nothing of the encounter. Both Morrison's reappearance and Jones's death seem oddly fortuitous.

Repeatedly Conrad seems to be striving to impose cosmic significance on an action which increasingly resembles a Hollywood melodrama: and this resemblance is verified by the fact that *Victory* was filmed not once but three times by Hollywood: by Paramount-Artcraft in 1919, by Paramount in 1930, and yet again by Paramount in 1941. The allegorising of characters conflicts in its explicitness with the predominantly realistic mode of the first half of the book. (Wang's habit of materialising and vanishing anticipates the devices of a film-cartoon.) To the numerous commentators who esteem *Victory* highly I offer two reminders of its techniques at their most lamentable. The first is a sample of the implausible dialogue. Here is Jones denouncing Heyst:

'I have a good mind to shoot you, you woman-ridden hermit, you man in the moon, that can't exist without — no, it won't be you that I'll shoot. It's the other woman-lover — the prevaricating, sly, low-class, amorous cuss!'

(387.)

And secondly, an example of the excessively allegorical habit of mind. Here are the instructions that Heyst gives to Lena when he tells her to go into hiding:

'Wait in the forest till the table is pushed into full view of the doorway, and you see three candles out of four blown out and one relighted — or, should the lights be put out here while you watch them, wait till three candles are lighted and then two put out. At either of these signals run back as hard as you can, for it will mean that I am waiting for you here.'

(372 )

The reader will perceive some over-ingenious covert plotting: the reason for Heyst's elaborate rigmarole is that these are allegoric candles. The four represent Heyst, Jones, Ricardo and Pedro. 'Four blown out and one relighted' means that Jones, Ricardo and Pedro have been dealt with and Heyst survives; 'three.....lighted and then two put out' means that Jones and Ricardo have been dealt with and Heyst survives. Yet all that the situation requires is that Heyst should undertake to light just one candle to signal that all is well; the specificity of four and one, or three and one, is needless and time-consuming; and as Lena never leaves the house, the device is technically redundant.

Thus, *Victory* illustrates a general rule about covert plots, and particularly covert plots with metaphysical implications, which is confirmed by other works of Conrad (and of other writers). The most effective co-ordination of different narrative dimensions is established when the dominant viewpoint is presented as that of a specific character (or is a combination of the observations of specific characters). The more the dominant viewpoint approaches the 'objectivity' and authority of an omniscient authorial perspective, the more the reader's sceptical questioning may be aroused; whereas the use of a localised narrator or narrators can allay such questioning, for the reduction in implied authority entails an increase in persuasiveness. This is one reason for the supremacy among Conrad's works of *Heart of Darkness*, in which Marlow tells his story to an anonymous fellow who reports it to us.

# CHAPTER 7

# *Some Structural Ironies of* The Secret Agent

To discriminate between a main plot and a covert plot is sometimes difficult. To the extent that a main plot is ironic, it tends to generate a narrative sequence which underlies and offsets the purported sequence; while to the extent that a main plot has gaps, ellipses and opacities which render it subject to strenuous acts of inference, it invites the kind of reading which is required by a covert plot. We are dealing with differences in degree, though these may properly constitute differences in kind.

The part of *The Secret Agent* that I consider here is covert in the sense that its coherence and its ironic qualification of the story of the overt are likely to elude due recognition at a first reading of the text. The overt plot of the novel shows how the forces of law and order in London prevail over the forces of anarchy, subversion and disruption. The covert plot, which is sustained by a series of ironic symmetries, resembles by inversion a mirror-image of elements of the main plot; and it suggests that if law and order prevail, the ostensibly right thing is often done for the wrong reason, and that there are troubling resemblances between the world of the authorities and the world of subversion. The relationship in the narrative between covert and overt is variable and shifting; they blend, part and blend again. My argument, if sound, should be cheerfully self-defeating: for if the covert, when pointed out, is recognised or remembered by the reader as he recalls or re-reads the text, it will steadily be subsumed by the overt. It is perhaps the same with various forms of exploration: if the territory opened by an explorer is of value, that territory will soon become a familiar, mapped and well-trodden part of the world; mysteries will be dispelled; subsequent travellers may be puzzled to think that what now seems so obvious once seemed arcane or hostile; and other voices may truly say, 'But *we* were here first'. The meaning of covert plots lies partly and importantly in the very resistances to decipherment that they offer. My experiences as reader and teacher suggest that the resistances have sometimes been encountered as unyielding barriers: therefore I describe the territory beyond them. If the territory eventually becomes familiar and readily accessible, it would be the critic's duty to emphasise those (formerly so effective) resistances. In exploring the meaning of the covert, we should not overlook the meaning of the covering.

The main plot of *The Secret Agent* seems to result in a triumph for the forces of law and order. The instigator of the bomb-attack on Greenwich Observatory — and thus of the explosion which kills Stevie — is Mr Vladimir, Secretary of an Embassy which is clearly meant to be the Russian Embassy. His purpose in instigating the attack is to cause such consternation in Britain that the authorities will become more repressive, less hospitable to political refugees and more like those in autocratic Russia. (The period of the story is around 1894, the date of an actual bomb explosion near the Observatory.)[1] Vladimir's foe is the Assistant Commissioner of Police. The latter astutely gains from Chief Inspector Heat the reluctantly-imparted information that the victim of the explosion wore a tag giving an address (Verloc's) in Brett Street; the Assistant Commissioner then leaves his desk to visit that address personally; he interviews Verloc, and learns from him that the instigator was Vladimir. The same evening, the Assistant Commissioner tells Vladimir that the game is up, that his rôle will be revealed at the subsequent trial, and that this will be the occasion of action by the authorities against various Embassies which employ *agents provocateurs*. Vladimir, alarmed and humiliated, prepares to leave England. Thus the villain has been rapidly identified and expelled. The Assistant Commissioner seems all the more astute, given that Chief Inspector Heat had attempted to conceal the link between the bombing and Verloc: and Heat had done this in the hope of protecting Verloc (a useful source of information) while pinning the responsibility for the outrage on Michaelis. Since Michaelis was ignorant of the affair, the Assistant Commissioner does indeed seem to have averted an injustice and eliminated the true source of evil. Britain has been safeguarded by a shrewd, enterprising and far-sighted leader of the police. Such is the effect of the main plot.

This positive effect is strongly qualified by the covert plot. The Assistant Commissioner may do the right thing, but his motives are mixed, and one of them is very dubious. Heat had sought to blame Michaelis in order to protect Verloc; but the Assistant Commissioner seeks out Verloc partly in order to protect Michaelis. And the Assistant Commissioner's motive for wishing to protect Michaelis is clearly indicated. This ex-convict has become a social celebrity; he has been befriended by a wealthy hostess in high society; and that hostess is a close friend of the Assistant Commissioner's wife.

> The lady patroness of Michaelis, the ticket-of-leave apostle of humanitarian hopes, was one of the most influential and distinguished connections of the Assistant Commissioner's wife, whom she called Annie, and treated still rather as a not very wise and utterly inexperienced young girl. But she had consented to accept him on a friendly footing, which was by no means the case with all of his wife's influential connections.....She herself was a great lady.....
>
> (*SA*, 104.)

His affection for the patroness stems largely from 'the instinct of flattered gratitude'; and he reflects:

> Her influence upon his wife, a woman devoured by all sorts of small selfishnesses, small envies, small jealousies, was excellent.....
>
> Appreciating the distinguished and good friend of his wife, and himself, in that way, the Assistant Commissioner became alarmed at the convict Michaelis' possible fate.....
>
> Though he judged his alarm sardonically he did not dismiss the improper thought from his mind. The instinct of self-preservation was strong within him. On the contrary, he repeated it mentally with profane emphasis and a fuller precision: 'Damn it! If that infernal Heat has his way the fellow'll die in prison smothered in his fat, and she'll never forgive me.'
>
> (111-12, 112, 113.)

This sequence of reflection is crucial to the action; for it is
his recognition that the well-being of Michaelis is essential to
his continued friendship with the wealthy patroness that leads
the Assistant Commissioner to cross-question Heat about the
link with Michaelis, which in turn leads to the mention of
Verloc, and thus in turn to the trail which leads to Vladimir.
Thus, at the fulcrum of the overt plot is a covert plot: behind
the proper intent to discover the true villain, Vladimir, lies the
'improper' motive of safeguarding one's domestic interests.

It is typical of Conrad's cunning Janiformity of outlook that
even in this, politically one of his more conservative novels, he
should so dextrously qualify the implication that British law
and order are generally admirable by indicating the dubious
motivation behind the main quest. And although this covert
plot does not fully endorse the idea, it does lend some support
to the idea of Verloc and his wife that the forces of law and
order exist to preserve the rights of property and the claims of
privilege. Verloc had reflected:

Protection is the first necessity of opulence and luxury. They had to be
protected; and their horses, carriages, houses, servants had to be protected;
and the source of their wealth had to be protected in the heart of the city and
the heart of the country; the whole social order favourable to their hygienic
idleness had to be protected against the shallow enviousness of unhygienic
labour.

(12.)

As Mrs Verloc succinctly puts it:

'Don't you know what the police are for, Stevie? They are there so that
them as have nothing shouldn't take anything away from them who have.'

(173.)

The covert plot of *The Secret Agent*, by showing an Assistant
Commissioner motivated to guard the tranquillity of an
affluent society-hostess, suggests that the views of Verloc and
his wife Winnie, if jaundiced, are not entirely false. It adroitly
suggests the inseparability of the political from the domestic
areas: the Assistant Commissioner speaks more truly than he
intends when, telling the Home Secretary about Verloc, he
remarks: 'From a certain point of view we are here in the
presence of a domestic drama' (222); and the unmasking of

Vladimir takes place not at the Embassy but at the salon of Annie's affluent friend.

It is characteristic of this ruthlessly sardonic novel that London, 'centre of the Empire on which the sun never sets' (214), is seen as a murky, slimy place, resembling a dismal stagnant aquarium in which move shoals of lonely and moribund people. It is also characteristic that though acts of altruism take place, they result in cruel disaster. Winnie's mother secures a place in a Charity Home in order to ensure that she is not a burden to Verloc, so that Verloc will be the more likely to look after her son, Stevie. Her altruism is not perceived by Winnie, who upbraids her for the kindly act; and by consigning Stevie so deftly to the continued care of Verloc, the mother is committing her son to the man who will cause his death. Winnie, so nobly loyal to her mentally-retarded brother, strives to create a bond of affection between Verloc and Stevie, by telling her husband, for instance:

> 'You could do anything with that boy.....He would go through fire for you.....
> I wish you would take that boy out with you.....'
>
> (184, 185.)

And it is those words which give Verloc the idea of using Stevie as an accomplice in the bomb-raid, as a result of which Stevie does literally 'go through fire' for him.

A further irony of *The Secret Agent*'s structure is that the interview in Chapter 6 which inaugurates the covert plot has artful parallels to the interview in Chapter 1 which inaugurated the overt plot. Vladimir's plan that Verloc should assail the Observatory with a bomb had been conceived during an interview at which Verloc was surprised by, and resentful at, the challenge offered to his *modus operandi* by an official whom he is inclined to regard as a theoretician inexperienced in the day-to-day practicalities of the work. The Assistant Commissioner's plan to protect Michaelis (related to his discovery of the link between the explosion and Verloc) was conceived during an interview in which Heat was surprised by, and resentful at, the challenge offered to his *modus operandi* by an official whom he, too, is inclined to regard as a theoretician inexperienced in the day-to-day practicalities of the work. On each occasion, the superior is a new arrival from abroad, interested in implementing a change of policy; and both superiors (Vladimir and the Assistant Commissioner) are 'gentlemanly' in speech, appearance and life-style; while both subordinates are lower-middle-class in speech and bearing. Verloc experiences embarrassment and apprehension: 'A slight perspiration had broken out on his forehead.....He had remained motionless, as if feeling himself surrounded by pitfalls' (18); 'The nape of his gross neck became crimson' (23), and he subsequently feels like a rider whose horse is about to fall dead beneath him (57). Heat has rather similar feelings: 'The Chief Inspector felt as if the air between his clothing and his skin had become unpleasantly hot.....The indignation of a betrayed tight-rope performer was strong within him' (124). Each, with the resentment of the old professional, notes that the previous superiors never caused the difficulty now being caused by the new man with strange ideas. The parallelism is increased when we see that Vladimir and the Assistant Commissioner belong to the same social circle, meeting at the same salon, while Heat and Verloc not only know each other but have a practical working relationship in which each provides useful information for the other.

Unlike geometrical parallels, fictional parallels may readily meet. Similarity is not identity; but these similarities, so carefully deployed by Conrad, do characteristically qualify the conventional sense of clear contrast between the realm of authority and the realm of subversion.

Conrad's interest in fictional parallelism, delayed decoding, and oblique and covert narrative procedures may partly have been engendered by a novel which his commentators seem to have overlooked and which bears a curious relationship to *The Secret Agent*. In a letter of 1898 which was not included in the Jean-Aubry collection of his correspondence,[2] Conrad mentions that his admiration for the work of Israel Zangwill dates back to the days of *The Premier and the Painter*, which he had read, he says, while sailing in the Indian Ocean. *The Premier and the Painter*, by 'J. Freeman Bell' (the pseudonym of Israel Zangwill, who wrote most of the book, and his co-author Louis Cowen), was published by Heinemann in 1888. The plot of this 'satirical, political, and philosophical fantasia' (as Zangwill subsequently termed the book) is based on a *Doppelgänger* situation. Arnold Floppington, a meditative Tory Prime Minister, changes places with his physical double: Jack Dawe, an energetic house-painter with radical opinions. As Prime Minister, Dawe transforms Tory policy so that it includes Liberal measures: suffrage is granted (at last) to women, and he is even planning to give Home Rule to Ireland; but he is then assassinated in a dynamite explosion arranged by Irish Nationalists who fear that the granting of Home Rule would deprive them of their cause and *raison d'être*. Not only does this novel have some thematic linkages, therefore, with *The Secret Agent*; but also *The Premier and the Painter* offers two related anticipations of Conrad's elliptical and evasive techniques. The centrally important scene in which the Premier and the painter first agree to exchange rôles is never presented directly to the readers: we have to infer it from later events. (In 1893 Zangwill, in his Preface to the third edition, gleefully pointed out that his oblique technique had baffled readers and reviewers alike.) In addition, there is no direct presentation of the exciting climactic event of the story, the assassination of Dawe; instead, there is an abrupt transition from the account of preceding events to the report of newspaper-headlines about the mysterious bomb-explosion. In *The Secret Agent*, we move abruptly from Chapter 3, in which Verloc is preoccupied with the prospective mission, to the dialogue of Chapter 4 in which Ossipon shows the Professor the newspaper-report of the bomb-explosion in Greenwich Park. (Incidentally, Conrad's Professor, who believes that some dynamite and the perfect detonator are worth more than all the theorising of Yundt, Ossipon and Michaelis, would have concurred fully with the claim made by the fanatical Captain, the chief assassin in the earlier novel: 'An ounce of dynamite is worth a ton of arguments.') In addition, the narrator of *The Premier and the Painter* often adopts the style of an ironic, humorously-pedantic, mock-heroic historian, so there are some anticipations of the distinctively sardonic narratorial style of *The Secret Agent*.

*The Premier and the Painter*, an accentric, whimsical, Gilbertian venture into political satire, may seem to have been a strange travelling-companion for Conrad in the Indian Ocean; but in its conception of political history as ironic farce and in its structural elisions it may have provided hints which *The Secret Agent* subsequently developed. Even *Under Western Eyes*, when it so incisively elides the conversation which persuades Razumov to become a spy, may own a debt to the conspicuously delayed decoding of Zangwill's novel.

# CHAPTER 8

# The Covert Plot and the Deceived Narrator: Heart of Darkness, The Shadow-Line and 'A Smile of Fortune'.

Conrad's sustained interest in covert plots is illustrated by the fact that a variety of his subsequent works maintain the ironic narrative strategy of *Almayer's Folly*: they have a central figure who is the victim of a plot (in the sense of 'an intrigue or deception') which he either fails to perceive or only tardily perceives, and which the reader may be slow to comprehend. Often this figure is the narrator.

Usually, in fiction, the distinction between plotting by characters and plotting by the author is quite clear. For example, Shakespeare's Macbeth and Lady Macbeth success-fully conspire to murder Duncan, and not until after the death is their plot suspected by other characters; but from its inception the reader has been fully aware of it. Conrad, on the other hand, distinctively strives to mesh the characters' and the authorial plots by approximating the reader's awareness to that of the person deceived.[1]

## (i) HEART OF DARKNESS AND THE SHADOW-LINE

In *Heart of Darkness*, the central figure who fails to perceive the plot of which he is a victim is Mr Kurtz. The narrator, Marlow, is also adversely affected by that plot and is slow to comprehend it, though his comprehension still precedes that of the text's commentators by about seventy years.

The plotter is the Company's manager at the Central

Station, and his motive is ambition; because Mr Kurtz, an influential and remarkably successful ivory-hunter, is his main rival for promotion. As schemer, he has one great asset: he enjoys an uncanny immunity from illness, despite the rule that in this 'white man's grave' the majority of Europeans soon succumb to disease, derangement or death. Kurtz has chosen to remain a long time at the Inner Station; the manager therefore contrives to delay his relief as long as possible. Just before Marlow arrives to take the steam-boat upstream, the manager and 'some volunteer skipper' take the vessel into the river and run it aground so that it is extensively damaged. Marlow then needs rivets for the repair, and asks for them to be sent from the Outer Station; but they are remarkably slow to appear, evidently because the secretary writes 'from dicta-tion': the manager decides which requests shall be sent. The repairs take three months, just as the manager had predicted to the incredulous Marlow; and by the time the steamer reaches the Inner Station, Kurtz, who has thus been isolated for well over a year, is mortally ill, and he dies during the journey downstream. Even when further years have elapsed and Marlow is recounting the tale, Marlow seems only gradually to be discerning the extent of the manager's Machiavellism; he reflects:

> 'I did not see the real significance of that wreck [of the steam-boat] at once. I fancy I see it now, but I am not sure — not at all. Certainly the affair was too stupid — when I think of it — to be altogether natural.'
>
> (*Y*, 72.)

Marlow himself, deceived and subjected to frustrating delays, was in large measure a victim of the manager's ruthless plan.

I have discussed elsewhere[2] the detail and the thematic implications of this covert plot, which formerly was rather neglected. Here, my concern is with the more technical linkages to two subsequent works, 'A Smile of Fortune' (in *'Twixt Land and Sea*) and *The Shadow-Line*, in both of which the hero's plight has a certain structural resemblance to that of Kurtz and Marlow in *Heart of Darkness*. In both these later tales, the hero is victim of a plot which he only tardily and gradually perceives; in *The Shadow-Line*, he eventually sees clearly what is happening; in 'A Smile of Fortune', he has a growing recognition but, like a somnambulist or a man drugged by sexual desire, becomes an acquiescent victim-cum-accomplice, and until it is very late never reacts lucidly against the situation. If, in each case, the recognition of the plot is for a considerable time withheld from the hero, it is similarly withheld from the reader. The main reason (as with Marlow's tale in *Heart of Darkness*) is that both narratives employ first-person narration: the hero is also the story-teller, so that the reader, looking through his eyes or at least over his shoulder, must largely share the hero's ignorance or puzzlement. There is delayed decoding of the situation by the narrator, and the reader's decoding of the narrative (which includes the narrator) is also delayed. Sometimes the reader may see what is impending before the narrator does, because the experienced reader of fiction may give keener scrutiny to the offered events (knowing that 'plotting' of various kinds is in progress as soon as a narrative starts) than may a character surveying events which he does not presume to be 'plotted'; on the other hand, the reader's initial uncertainty about the narrative's direction, the presence of 'false trails' and interesting distractions, and the natural fallibility of memory, may cause his perceptions to lag behind the narrator's. Obviously enough, the lagging comprehension is more likely at a first reading of the tale; the proleptic comprehension more likely at a second reading. And there is an intermediate comprehension: when we reach the point of clarification or dénouement, we may without re-reading the text cast our minds back over it, perhaps mentally or physically thumbing back through the pages, correcting our responses to make our sense of the tale's logic tally with the new recognition. Critical commentaries frequently misrepresent the negotiation of the text by the reader, for they tend to telescope these stages and impose too rapidly the achieved understanding upon the initial uncertainties.

The part of *The Shadow-Line* which is instructive here is the long opening sequence. In a previous chapter, we have considered the 'covert plotting' of the sea-journey; but before the hero embarks on that journey there is a sequence ashore which takes up a third of the book (two parts of the six into which the novel is divided: 51 of 133 pages in the standard Dent edition). Both this 'shore' section and the narrative of the voyage contain covert plots in which the hero is the suffering victim, tardy in his comprehension, and dependent on the friendly help of an attentive advisor. This ironic parallelism increases the co-ordination of a novel which at first may seem to consist of two weakly-related narratives: an over-long preamble ashore and a more highly-charged story of the voyage.[3]

We have seen that within a Conradian novel or tale, a sequence of delayed decoding generally has three stages. First stage: the relatively raw, undeciphered impingement of experience upon the observer's senses. Second stage: false or incomplete decoding. Third stage: true or largely complete decoding (though perhaps with an after-sense that reality has proved rather more recalcitrant and troubling than rational orthodoxy likes to maintain). The covert plot in Chapters 1 and 2 of *The Shadow-Line* offers the same sequence, though the 'false' and 'incomplete' decoding are sufficiently distinct to be regarded as *two* stages in a sequence of *four*. The revised sequence applies in this way to the text. First stage: the narrator sees strange occurrences but does not understand them. Second stage: false decoding: the narrator decides that Captain Giles, who does understand them, is a fool. Third stage: inadequate decoding: the narrator understands only part of the plot. Fourth stage: he sees the whole, and Giles is vindicated.

Initially, the narrator is aware that the steward and Hamilton are behaving in odd ways, but he makes no sense of their actions. Next, Captain Giles offers a number of veiled hints about what is happening, but instead of recognising the astute benevolence of Giles, the narrator deduces that he is either half-mad or a fool:

[I]t flashed upon me that high professional reputation was not necessarily a guarantee of sound mind.....
I came to the conclusion that he was simply the most tactless idiot on earth.....
Such perfect stupidity was almost interesting.....
Here was a man of recognised character and achievement disclosed as an absurd and dreary chatterer.....
Everything was stupid and overrated, even as Captain Giles was.

(21, 22, 23.)

The third stage tardily comes when the hero, still not understanding what Giles is suggesting, accepts his advice to the extent of accosting the Steward and asking him whether the Harbour Office had sent a letter to the Seamen's Home. The Steward's response surprises him:

> Instead of telling me to mind my own business, as he might have done, he began to whine with an undertone of impudence. He couldn't see me anywhere this morning. He couldn't be expected to run all over the town after me.
>
> 'Who wants you to?' I cried. And then my eyes became opened to the inwardness of things and speeches the triviality of which had been so baffling and tiresome.
>
> (26.)

Even here, when he thinks his eyes are 'opened to the inwardness of things', they are only just beginning to open. He senses that the diverted letter concerns himself, but is still surprised to learn from the Steward that the letter offers the command of a ship. The hero indignantly says to Giles (who has been fully aware of the real situation):

> 'You would never believe it..... It was a notification that a master is wanted for some ship. There's a command apparently going about and this fellow puts the thing in his pocket.'
>
> (27.)

He then thinks 'This was to be the end of the incident — for me', but he is quite wrong. Again Giles presses him to act, this time by going to the Harbour Office; and there the hero learns that the letter was no general notification but had been sent specifically to himself to offer him the command of a ship at Bankok whose master had died. Having signed the agreement to take command, the hero walks back — passing Hamilton, who is heading for the same office and is shocked to see him: 'I verily believe he staggered, though as far as I could see he didn't actually fall.' (35.)

There is still a delay before the occurrence of the fourth stage, complete decoding. The hero tells Giles that he can't understand why the Steward had withheld the letter 'for no reason at all'. Giles then explains:

'Don't you see that what he wanted was to get rid of our friend Hamilton
by dodging him in front of you for that job? That would have removed him
for good, see?'

(41.)

The Steward had withheld the letter from the hero but had
shown it to Hamilton because he wanted Hamilton to get the
command. And his reason for wishing Hamilton to suceed
was that the latter had not been paying his bills at the Home:
he has been a worrying, parasitic encumbrance. The covert
plot involving the Steward and Hamilton at last becomes overt
to the narrator — and overt to the reader with a good memory
for detail. However, there remains an important aspect of the
plot and of Giles's vigilant rôle as detective which the hero
never fully recognises.

If we consider the natures of the other characters at the
Home and also the implications of Giles's enquiries about the
hero's plans, we see that Giles has been doing more than
outwitting tricksters and averting an act of dishonesty; he has
been saving the hero's soul — his maritime soul, at least. For
the Home is presented as a kind of limbo in which men may
sink into slothful failure and stupefied demoralisation. The
Steward is a fretful, despondent drug-addict. Hamilton is a
surly parasitic loafer. Another resident is a moribund alcoholic:

He, poor fellow, not because he was hungry but I verily believe only to
recover his self-respect, had tried to put some of that unworthy food into his
mouth. But after dropping his fork twice and generally making a failure of it,
he had sat still with an air of intense mortification combined with a ghastly
glazed stare.

(15-16.)

As the Sargasso Sea is the graveyard of sailing ships, so this
Seamen's Home in the balmy air of an eastern port is a
graveyard of ambition and effort; and the hero has run the risk
of becoming just such an apathetic ex-voyager. For no clear
reason, he had abandoned a post as mate on a good ship; he is
suffering a vague malaise, an acedia — or, as he terms it, the
'green sickness':

One day I was perfectly right and the next everything was gone — glamour,
flavour, interest, contentment — everything..... The green sickness of late

youth descended on me and carried me off.....

(5.)

At the Home, Giles points out that Hamilton had seemed 'a nice boy' when he came ashore there — but that was 'some years ago'; and his questions to the hero imply that Giles is apprehensive that the new 'nice boy' may take a similar downward path after abandoning his vessel.

Thus, a covert plot which extends around and far beyond the Steward's intrigue is one in which first Giles and later Ransome help the hero to resist the temptation of various kinds of moral paralysis. The point is emphasised at the very end of the purgatorial voyage, when the hero again meets Giles.

> 'Are you leaving soon?' [Giles asks.]
> 'I am going on board directly,' I said. 'I shall pick up one of my anchors and heave in to half-cable on the other as soon as my new crew comes on board and I shall be off at daylight to-morrow.'
> 'You will?' grunted Captain Giles approvingly. 'That's the way. You'll do.'
> 'What did you expect? That I would want to take a week ashore for a rest?' I said, irritated by his tone.
>
> (132.)

That the hero is 'irritated' by Giles's tone and fails to see the irony of his own sarcasm about going ashore for a rest shows that even now, at the end of the narrative, he has still not perceived the full extent of Giles's very successful plan to redeem him. It is the realism of presentation of this mild friction between the impatient young hero and the elderly, slowly-ruminative Captain which helps to make this one of the most subtle and quietly successful covert plots in Conrad's fiction. Conrad was always affectionately interested in the wisdom of the reticent; hence, in part, his devotion to wisely reticent plot-structures.

## (ii) 'A SMILE OF FORTUNE'

This long tale is one of Conrad's most subtle, neglected and underrated works, and what makes it subtle is probably what has made it neglected and underrated. The work as a whole is enigmatic. The overt plot, concerning a sea-captain's sexual infatuation (with a rather gauche, immature young woman) which leads to an unsavoury business-transaction, is unconventional. There is a minor covert plot concerning the deception of the captain; as it gradually emerges, so it blends into the overt plot. There are also, however, indications of a major covert plot which is hard to define. This covert plot is not an elliptically-presented realistic sequence; rather, it exists as a ghost overshadowing and encompassing the main narrative. By 'ghost', I do not mean that it is vague in presentation, or murky, or a matter of 'inconceivables' and 'inscrutables'; on the contrary, the details which evoke it are highly specific, presented with documentary clarity and glowing precision. It is as if, in a film, an apparently straightforward story had been accompanied by a wealth of carefully-focused shots which initially seem superfluous or digressive: strange scenes and details which surround and accompany the patently narrative scenes. The enigma lies in their logic, which is hard to see at first; yet the connections between some of them are so deliberately deployed that one senses further connections which would vindicate the whole. I first discuss the minor covert plot; next, I discuss the enigma which may indicate a major covert plot.

*(a) The minor covert plot*
In some respects 'A Smile of Fortune' resembles the shore-sequence of *The Shadow-Line*, because a covert plot gradually emerges and blends with the overt material as the protagonist tardily recognises the extent to which he is the object of machinations by another man. The hero of the tale (again, a sea-captain who is the supposed narrator) is a person cleverly being decoyed into ambush; and though he gradually perceives most of the ambush, he is unable to make a clean break from it; he extricates himself awkwardly and feels sullied. The schemer is Alfred Jacobus. As a ship's chandler on Mauritius,[4] Jacobus has the general aim of ingratiating himself with visiting sea-captains in order to increase his business; but he is particularly attentive to the hero, partly in the hope of selling him a huge load of potatoes and largely to fulfil his long-term aim of finding a respectable husband for his illegitimate

daughter Alice. The captain is slow to see that he is being manoeuvred into the position of being compromised with Alice so that he will be tempted to accept either her or the potatoes or both. The reader also, though to a lesser degree, will at first fail to see the full extent of Jacobus's wiles.

An ambiguous term which is recurrently applied to Alfred Jacobus is 'procurer'. He is a procurer in the mild sense, being an adept at obtaining, for the sake of trade, things needed by visiting captains (provisions, sugar-bags and even funeral arrangements); but he is also a procurer in the sexual sense, through his cleverness in bringing together the hero and Alice. His astuteness lies behind the apparently trivial incidents of his first meeting with the captain, on his ship. Initially he exploits a confusion of names (he is confused with his brother Ernest Jacobus, the rival merchant to whom the captain was actually commended by the ship's owners); he draws attention to the merits of the potatoes on the breakfast-table (before the captain discovers that these have been furnished by Alfred himself to advertise his wares); and he is quick to ascertain that the captain is neither married nor engaged. On a subsequent visit to the vessel, Jacobus presents the captain with a bunch of flowers and offers to 'procure' him several such plants: another trade-advertisement which also serves to introduce the subject of his beautiful walled garden, where the lonely Alice is to be found. Eventually, on the understanding that a difficult negotiation about sugar-bags will thus be facilitated, the captain is persuaded to visit that walled garden; and there, as Jacobus had planned, he meets and becomes infatuated by the gauche, ignorant, inhibited but physically seductive girl. 'What she had on under that dingy, loose, amber wrapper must have been of the most flimsy and airy character. One could not help being aware of it. It was obvious..... I did not avert my gaze from Alice.' (*TLAS*, 44-5.)

The captain becomes a frequent visitor to the garden as his infatuation with Alice grows; he feels that he is becoming 'the slave of some depraved habit' (59), an addict of 'a secret vice....., like the habit of some drug or other which ruins or degrades its slave' (62). At last he embraces Alice, only to find that he has been observed by her father; and in order to placate Jacobus and gain the opportunity for a final meeting with

Alice before he returns to sea, the captain now acquiesces in the unethical potato-deal, paying with every penny he has. He sets sail for Australia; many of the potatoes rot on the voyage; but at landfall he is able to sell the remainder at a huge profit. After failing to persuade the vessel's owners to change the route so that he will never again have to visit Mauritius, the captain resigns his command, thus jeopardising his career. The kiss which the girl had given him at their last encounter 'had to be paid for at its full price' (87).

### (b) The covert enigma

The tale is lucid, vivid and yet strange: as we have seen, Jacobus's stratagems gradually become overt enough to the captain and to us; but there remain various mysteries which haunt the narrative. The sense of a larger covert plot is evoked partly by the series of symmetrical contrasts that the work establishes. For example, after the first landfall on Mauritius, the captain encounters two mourning fellow-captains. One mourns the loss of an infant son, who died at sea and is to be buried on land; the other mourns the loss of his figure-head, a beautiful woman with extended arms, which vanished during a voyage: two contrasting loves, a father's love for a real child and a bachelor-captain's love for a woman of wood, yet interlinked in mourning. And near the end of the tale this theme of death and burial is completed when the hero has a strange dream: 'I dreamt of a pile of gold in the form of a grave in which a girl was buried, and woke up callous with greed.' (84.)

Another symmetrical contrast is provided by the brothers Jacobus: Alfred is patient and ingratiating; Ernest is impatient and irascible. Alfred has the illegitimate daughter whom he guards and keeps in sheltered idleness at home; Ernest has an illegitimate son whom he bullies and treats as a contemptible servant at his office. The central image of the tale is that of the lush, perfumed flower-garden; but from the transaction in the walled garden results a cargo of rank, decaying potatoes.

My bargain with all its remotest associations, mental and visual — the garden of flowers and scents, the girl with her provoking contempt and her tragic loneliness of a hopeless castaway — was everlastingly dangled before my eyes, for thousands of miles along the open sea. And as if by a satanic refinement of irony it was accompanied by a most awful smell. Whiffs from decaying potatoes pursued me on the poop, they mingled with my thoughts, with my food, poisoned my very dreams. They made an atmosphere of corruption for the ship.

(82.)

The potatoes are literally decadent — decaying; both passively and actively corrupting; and the tale is largely about modes of quiet decadence: the torpidly decadent society of Mauritius, and the kinds of mild corruption which sexual desire may induce; it is about the ways in which the moral fibre of seamen may be softened by emotional entanglements, and friendships may be corrupted by concerns of trade.

The narrative as a whole has a resonance and symbolic glow which result from its combination of precise realism with glints and half-echoes of ancient myths and archetypes — glints and half-echoes rather than allegoric tableaux and rhetorical insistences. A beautiful and lethargic girl confined to a walled garden; guarded by a shrewish harridan and watched by a schemer, yet capable of liberation by a stranger from the seas; a girl on an island who offers a form of temptation and seduction to a voyager; a daughter who is offspring of a circus-rider and of a merchant who 'apparently travelled at the tail of that beastly circus to other parts of the world, in a most degrading position', being treated 'worse than a dog' by the woman. The story thus evokes half-echoes of numerous folk-tales and legends: for example, of the Sleeping Beauty (who slept in the enchanted palace within the overgrown garden, waiting to be awakened by a kiss), and of Cinderella (confined and jealously watched over; in 'A Smile of Fortune' much is made of Alice's lost slipper, and the final embrace occurs when she has sought it and the captain 'put on the shoe, buttoning the instep-strap' after he has 'groped for her foot under the flounces of the wrapper'). Folk-tales of tainted transactions, blighting erotic enchantment and of a seductive girl controlled by a mage, these briefly beckon. The central situation and the emphasis on Jacobus as 'procurer' evoke memories of the legend of Troilus and Pandarus. The story of Odysseus and Calypso, voyager and seductress, is evoked too; and, as we have seen, the account of Jacobus's infatuation with the circus-woman is so phrased as to recall the legend of Circe and her men-beasts. And all these echoes are distorted parodically in this world of mundane nineteenth-century actualities. As the narrator reflects on hearing of Jacobus's enchantment by the equestrienne:

> The grotesque image of a fat, pushing ship-chandler, enslaved by an unholy love-spell, fascinated me; and I listened rather open-mouthed to the tale as old as the world, a tale which had been the subject of legend, of moral fables, of poems, but which so ludicrously failed to fit the personality. What a strange victim for the gods!
>
> (36.)

'A Smile of Fortune', like numerous other tales by Conrad, is a first person narrative which purports to be reminiscence by the captain. It is based to some extent on Conrad's own brief love-affair on the island of Mauritius in 1888, but there are marked differences from actuality (for example, although Conrad envisaged marriage to Eugénie Renouf, the girl who was one of the counterparts of the fictional Alice Jacobus, he found that she was already engaged).[5] The tale, then, has the ostensible flexibility of personal reminiscence in which the anecdotal and the apparently incidental blend with the symmetries of a structured narrative. Again, as a tale in a realistic mode, it offers us vivid glimpses and fragments of life; deployed inconsequentiality. But lurking behind and co-ordinating the material which gathers with seeming looseness around the central tale of the muted courtship and the tainted transaction is a new, partly-ironic working of an ancient cluster of material from legend and folk-lore. Dream and fact, myth and circumstantiality, symbol and mundane recollection, all move and shimmer there; and that the greater covert narrative of this tale eludes comprehensive summary is, perhaps, a sign of its quiet originality and dexterity.

The solution to the enigma of 'A Smile of Fortune' is indicated by those words I quoted just now: 'a tale which had been the subject of legend, of moral fables, of poems, but which so ludicrously failed to fit the personality'. Legends, moral fables and poems are beckoned by 'A Smile of Fortune', mock it and are mocked by it. They are evoked by a tale which yet preserves the ironic distance of the mundane. To a would-be Prince Charming (and a Freudian interpreter) it offers not a magical shoe but a worn slipper; to the would-be Jason of the Golden Fleece (and a Jungian analyst) it offers fifty tons of stinking potatoes. This is a story of metamorphoses: boy into dust; wooden figurehead into object of love and mourning; a colonial society into decadent torpor; girl into woman; girl into stupor and a brief awakening; businesslike captain into an addict of the sensual; a kind of love into a business transaction; a ship-chandler into the slave of a circus-rider; the walled flower-garden into a ship laden with potatoes; potatoes into a smell of decay which poisons dreams; a dream of gold which forms a girl's grave. In very appearance, Alice is partly a slatternly adolescent and partly 'a seated statue': 'She was like a spellbound creature with the forehead of a goddess crowned by the dishevelled magnificent hair of a gipsy tramp' (59). And if she seems caught in mid-metamorphosis between goddess and tramp, statue and human, even sexually her metamorphosis from male stock into female seems incomplete:

Her attitude, like certain tones of her voice, had in it something masculine: the knees apart in the ample wrapper, the clasped hands hanging between them, her body leaning forward, with drooping head.

(65.)

She.....took her chin in her hand — a Jacobus chin undoubtedly. And those heavy eyelids, this black irritated stare reminded me of Jacobus, too — the wealthy merchant, the respected one. The design of her eyebrows also was the same, rigid and ill-omened. Yes! I traced in her a resemblance to both of them. It came to me as a sort of surprising remote inference that both these Jacobuses were rather handsome men after all.

(47.)

The very stock of the Jacobus family is caught in protean transition: it has produced both the sleepy-eyed Alfred and the seductive Alice; both the irascible Ernest and his wretched son.

Metamorphosis is not merely a theme of the tale. The central narrative strategy of 'A Smile of Fortune' aspires to the enactment of metamorphosis. Through allusion, echo and strange symmetries it beckons the reader from the overt plot to potential plots which partake of past myth, legend and folk-tale; but the resistant disparities between the ancient material evoked and the modern material presented deflect us back towards the realistic surface. A cyclical process is generated. As though watching the nymph Daphne changing and dwindling, largely but not entirely transformed into laurel-bush, so when reading 'A Smile of Fortune' we sense a body of legend of magical metamorphoses largely but not entirely transformed into a secular, mundane, realistic narrative.[6]

The covert plot of 'A Smile of Fortune', then, consists not of a determinate sequence but rather of a cluster of narrative possibilities evoked by allusions to some traditional and ancient literary material. Some of the allusions are relatively explicit; others are implicit in the situations and patternings which invest the overt plot. In some of the traditional material, the story ends happily. the hero rescues a heroine from her place of confinement and takes her away to a new life *(as in Cinderella, The Sleeping Beauty* or 'The Eve of St. Agnes'). Alternatively, the story is relatively unhappy, the hero emerging from an encounter with an enchantress who has seduced, impeded or blighted him (we recall the encounters with, say, Calypso, Circe, Morgan la Fay, Lamia or La Belle Dame). But all such narratives relate sexuality to magical transformations, and it is the theme of sexuality and metamorphosis which centrally links the covert matter to the overt plot of 'A Smile of Fortune'. The reader's recognition, as the tale proceeds, that a protean, shifting complex of magic-invoking narratives is itself being invoked by, yet largely subordinated to, a non-magical realistic narrative, means that the very process of metamorphosis is being generated and enacted by the reader. Here theme, technique and process are one.

# CHAPTER 9

# *Transtextual Narratives*

## (i) FICTIONAL SYMBIOSES

Just as there are logical relationships between delayed decoding and covert plots (for in each case the observer or reader supplies the delayed or suppressed causal connections), so there are logical relationships between delayed decoding and what I term transtextual narratives. A transtextual narrative is one which exists in, across and between two or more texts.[1] It is covert in proportion to the reader's unawareness of the relevant material. The reader needs both a microscopic and macroscopic eye — an eye for small significant detail and an eye for vast patternings of which, for example, one novel or even two novels may be just a part.

Sometimes, though not always, a transtextual narrative is an example of large-scale *hysteron-proteron*: inverted order. In delayed decoding, we encounter first the later and subsequently the earlier. The later event is thrust at us; subsequently we learn of the preceding causal events. This is the case with some of Conrad's transtextual plots (as with Shakespeare's dramatisation of English history from Richard II to Richard III), in which the later stages of the narrative may have been written and published years — sometimes decades — before the earlier.

Transtextual narratives may be small, medium, large or vast in scale. To give a simple case, I begin with a small example which is generally overlooked: the story of Hamilton. In my

previous discussion of *The Shadow-Line* (in Chapter 8), I dealt
with the affair of Hamilton, the unpopular sponger at the
Seamen's Home. We saw how the Steward's endeavour to get
rid of this parasite entailed his attempt to defraud the hero of
his chance of a first command. The story of Hamilton, this
earlier part of which was thus inaugurated in that later work
(for *The Shadow-Line* was first published in *Harper's Magazine* in
1916), had actually been completed in an earlier work, the tale
'The End of the Tether', first published in *Blackwood's Magazine*
in 1902. In 'The End of the Tether', we learn how Hamilton
was finally sent packing, when Captain Elliott ( a counterpart
of Captain Ellis in *The Shadow-Line*) tells Whalley:

'You would think they would be falling over each other. Not a bit of it.
Frightened to go home. Nice and warm out here to lie about a verandah
waiting for a job. I sit and wait in my office. Nobody. What did they suppose?
That I was going to sit there like a dummy with the Consul-General's cable
before me? Not likely. So I looked up a list of them I keep by me and sent
word for Hamilton — the worst loafer of them all — and just made him go.
Threatened to instruct the steward of the Sailors' Home to have him turned
out neck and crop. He did not think the berth was good enough — if you —
please. "I've your little record by me," said I. "You came ashore here
eighteen months ago, and you haven't done six months' work since. You are
in debt for your board now at the Home, and I suppose you reckon the
Marine Office will pay in the end. Eh? So it shall; but if you don't take this
chance, away you go to England, assisted passage, by the first homeward
steamer that comes along. You are no better than a pauper. We don't want
any white paupers here." I scared him. But look at the trouble all this gave
me.'

(*Y*, 199-200.)

Thus, Conrad ends the yarn about Hamilton — approximately
*fourteen years* before starting it; and thus our inference of the
official's concern for the hero of *The Shadow-Line* is further
verified by this earlier and quite different tale.

Conrad's very first novel, *Almayer's Folly*, inaugurates various
transtextual narratives. It gives, for example, later stages of
intrigues which were engendered in the past and whose
engendering will be revealed in a later novel or novels. We saw
that the most important covert plot in *Almayer's Folly* concerns
the stratagem of Abdulla, the Arab trader, who secures the
downfall of Dain and Almayer. If we ask how the Arab traders
came to be established in Sambir in the first place — if, that is,

protégés disappointed or destroyed. What is true of the 'adoption' of Almayer and Willems by Lingard is largely true of the 'adoption' of Jim by Stein and Marlow. The fictional Tom Lingard is finally swallowed up in Europe, whither he had returned in the hope of raising funds for his gold-prospecting schemes; and the real Lingard (William Lingard) on whom Conrad had based the character similarly travelled far away from his familiar trading area in the Malay Archipelago to England, and died at Macclesfield in 1888.[2] (The real Almayer, Charles Olmeijer, in 1890 petitioned the Governor-General of the Dutch East Indies to be permitted to prospect for gold in Berau:[3] another link with his gold-seeking fictional counterpart, whose location Conrad spelt phonetically as 'Brow'.)

Transtextual narratives generate proleptic and analeptic ironies. These affect not only major characters but also minor characters, who accordingly gain in significance. A good example is provided by the characterisation of Jim-Eng, the Chinaman. In *Almayer's Folly* he is seen as a decadent opium-addict who helps Almayer on the downward path into drug-addiction and death; and he is a living instance of the larger thematic conflict between the world of consolatory dreams (and ideals and hopes) and the world of harshly frustrating realities — the conflict invoked by the very epigraph of Conrad's first novel: 'Qui de nous n'a eu sa terre promise, son jour d'extase et sa fin en exil?' ('Which of us has not known his promised land, his day of ecstasy and his end in exile?')[4] When we read the subsequent novel, *An Outcast*, we find that Jim-Eng is there presented as a relatively young, fit, active and courageous fellow. ' "I brought him here," exclaimed Lingard. "A first-class Chinaman that." ' (He is also another doomed protégé.) Lingard learns that when Abdulla hoisted the Dutch flag, Jim-Eng had the courage to defy it.

'[T]hey were after him because he wouldn't take off his hat to the flag. He was not so much scared, but he was very angry and indignant. Of course he had to run for it; there were some fifty men after him — Lakamba's friends — but he was full of fight. Said he was an Englishman, and would not take off his hat to any flag but English.....Says he: "They are only black fellows. We white men.....can fight everybody in Sambir." '

(182.)

This vivid depiction of Jim-Eng in *An Outcast* clearly helps to point many of the racial and national ironies of the text. The Chinaman is patriotically 'English' and braver than Almayer in defying those who have hoisted the Dutch flag. Almayer the Dutchman, who works under the British flag of Lingard, is being defeated by an alliance of Arabs and Malays who help their cause by hoisting the flag of the European nation from which their enemy is descended; while the Chinaman defies that flag and claims common cause — and common race and prejudice — with the British. A powerful proleptic irony operates: those readers who remember the older, dope-sodden Jim-Eng of *Almayer's Folly* will see in a poignant light the younger, active and absurdly pugnacious Jim-Eng of *An Outcast*; and there is analeptic irony, too, for on looking back at that older Jim-Eng of the earlier text we have to revise our former opinion of his apparent worthlessness, as we now know the spirit that was crushed. Transtextual recollection also gives new emphasis to an apparently incidental detail of *An Outcast*:

'They released Jim-Eng the next day, when the [British] flag had been hauled down. He sent six cases of opium to me for safe keeping but has not left his house. I think he is safe enough now.'

(186.)

Jim-Eng's opium, to which Almayer refers so casually here, will (we know) prove to be the death of Almayer himself.

Transtextualities are not always examples of *hysteron-proteron*. One transtextual biography which largely proceeds in normal chronological order through the fiction is the most important in the whole range of Conrad's work: the biography of Captain Charles Marlow, presented in 'Youth', *Heart of Darkness*, *Lord Jim* and *Chance*. (The publications span fourteen years, from 'Youth' in 1898 to *Chance* in 1912; the main fictional events span perhaps fifty years, from the action of 'Youth' to the narration of *Chance*.) It is a sad story, for as Marlow ages we hear him gradually become less intelligent and more garrulous: in the later part of *Lord Jim* and for much of *Chance* he is too facile and waffling as philosopher-raconteur, and we regret his ageing. It is a sad story in another respect, too, for this man who had once felt love for Kurtz's fiancée never marries but settles into a long and lonely bachelorhood. In this vast biographical narrative, one crucial piece of covert plotting is indeed the muted, abortive love-relationship in *Heart of Darkness*. Again, this has been neglected by commentators; but there is clear evidence of its presence and central importance in the story of Marlow.

His extreme embarrassment at the interview with Kurtz's Intended stems from his knowledge of Kurtz's true character; but it is compounded by the fact that when he had first seen her portrait, he had experienced a stirring of emotions which included not only curiosity, not only a sense of responsibility, but also love: love for a young woman whose beauty seemed so perfectly expressive of truth in a world of falsehood, and of trust amid a world of betrayals.

'She struck me as beautiful — I mean she had a beautiful expression. I know that the sunlight can be made to lie too, yet one felt that no manipulation of light and pose could have conveyed the delicate shade of truthfulness upon those features. She seemed ready to listen without mental reservation, without suspicion, without a thought for herself. I concluded that I would go and give her back her portrait and those letters myself. Curiosity? Yes; and also some other feeling perhaps.'

(154-5.)

Thus there is a personal romantic aspect to Marlow's visit to the Intended. He is meeting an intriguingly beautiful, bereaved young lady, who is eager for companionship in mourning and the comfort that her fiancé's friend can supply; and Marlow is in a position of power, for whether he tells her the truth or not, she is in an emotionally-exploitable situation. But his embarrassment grows with the recognition that the preservation of her beauty of 'truthfulness' depends on his connivance in the extension, by falsehood, of ignorance; and he chooses to preserve her fidelity to the unfaithful Kurtz.

There is no doubt that Conrad deliberately planned this brief, delicate excursion by Marlow into unrequited love; for, in a letter to David Meldrum at the publisher's office, Conrad remarked of *Heart of Darkness* (which he was then completing): 'A mere shadow of love interest just in the last pages — but I hope it will have the effect intended.' (*BBL*, 38.) So, briefly in *Heart of Darkness*, Conrad hints at an amatory tragedy of 'what might have been' for Marlow; and the implications of that frustrating brief encounter expand throughout his subsequent transtextual biography. Just as it can be inferred from the adoptions of Tom Lingard, who also remains unmarried, a need to gratify a frustrated paternal instinct can be inferred from Charles Marlow's recurrent adoptions of various protégés, most notably Lord Jim (who is twenty years younger than he). Furthermore, that long-past meeting with Kurtz's fiancée, who was trapped in the memory of previous love, lends a poignant irony to the ending of *Chance*. There Marlow, on behalf of his protégé Powell, intercedes with Flora Anthony, the young widow who, like Kurtz's bereaved fiancée, cherishes loyally the memory of the man she loved. She mentions that Powell has been a comfort to her in the past, and enquires: 'You like him? — don't you?'. Marlow reports the subsequent exchange:

> ' "Excellent fellow," I said warmly. "You see him often?"
> "Of course. I hardly know another soul in the world. I am alone. And he has plenty of time on his hands. His aunt died a few years ago. He's doing nothing, I believe."
> "He is fond of the sea," I remarked. "He loves it."
> "He seems to have given it up," she murmured.
> "I wonder why?"
> She remained silent. "Perhaps it is because he loves something else better," I went on. "Come, Mrs. Anthony, don't let me carry away from here the idea that you are a selfish person, hugging the memory of your past happiness, like a rich man his treasure, forgetting the poor at the gate."
> ....."Do you think it possible that he should care for me?" '
>
> (445-6.)

Marlow's words take effect, and the novel concludes with a confident prediction of the marriage of Flora Anthony and Powell. A balance has been redressed: a pattern begun so long ago in *Heart of Darkness* has at last been vicariously completed. *Chance* is not a major novel, but, for those who hear them, the echoes of the earlier tale sometimes enhance it.

Not only Lingard and Marlow but numerous other characters, major and minor, recur in Conrad's pages, figuring in two or even three of his works. As we have seen, Almayer, Abdulla, Lakamba, Babalatchi and Jim-Eng appear in both *Almayer's Folly* and *An Outcast*. The presentation of Nina

Almayer as a happy child in *An Outcast* lends retrospective irony to her less happy self in *Almayer's Folly*, just as the presentation of her father's doting love for her in the later novel magnifies retrospectively our recognition of his crushing sense of loss at her elopement, recorded in the earlier one. Schomberg, the rascally hotel-keeper, figures briefly in *Lord Jim* and prominently in 'Falk' and *Victory*, becoming predictably slanderous. Captain Ellis, Master-Attendant at Singapore, appears in *Lord Jim*, 'The End of the Tether' and *The Shadow-Line* as a consistently brusque professional; in the two earlier works he is called 'Elliot' and 'Elliott'. His real-life counterpart, Captain Henry Ellis, died in 1908, so that by the time *The Shadow-Line* was being written (circa 1915) there was less need for Conrad to conceal the debt by modifying his surname. The rather surly first mate, Burns, appears in *The Shadow-Line*, 'A Smile of Fortune' and (un-named but clearly identifiable) in 'Falk' and 'The Secret Sharer'. The old seaman, Gambril, appears in *The Shadow-Line* and 'Falk'. There is even continuity among the listeners to tales: the anonymous primary narrator of *Heart of Darkness* reminds us that the very same group of men (including a lawyer, an accountant and a company director) had listened to Marlow telling the tale of 'Youth': 'Between us there was, as I have already said somewhere, the bond of the sea': and the 'somewhere' was the opening of that earlier tale. And as my subsequent list shows, there are many other examples of transtextual characterisations.

This large network of recurrent characters and their transtextual biographies gives a special quality to Conrad's fiction. First, and obviously enough, this network enhances the realism, for we know that such recurrences (particularly of ageing characters)[5] are likely to arise when an author is drawing closely on memories of actual encounters in life. Sometimes the reason for the recurrence is that Conrad is indeed recalling a real person (Burns is based on the real mate, Born; Tom Lingard on the real William Lingard; Almayer on the real Olmeijer); but sometimes the reason is that he is re-using a convenient fictional construct, though one based, no doubt, on several real acquaintances (as seems to be the case with Charles Marlow). While one effect is to give an apparent warrant of authenticity to the fiction, another is to give a peculiar spaciousness to the fictional world: for, as tale is linked to tale, novel to novel, tale to novel and novel to tale by means of these recurrent characters (and recurrent vessels and locations), we sense behind the individual works a *meta-narrative* — one huge imaginative territory closely related to actuality (however diversely modified) and from which all the individual existent fictions can be seen as selections. With most other major writers, we move from separate work to separate work, and though we gain cumulative knowledge of each writer's habits of imagination and technique, we do not encounter that Conradian sense of the symbiosis of fictional and actual worlds and lives, or of a greater unrecorded world from which these beings have emerged into the light of utterance and literary history.

A second obvious advantage is that transtextuality provides a gain not only in realism but also in economy. Conrad can invoke in one tale our recollection of matters given, perhaps more fully, in a previous tale (as when the description of the Director of Companies in 'Youth' is invoked by the opening of *Heart of Darkness*); and this suggests in turn that any reading of a single Conradian work which is not 'contextual' in its range may drastically impoverish that work. If it be argued that to evaluate a literary text we should regard it as a single entity, isolated from its fellows, the answer is that in deciding on the content and meaning of that text we naturally and properly take account of those parts of its context which seem appropriately to enrich it, rather as we relate to a Shakespeare sonnet or a Blake poem others in their respective sequences; and there are obvious grounds for considering as one entity a narrative which extends across two or more tales or novels, just as, for some critical purposes, we may deem the tetralogy of Shakespeare's histories from *Richard II* to *Henry V* to be one entity. Incidentally, we should beware of the temptation to talk of fictional characters as though they were *not* real people. From time to time literary theorists advocate this temptation: L.C. Knights did so in the 1930s and post-structuralists did so in the 1970s, though they were seldom able to practise consistently what they preached. As Dr Johnson long ago pointed out, 'Imitations produce pain or pleasure, not because they are mistaken for realities, but because they bring realities to mind.'[6] To speak of Marlow as an ageing, lonely man (instead of, say, 'an assembly of semes' or 'the subject of the enunciation') can be a courteous, concise and cogent way of addressing the realities which the fiction brings to mind.

Conrad's transtextual narratives generate a keen sense of Joseph Conrad as a living, responsive author, responsive to the reader's curiosity: his narratives, apprehended as groups or clusters, invite and reward our interrogation. For example, near the beginning of 'A Smile of Fortune', the narrator discusses the character of the mate, Burns:

> Meantime the wind dropped, and Mr. Burns began to make disagreeable remarks about my usual bad luck. I believe it was his devotion for me which made him critically outspoken on every occasion. All the same, I would not have put up with his humours if it had not been my lot at one time to nurse him through a desperate illness at sea. After snatching him out of the jaws of death, so to speak, it would have been absurd to throw away such an efficient officer. But sometimes I wished he would dismiss himself.
>
> (*TLAS*, 4.)

We interrogate this statement in various ways. One is by asking the narrator to tell us more about this interesting love-hate relationship — and he subsequently will do so in this tale. Another is by asking for more information about the dramatic incident mentioned ('snatching him out of the jaws of death'): and this second question will be answered not in 'A Smile of Fortune' but five years later in *The Shadow-Line*, which gives a full account of Burns's feverish illness and of the captain's care for him. A further general consequence ensues for the readers: not only a sense of entry into an extensive and consistent fictional universe in which we have freedom to roam — and to re-encounter interesting landmarks and acquaintances — but also a sense that the narrator, where he is the anonymous presenter of a tale (and particularly when he is a naval figure) has a remarkable resemblance to an author who is intelligently responsive to our enquiries and who is an astute friend in evoking and eventually gratifying our curiosity: an olympian yet intimate raconteur. Recent critics who have claimed that literature is merely about itself shun many friendships and much wisdom.[7]

Although the majority of writers do not offer transtextualities, those who do so constitute a very large and varied minority; and they vary from the august and ancient to the popular and recent. Characters with transtextual biographies include Odysseus of *The Iliad* and *The Odyssey* (who is transauthorial too, his life being extended by numerous authors from Sophocles to Ezra Pound), Chaucer's Pardoner (of the General Prologue, Pardoner's Prologue and Pardoner's Tale) in *The Canterbury Tales*, Stalky in Kipling's tales, Allan Quatermain in Rider Haggard's novels, and the Brangwens in Lawrence's *The Rainbow* and *Women in Love*; and there are numerous other examples, some as recent as Wilt in Tom Sharpe's satires. Yet, though various similarities can be found, there is nowhere a really close equivalent to the transtextual world of Joseph Conrad. One reason is obvious. Conrad was drawing on the remembered experiences of a very distinctive life-pattern: that of a Pole who became a British citizen; of a seafarer who was an introspective student of literature and philosophy; of a Romantic and a sceptic. Technically, his transtextualities often constitute a fruitful paradox: they are narratives which arise with the seeming spontaneity and vagrancy of reminiscence, but which are constructed with minute attention to irony, allusion, symbolic ambiguity and literary precedent; they have the freedom of ample autobiography yet the discipline of a highly sophisticated creative imagination.

## (ii) TRANSTEXTUALITY BETWEEN FACT AND FICTION

Our sense that Conrad offers a distinctively spacious imaginative realm results partly from our awareness that his transtextual narratives extend strongly into autobiographical reality as well as into the compressed, charged, formalised and symbolic modes of fiction.

Most, though not all, of his fictional works deal with events which, chronologically, lie within the life-time or memory-span of the writer: Conrad generally describes what is recognisably the world in Conrad's time, not Homer's or Dr Johnson's. We gain the impression that generally the locations were known to the author personally, and this impression is

usually confirmed by the facts of Conrad's biography. Even in
the case of *Nostromo*, Conrad had had some glimpses of South
and Central America; and when events are set in a pre-
biographical past, as in *The Rover* and *Suspense*, the French
locations are those known well by him. Furthermore, as we
have seen, the recurrence of particular characters (and ships)
in different fictional works tends to imply the presence of a pre-
fictional pool of remembered actuality; and the narratorial
habits of Conrad's fiction often imitate closely the circling and
homing procedures of our friends' oral reminiscences. (We
recall conversations that turned into stories: 'Yes, certainly I
remember Robinson. But did you hear about the terrible
thing that happened to him when he tried to get to Paris? Well,
three years ago.....') Another reason is obvious but important.
People named and described in the 'fictional' works of Conrad
recur in his ostensibly 'non-fictional' and autobiographical
factual works, notably *The Mirror of the Sea* and *A Personal Record*.
What my inverted commas here imply is that the blurring of
orthodox distinctions between the fictional and non-fictional
is one of the most interesting qualities of Conrad's *œuvre*. The
mundane term 'yarn' is little used by today's critics; but it is a
useful generic term for stories which are often presented as
factual and autobiographical but which are likely to have
exaggerations and 'poetic licence' in the telling. The period
1860-1920 was the period in which the literary genre of the
yarn had its heyday, and no writer developed more fully than
did Conrad its capacity for registering truths of experience. In
that period proliferated literary narratives using oblique form:
tales within tales, and narratives introduced within ostensibly
personal reminiscence whether by the author or a character.

In Conrad's work, the relationship between the fictional
and the non-fictional territories is often highly problematic.
Here is a characteristic example. In the novel *The Arrow of Gold*
(1919), the first-person narrator, George, says that long ago in
Marseilles he was engaged in smuggling arms to a Royalist
group in Spain. One day he and his crew were ambushed by
'rascally carabineers' but escaped; soon afterwards the vessel
was again ambushed and pursued. Then, on the Spanish
coast, the craft was lost: this was

a shipwreck that instead of a fair fight left in me the memory of a suicide. It took away all that there was in me of independent life, but just failed to take me out of the world.....

I had nearly lost my liberty and even my life, I had lost my ship, a money-belt full of gold, I had lost my companions, had parted from my friend.....

(Dent, 1947; 256-7.)

Dramatic events, but presented in summary form over four pages, with the emphasis on the return rather than on what happened during the adventure. Now the problem begins. In the autobiographical and ostensibly non-fictional volume *The Mirror of the Sea* (sections 40-46), Conrad states that during his early days in Marseilles he was engaged in smuggling arms in a small sailing-vessel (the *Tremolino*) to Royalists in Spain. The crew included the admirable Dominic Cervoni and Dominic's unsavoury nephew César. On one voyage the vessel was ambushed by coastguards who had been alerted by an informer, evidently César; and, so as to elude the ambush, the smugglers took the *Tremolino* close in to the shore and deliberately wrecked her on the rocks. Just before the collision, Conrad went to his cabin to retrieve a money-belt laden with gold; he found that the cupboard had been broken open and the money-belt stolen. As the vessel foundered, Dominic, enraged by this further treachery by his nephew, knocked César overboard; and César, weighted by the stolen money-belt round his waist, drowned in the foaming sea.

The striking difference between these two accounts is that the autobiographical version gives a fuller, more dramatic, more fully characterised and explanatory sequence of events; it resembles a piece of melodramatic fiction far more than does the less eventful and less ironic account in *The Arrow of Gold*. Now an ingenuous reader may easily explain the similarities and the differences. He may say: 'The account in *The Mirror of the Sea* is factual autobiography, for this is the non-fictional work. Naturally, when writing his fictions Conrad drew on his actual experiences, and therefoe in *The Arrow of Gold*, which is set in Marseilles, he recalled the earlier incident. He condensed and simplified it, however, so as not to distract attention from the main fictional matter in hand, the story of George's love for Rita.' A more sceptical reader, though, may say: 'There's something odd about this supposedly autobiographical reminiscence in *The Mirror of the Sea*. It is very like a fictional tale in its presentation and plot, and not a very plausible one, for it resembles a sequence from romantic fiction or a boys' adventure-story. The very neatness of the fatal irony (the traitor destroyed by his own treachery; the thief dragged to a watery death by the weight of the gold he had stolen) raises suspicions that this is really fiction.' The researches of Norman Sherry prove that Dominic and César Cervoni actually existed and sailed with Conrad; furthermore, Dominic was known to be a smuggler; all three were in Marseilles around the same time and might have smuggled arms to Royalist forces in Spain, even though the date Conrad suggests for the incident does seem to coincide with a time when he and Dominic were engaged on lawful enterprises and on a large ship. What is most remarkable is that César lived on to marry and have a son. He was not drowned at sea in the circumstances that Conrad relates, but died at a ripe age in 1926.[8] The most fictional-sounding part of the *Tremolino* reminiscence does indeed prove to be fiction.

The most dramatic incident of Conrad's actual period in Marseilles is one which, understandably enough, he does not describe in his autobiographical non-fiction: and that is his attempt at suicide after he had gambled away a lot of borrowed money at Monte Carlo. This suicide-attempt is fully attested by his uncle's private correspondence at the time, which was eventually published (by Jocelyn Baines and Zdzislaw Najder) long after Conrad's death. When, in the light of this, we look again at the two accounts of the *Tremolino* episode, we may understand them more fully. A form of psychological displacement and substitution is taking place. (An earlier literary example of such displacement is Wordsworth's treatment, in *The Prelude* and related poems, of his predicament with Annette Vallon.) Instead of describing a suicide attempt which brought him perilously close to death but did not kill him, Conrad describes a risky deliberate shipwreck which he survived — an event which *The Arrow of Gold* terms, we remember, 'a shipwreck that instead of a fair fight left in me the memory of a suicide'. Furthermore, instead of talking in the autobiography about the borrowed wealth that he had gambled away at Monte Carlo, he tells a story of stolen wealth lost at sea by someone who drowned as a result of the theft: a transformation which could be one way of imaginatively purging guilt. In *Nostromo*, as if to confirm this interpretation, the linkage recurs: the linkage of smuggled arms, suicide, and death by water of someone weighted down with wealth that is not his.

The 'Author's Note' to *Nostromo* makes clear that the character of Decoud is based in part on the young Conrad. In that novel, Decoud is engaged in smuggling arms by water to a conservative régime, as Conrad claimed to have done and might well have done. At a crisis of isolation, Decoud commits suicide on a boat by putting a pistol to his chest and pulling the trigger (Conrad too had shot himself in the chest), and he falls into the water, his body being carried down into the depths by the weight of the bars of silver he had first put in his pockets. Circularly, the motif of 'corpse dragged down by purloined precious metal' leads us back to suicide and to Conrad: the author has found a way of revealing and concealing, of confessing yet exculpating himself.

So it appears to me. Such explanations as I have offered here are tentative, necessarily; and they are not intended to 'explain away' the problematic relationship between Conrad's 'facts' and 'fictions' or between the good and the less good parts of his writing. It is, however, significant that the 'autobiographical' account of the *Tremolino* episode in *The Mirror of the Sea* is more conspicuously 'fictional' in presentation, and less plausible, than the more cursory and reticent account in the novel *The Arrow of Gold*, and that neither rendering has the power of the rendering of Decoud's death in *Nostromo*, a *locus classicus* of the Conradian evocation of mortality, isolation, and human littleness in the face of nature. A man who wears a mask may behave less inhibitedly than a man who does not; and autobiography has its own devious covert plots. By means of the fictional Decoud, Conrad may actually convey more of his personal experience (in terms of attitude, belief, and perhaps in fact) than in the supposedly factual *Mirror of the Sea*. Conradian fiction and non-fiction are not distinct but merge, blend and separate in the most complex of ways, constituting one great Conradian imaginative territory. A fictionalised César Cervoni appears in the autobiographical *Mirror of the Sea*; the historic Nelson appears in the novel *The Rover*; and the story 'Prince Roman' describes a real Prince Sanguszko. In the 1970s, when the Joseph Conrad Society appealed for funds for its Library, a Prince Sanguszko 'phoned the Chairman and sent a large donation: he had not forgotten Conrad's story of his patriotic ancestor. Conrad's work offers a majestically complete answer to recent theorists who would uphold the autonomy of literature by denying its relationship to empirical reality.[9] 'That conscientious rendering of truth in thought and fact', said Conrad, 'has always been my aim.'[10]

## (iii) LIST OF TRANSTEXTUAL CHARACTERISATIONS IN CONRAD'S WORKS

| *Characters* | *Texts* |
| --- | --- |
| Abdulla (Abdullah) | *An Outcast, Almayer's Folly*, 'Because of the Dollars', *A Personal Record*. |
| Allen (Dawson) | 'Freya', *The Rescue*. |
| Almayer, Caspar | *An Outcast, Almayer's Folly, A Personal Record*. |
| Almayer, Nina | *An Outcast, Almayer's Folly*. |
| Anonymous captain and narrator whose ship resembles Conrad's *Otago* | 'Falk', *The Shadow-Line*, 'The Secret Sharer', 'A Smile of Fortune' |
| Babalatchi and Lakamba | *An Outcast, Almayer's Folly*. |
| Blunt | *The Mirror of the Sea, The Arrow of Gold*. |
| Burns (sometimes nameless) | 'Falk', *The Shadow-Line*, 'A Smile of Fortune', *The Mirror*. |
| Cervoni, Dominic | *The Mirror, A Personal Record, The Arrow of Gold*. (As Nostromo:) *Nostromo*. |
| Daman | 'The End of the Tether', *The Rescue*. |
| Davidson | 'Because of the Dollars', *Victory*. |
| Ellis (Elliot, Elliott) | *The Shadow-Line, Lord Jim*, 'The End of the Tether'. |
| Ford | *An Outcast, Almayer's Folly*. |

| | |
|---|---|
| Gambril | 'Falk', *The Shadow-Line*. |
| Hamilton | *The Shadow-Line*, 'The End of the Tether'. |
| Hollis | 'Karain', 'Because of the Dollars'. |
| Hudig | *An Outcast, Almayer's Folly, The Mirror*. |
| Jim-Eng | *An Outcast, Almayer's Folly*. |
| Lingard | *The Rescue, An Outcast, Almayer's Folly*. |
| MacWhirr (MacW—) | 'Typhoon', *The Mirror*. |
| Marlow | 'Youth', *Heart of Darkness, Lord Jim, Chance*. |
| Nelson | *The Rover, The Mirror*. |
| Ortega | *The Sisters, The Arrow of Gold*. |
| Rita | *The Sisters, The Arrow of Gold*. |
| Roman galley-commander | *Heart of Darkness, The Mirror*. |
| Schomberg | *Lord Jim*, 'Falk', *Victory*. |
| Thérèse | *The Sisters, The Arrow of Gold*. |
| Vinck | *An Outcast, Almayer's Folly*. |
| Violin-playing captain | 'Falk', *The Shadow-Line*. |

*Part Three:*

*Covert Plots in Works by Other Writers*

CHAPTER 10

# *General Survey*

So many important and interesting works arguably contain
covert plots that in this chapter I will offer only a rapid survey
of some of the main possibilities; in the subsequent chapter I
will look closely at two of the best examples.

Sterne's *Tristram Shandy* is exuberantly chaotic and seems to
be ostentatiously 'plotless', apart from the obvious story of the
narrator's attempt to write an autobiography. But beneath this
surface lies a plot which is co-ordinated with remarkable
efficiency. This plot is the conspiracy of events to impose a
double impotence on Tristram. Just as events repeatedly
conspire to render Tristram impotent as one who would
'father' a literary offspring, a completed autobiography, so
events conspire to render Tristram impotent as one who might
maintain the family-line of Shandy by fathering a child.
Whether it be the dispersal of the vital energies in the moment
of his conception, the crushing of his nose (which the text so
insistently proposes as a phallic index), the accidental substitution of an ill-omened name for a promising one, the
circumcision by falling window-frame which almost castrates
him, or, in the childless adult, the onset of mortal illness,
everywhere the world threatens potency. Uncle Toby is almost
emasculated in battle; when Phutatorius drops a hot chestnut
it inevitably falls into his flies; and even Toby's bull proves
impotent. This is indeed, leeringly, a *cock* and bull story: and
just as the bull cannot sire a calf, Tristram will not produce a
son, nor will he even father the projected complete Life of
Tristram.

Another outwardly chaotic novel, James Joyce's *Ulysses,* offers a covert plot with a kindred theme of frustrated parenthood. In the overt plot, the climactic event (in two senses) is the afternoon's adultery between Molly Bloom and Blazes Boylan. Molly's husband, Leopold Bloom, has reluctantly connived at the adultery, knowing that it will ensure Molly's concert-tour with Boylan, who is a prosperous impresario. Years ago Bloom and Molly had a son who died in infancy; since the death, Bloom has become sexually inhibited as a husband; and both Molly's account of his sexual habits and the text's reportage of them imply that he is unlikely to father another son. The covert plot offers a story of potential but unfulfilled compensation for frustrated paternity. We see that Stephen Dedalus, a son alienated from his own father and in some need of a congenial father-figure, is repeatedly crossing the path of Leopold Bloom, the bereaved father still sadly remembering the son who died in infancy. Eventually, Stephen and Leopold meet, talk, get drunk together; Bloom takes him home, and offers him lodgings at his house; but Stephen declines the offer, and after the short visit goes on his way. In *The Odyssey*, Ulysses and his son Telemachus were at last reunited; characteristically, the covert plot of *Ulysses* invokes yet finally rejects the traditional story of a family restored. As in *Tristram Shandy*, there is a sense that the author links the ideas of literary and familial fatherhood. Stephen is something of an aesthete, a connoisseur of words, fluent as a literary theorist; but in his rather egoistic aloofness from life he seems unlikely ever to be able to produce a novel with the richness of *Ulysses*. Bloom, who has no literary ambitions or artistic manifestoes, has a voracious curiosity and a keenly sympathetic interest in the life around him. The combination of Stephen's ambitious dedication and Bloom's humane curiosity might engender a novel like *Ulysses*. In retrospect, Joyce's *A Portrait of the Artist as a Young Man* resembles *A Portrait of the Aesthete as a Young Egotist.*[1] Not until Stephen's spirit could be given hospitality by that of the genial Bloom could Joyce's mature masterpiece, *Ulysses,* be fathered.

We have seen that the sceptical Joseph Conrad sometimes offers 'metaphysical' or supernatural covert plots. This is a frequent structural phenomenon in novels. E.M. Forster was a sceptic, but in *A Passage to India* there is undoubtedly a covert supernatural plot: the spirit of Mrs Moore exerts an uncanny harmonising influence when she is present, when she is absent, and even when she is dead, as though by a form of telepathy which can continue after this life; she seems to aid Aziz at his trial and, subsequently, to induce moments of reconciliation between various people. (Mrs Wilcox, in *Howards End*, was similarly gifted in benign posthumous telepathy, and in *Maurice* telepathy between the living promotes the sentimentally happy ending.) In this respect, Virginia Woolf may partly have learned from Forster, because in *To the Lighthouse* the spirit of Mrs Ramsay, long after her death, seems able to convert to moments of harmony the discords in the lives of Mr Ramsay, Cam, James, Lily Briscoe and Mr Carmichael; and the text's recurrent allusions to the myth of Demeter and Persephone, deities of seasonal nature which dies to live again, help to maintain this supernatural covert plot.

While Modernist writers often looked nostalgically to ancient Greece and Rome, writers in the 'existentialist' and 'absurdist' traditions frequently compromised their purported radicalism of belief by smuggling into their texts some rather traditional plot-patterning. In Sartre's *La Nausée* (*Nausea*) the overt plot presents the hero as an extreme philosophical rebel who truly perceives that all is meaningless, 'meaning' being a bourgeois illusion. The covert plot, however, ingratiatingly suggests that the hero is a Romantic with liberal sympathies (he sides with a bullied homosexual and two imagined victims of oppression, a Jewish song-writer and a Negress who sings jazz): a bourgeois scholar on a private income, unlucky in love, who bravely battles against waves of incipient madness and achieves at least a local victory in his final decision to write a brilliant novel. Those 'insights' into senseless contingency which Sartre and various commentators have (perhaps paradoxically) deemed highly meaningful are intermittently diagnosed by *La Nausée* as a nasty malaise amenable to a variety of helpful therapies.[2] In addition, this text has a 'metaphysical' covert plot that depicts a world divided between things benign, which are abstract and mineral (and preferably cold, hard and dry), and things malign, which are animal and vegetable (and at their worst warm, moist and sticky). The salutary music emerges from a shellac disc and a steel needle; the projected novel will be 'beautiful and hard as steel'; and Sartre subsequently claimed that when writing *La Nausée,* he was 'a photomicroscope of glass and steel bent over my own protoplasmic juices'.[3]

There are some parallels to this in Camus's *L'Etranger* (*The Outsider*).[4] Here the main plot suggests that the hero is a likeable philosophical rebel who rightly senses the radical absurdity of life and who therefore exists as an honest stoical hedonist until he is cruelly tried and sentenced to death by society for a murder which he did not intend to commit. The covert plot elegantly suggests, however, that the world, far from being absurd, is truly a world of cause and effect in which actions have their appropriate consequences: the hero is callously irresponsible in firstly helping a pimp to bully an Arab girl and secondly (through the consequences of that first action) in murdering another Arab: his own actions have led him to a death-sentence. The trial ingeniously unites people and events which Meursault had deemed to be unconnected; and his myopic belief in living for the present moment is shown to deprive him of a vast number of future 'present moments'. In the same text, a metaphysical covert plot offers the contrasting suggestion that Meursault has been victimised by the hostile father-principle of the universe, symbolised by the oppressive sun which shines on the funeral of his mother and glares at him from the Arab's knife (forcing him to fire the fatal shots). This hostile, death-dealing father-principle is in perennial conflict with the kindly mother-principle of the universe, symbolised by the serene and refreshing sea in which Meursault likes to bathe. (Sun and sea have closely analogous rôles in *La Peste*, the sun associated with the spreading of disease and death, the sea with life and restoration.) Behind this symbolic dichotomy lie the experiences of Camus's early upbringing: a loving mother, an absent father; the blue Mediterranean and the arid Algerian landscape.

Behind it lies, too, the familiar antipathetic fallacy of much modern writing, in which the author slides between implying that the universe is Godless and neutral to man and, on the other hand, implying that it is actively hostile to man. To humane humans the non-human may seem inhuman. Thomas

Hardy's *Tess of the d'Urbervilles* and *Jude the Obscure* clearly offer (Hardy's subsequent disclaimers notwithstanding) antitheistic covert plots: the dice are so consistently loaded against the thoughtfully sensitive that the reader may reasonably infer the presence of a cruel omnipotent gambler against human dupes, or alternatively the presence of a blundering Creator who has not yet evolved into responsible awareness; and both inferences are supported by Hardy's more sardonic asides, by poems like 'Hap' and by the depiction of the Creator in *The Dynasts*. This tradition continues: Hardy's antitheism is maintained covertly by Samuel Beckett. In *Waiting for Godot*, against the overt plot which suggests that Estragon and Vladimir inhabit a meaningless and Godless universe plays the covert plot which suggests that they are preserved in life, in futile waiting, by an observant but hostile God. 'At me too someone is looking', the wretched Vladimir recognises in a moment of insight.[5] For Berkeley and Beckett, *esse est percipi*; but to Berkeley's philosophy Beckett gave his own sinister reading.

There is an antitheistic quality about much of Kafka's work, particularly *Der Prozess* (*The Trial*) which ends with the execution of K. at the hands of the vindictive 'Law'. *Das Schloss* (*The Castle*) is more open and indeterminate; being patently incomplete, it seems to be more consistently and uncompromisingly Kafkaesque. The overt plot dramatises the belief of K., and of those he consults, that he is moving in a static labyrinth. The covert plot indicates that he is moving in a dynamic labyrinth. A static labyrinth, though tortuous, is fixed and stable; its goal, though hard to attain, is definite and unmoving. (On that assumption, ultimate authorities exist in the castle, which is real.) A dynamic labyrinth, however, is mobile and protean, as in a dream or nightmare: the more the quester strives to penetrate it, the more it extends itself, in proportion to his efforts. If he ceases to strive, it diminishes; when, encouraged by this, he resumes the striving, it resumes its extension. (There may be no ultimate authorities; the castle may be illusory.) The dynamic labyrinth is open to an antitheistic interpretation if one assumes that a hostile deity is ordaining the tantalising circumstances; or to an anti-rationalist interpretation if one assumes that the quest satirises the search for a merely mentally-conceived certitude and ultimate significance. A peril for interpreters is that of allegorising the work to make it appear a story of a static rather than a dynamic labyrinth: for then they fall into K.'s error and mimic his ambitions.

One of the reasons why novels commonly have covert plots and plays seldom do is that novels frequently have fictional narrators and plays hardly ever do; Arthur Miller's *A View from the Bridge* is unusual in this respect. When a fictional narrator tells the story, his narrative generates a covert plot to the extent that we deem his perceptions to be distorted. They may be distorted by jealousy, apathy, vanity, stress, sickness; commonly by some degree of mental illness. *La Nausée* was one example; two others are Nabokov's *Pale Fire* and Robbe-Grillet's *La Jalousie (Jealousy)*. In *Pale Fire* the narrator purports to be a king in exile, pursued to his American retreat by an assassin serving his political enemies; the assassin's shot misses the king but kills John Shade, a distinguished poet. The book's comedy depends largely on our easy inferences that the narrator is a half-crazed fantasist and the 'assassin' a local lunatic who had shot Shade in a deluded act of revenge. The 'overt' narrative is so transparently fantastic and the 'covert' so conspicuously plausible that much of Nabokov's ingenuity is devoted to the ironic comedy of their intersection and imaginative interchange; and in a characteristic final flourish the narrator envisages writing 'an old-fashioned melodrama' about 'a lunatic who intends to kill an imaginary king, another lunatic who imagines himself to be that king, and a distinguished old poet who stumbles by chance into the line of fire, and perishes in the clash between the two figments'.

A novel may have a covert plot and no overt plot at all: the proof is Robbe-Grillet's *La Jalousie*. A credulous reader would deem the work to be ostentatiously plotless and systematically self-contradictory: events are specified, contradicted, re-specified, contradicted, a centipede is crushed, lives, crushed, lives, has its stain erased, leaves its stain; a man and woman return from a journey, set out for the journey, return, set out; less a story than a repetitive incantation of disordered pages by a pedantic precisian.[6] The covert plot, nevertheless, is a very traditional tale (resembling in outline some of W. Somerset Maugham's)[7] of an adulterous liaison in the tropics. A beautiful wife is having an affair with a married man, Franck, who lives on a neighbouring plantation. The husband watches as she furtively passes a letter to Franck; notes their plan to spend a day at the port; passes a sleepless night during their absence; and when they return the next morning he notes suspiciously their claim that they were delayed overnight by a mechanical fault in their car. The covert plot is easily reconstituted from the jumbled materials by postulating that the central observer is the jealous husband, on the verge of breakdown, who is obsessively reliving his tormented experiences: this would account for the disordered time-scale, the apparent inconsistencies, his manic repetitions, and his obsession with the precise denotation of apparently trivial minutiae. As is customary in radically experimental novels, the initial effect is one of anarchic distruption of the familiar, and ingenuous commentators traditionally attempt to vindicate such unconventionality by alleging that it is somehow truer to life than was the previous conventionality. (This example may tempt them to postulate modern 'alienation' and 'reification'.)[8] The readers who reconstitute the covert plot will see that the work as a whole is scarcely an 'anti-novel' but rather a text that maintains the long and protean tradition of the realistic novel, which has always been concerned to gratify and reconcile in one narrative two conflicting demands: the demand for a reflection of the apparent untidiness of experience, and the demand for a tidily purposeful selectivity. The ambiguity of the title *La Jalousie* points (like Janus) in both directions. It means 'The Venetian Blinds or Slatted Shutters', and thus inaugurates the novel's unconventionally attentive denotation of apparently trivial nonhuman details; but it also means 'Jealousy', and thus inaugurates the covert plot's conventional concern with human relationships in general and the adulterous triangle in particular. Each level depends on the other. To reconstitute the covert plot is not to 'recuperate' (i.e. reduce to orthodoxy) the text, because without such reconstitution one cannot gauge the extent and implications of the deformations (which in this case challenge and question the traditional novelists' emphasis on the orderly exposition of characters' motives and feelings; perspectival geometry, locational incantation and textual autonomy may have been neglected).

Covert plots can thus be found in both traditional and non-traditional texts, both 'realist' and 'anti-realist' novels. In works of art, whether novels or films or paintings, the sense of 'realism' is normally generated by the artist's inclusion of details which the reader or observer will have been aware of in life but will not previously have regarded as worthy of the particular scrutiny which the artistic presentation now solicits. For realism to be vivid, it must not merely tally with experience; it must tally surprisingly: the familiar may be seen with new precision or have its significance extended by unfamiliar analogies. In this respect, the traditional distinction between realist and non-realist works may be misleading, because this same principle links vivid realism and effective experimentalism.

Readers in the twentieth century have often responded with increasing hospitality to works which appear to be radically disordered. Sometimes this is because such readers have less faith in divine, social or private order than had past generations. The detection of covert plots may suggest not only that the 'disordered' works are more dependent on traditional conceptions of order than at first appears, but also that there are both logical and practical failings in various kinds of philosophical radicalism — the kinds, for example, that advocate solipsism or the 'arbitrariness' of language and meaning. Since, historically, such epistemological radicalism has been linked at least as frequently with right-wing as with left-wing politics, there is no sound basis for the common critical assumption that the dogged resilience of traditional plot-structures entails a political conservatism implicit in form. Nobody is more conservative than the solipsist. If the searching power of art lies mainly in its ability to challenge habitual perceptions, a particular work may, according to its context, challenge the world's disorder by its own order quite as fruitfully as it may challenge the world's imputed order by its own apparent disorder.

# CHAPTER 11

# Two Major Examples: Ibsen's The Wild Duck and Mann's Death in Venice

## (i) EKDAL'S SUICIDE IN THE WILD DUCK

I argue that the covert plot of Henrik Ibsen's *Vildanden (The Wild Duck*, 1884) is the story of Old Ekdal's tipsy progress towards his suicide. It seems to me that the action of this play culminates in not one suicide, but two: Hedvig's death provokes the death of Old Ekdal, which takes place in the closing minutes of the drama, behind the attic doors at the rear of the stage. This second death gives the work a bold thematic symmetry: as Hedvig's suicide had implied a sardonic authorial comment on the élitist idealism of Gregers, so Ekdal's suicide implies a similarly sardonic comment on the élitist cynicism of Dr Relling. That the play's final catastrophe has gone unnoticed gives the text an extensively ironic self-validating quality, for this fact validates the play's sceptical observations on the limitations of human perceptiveness and sympathy. If the 'philosophers', Gregers and Relling, had drawn the appropriate conclusion from Hedvig's death, they would have thought less about the claims of their respective philosophies and more about the claims of other people, and they might have saved a life. However, like these commentators *within* the play, commentators *on* the play have let Ekdal die unnoticed. Raymond Williams, after quoting Ibsen's remark that *The Wild Duck* occupies 'a place apart among my dramatic productions; its method of progress is in many respects divergent from that of its predecessors', comments 'This has never been satisfactorily explained'.[1] My theory offers an explanation.

The premise of the theory is the uncontroversial observation that *The Wild Duck* is meticulously written and constructed. Repeated readings demonstrate that Ibsen has constantly striven to combine the immediacy of naturalism with the general resonance of symbolism by means of economy and compression which charge even apparently-trivial stage-directions and sequences of dialogue with both local and extensive significance. A typical example of this principle is provided by the stage-direction at the beginning of Act II which tells us that when we first see Hedvig she is reading a book 'with her hands shielding her eyes' (*med hænderne foran ø jnene*). The intent posture, with the hands before the eyes, is natural enough; but to the alert observer it may also hint at a connection between Hedvig and Mr Werle, who in the previous act had been warned by Mrs Sørby of the danger of bright lights to his eyes. The hint is fulfilled when we learn of the probability that Mr Werle is Hedvig's true father and that Hedvig may resemble the wild duck in being 'the maimed trophy of Mr. Werle's sporting prowess',[2] for Hedvig, like Werle, is threatened by impending blindness. A further implication of the stage-direction is that Hedvig may be damaged by the light of truth which Gregers brings to the household: indeed, in Act IV Gina makes a bitter joke of this connection between the lamplight and truth, between the two senses of illumination and enlightenment:

Gregers: 'I was so sure that, when I came in at the door, I should be met by the transfiguring light of understanding in both your faces. And yet I see nothing here but this dull, gloomy, sad —'
Gina: 'Oh, well —' [Takes the lamp-shade off.][3]

This reminder of Ibsen's meticulous attention to detail in the play may serve to draw attention to the significance of the stage-direction which tells us that when Old Ekdal makes his last appearance in the play he is wearing full military uniform which includes a sabre (*han er i fuld uniform og har travlt med at spænde sabelen om sig*). We know that since the scandal over the tree-felling, which had resulted in his being jailed, he has been ashamed to wear his uniform in public; but he has chosen to wear full uniform on this morning in honour of Hedvig's fourteenth birthday. When he enters, the others realise that he could not have fired the shot in the attic: the dead Hedvig is then rapidly discovered and brought on stage. While the other characters gather about the corpse in horror and consternation, Ekdal inwardly resolves to kill himself by means of that sabre and, unnoticed, goes into the attic and shuts the door behind him. This intention of suicide is made evident, I believe, in his otherwise inexplicable last words: 'The forests avenge themselves. But I'm not afraid, all the same.' (*Skogen hævner. Men jeg er ikke ræd alligevel.*)[4] The process of reasoning proceeding in the recesses of his not-entirely-befuddled mind seems to be on these lines: 'Once, because of my mistakes in surveying the forests, the trees that were Crown property were felled. The forests have taken their revenge, firstly through my disgrace at the trial, and secondly through the disaster which has now befallen Hedvig — and befallen her in that attic where the forests are vestigially present in those stunted fir-trees among which I do my "hunting". At the time of my disgrace I tried to kill myself, but I was too frightened to go through with it. Now, at last, I've learnt my lesson: it's clear that the forests won't be placated until I've made the sacrifice they demand; and this time I'm not too frightened to die.'

Ekdal's furtive alcoholism has provided comic relief in the play; but commentators who regard him as simply a comic character, a pathetic buffoon, are making Relling's kind of reductive misjudgement.[5] We know from Hjalmar that at the time of the trial Ekdal had thought of killing himself; and Ekdal's tipsy progress through the play can be judged as the progress of an ageing, dishonoured man who has been trying unsuccessfully to silence with alcohol those inner voices which seem to be demanding of him a final atonement.

The orthodox view is that when Ekdal withdraws into the attic, he is merely going to potter about there dreamily as usual. Nevertheless, if Ibsen had not envisaged his off-stage suicide, the direction that Ekdal bears a sabre with him would be redundant (and in Ibsen's plays lethal weapons, when specified, are used); Ekdal's last words would remain a mere enigma; his conspicuous absence when all the other people of the household are on stage would be less explicable;[6] and the detailed presentation of his past life-history, with its particular emphasis on his sense of dishonour and desire to atone for disgrace, would not bear the weight of examination which, in this highly-compressed and multiply-layered work, it clearly requires. That his absence should go unremarked by the others is natural enough, given their immediate preoccupation with the tragedy of Hedvig; but at a thematic level the ironic implication of this unnoticed absence is entirely consistent with the warnings that Ibsen has been offering, in the play, about the limitations of human perception and about the tendency of men to see only a reality which has been distorted by their private needs, fears and guilts.

Such distortion clearly affects the outlook of Gregers, whose determination to make others face up to 'the claims of the Ideal' proves to be largely a compensation for his failure to face up to those claims in his own past life. The exchange between Gregers and his father in Act III had shown that Ekdal had virtually been framed — inveigled into apparent guilt — by Werle: who, well aware that errors were being made in the mapping of the forests, continued to profit by them, knowing that when they were discovered Ekdal would be the scapegoat. Gregers had evidence of his father's scheme, but lacked the courage to take it to the authorities.

Gregers: 'I should have stood up to you when the trap was laid for Lieutenant Ekdal. I should have warned him. For I guessed well enough how it would end.'
Werle:    'Yes. You should certainly have spoken then.'
Gregers: 'I dared not do it. I was such a coward.'[7]

So instead of facing the claims of truth in his own life, Gregers withholds his evidence from the authorities and compensates for his inner cowardice by urging others (first the workers in the mountains, and now Hjalmar) to face up to the truth in their own lives. The truth that he brings to Hjalmar is, of course, cruelly disruptive and, given Hjalmar's self-pitying, self-dramatising nature, destructive to Hedvig.

When we see how Relling initially warns Gregers not to tamper with the family, we may be tempted by the view (expressed by Halvdan Koht, among other commentators)[8] that Relling is Ibsen's spokesman. Nevertheless there are grounds for believing that the biblical question, 'Why beholdest thou the mote that is in thy brother's eye, but considerest not the beam that is in thine own eye?' (Matthew 7, verse 3), may apply to Relling, too. In Act IV we learn that Relling had once been a suitor to Mrs Sørby; he was unsuccessful, and, she implies, has since been dissipating the best that was in him. It seems that Relling has, like Gregers, in assuming the rôle of counsellor-mentor, been compensating for some inner deficiencies; and as a result he has become rather like a perverse physician who cures a patient of an addiction to tobacco by encouraging an addiction to heroin. This is shown by the way in which his doctrine of the 'life-lie' or 'saving illusion' works in practice. His provision of the life-lie of demoniac possession is bound to accelerate Molvik's alcoholism; and without the life-lie of the great invention, the illusion which Relling has fostered in Hjalmar, Hjalmar might have been more inclined to face up to his domestic responsibilities. Gregers and Relling could almost be regarded as joint participants in destruction: for any truth that Gregers brings is likely to be the more destructive to people who have been progressively insulated from reality by life-lies. Relling errs in cynicism, as Gregers in idealism. Hjalmar had less dignity than Gregers supposed, and disaster follows from this misjudgement. Ekdal, beneath his eccentricities, has more dignity than Relling supposes, and he proves it by his death.

Such symmetry in disaster is predicated by the play's balanced discussion of a philosophical problem which is implicit in the presentation of the 'wild' duck itself. The problem is that of how to reconcile the often-conflicting demands for a life of dignity and for a life of contentment. Ibsen had read, with crusty suspicion, J.S. Mill's *Utilitarianism* (1861),[9] which summarises the Utilitarian thesis that 'actions are right in proportion as they tend to promote happiness' but argues that 'It is better to be a human being dissatisfied than a pig satisfied; better to be a Socrates dissatisfied than a fool satisfied'. The play's ironic title epitomises the problem. When the duck was truly a wild duck, able to fly in the open air, it had its own kind of dignity, but it was vulnerable and was shot down. Now, in the attic, it waddles contentedly, has its water changed every other day, and is plump and well-tended; but it is de-natured: it has become a domestic fowl, a child's pet. If the bird's past vulnerability and present security mutely criticise Gregers' outlook, its de-natured state warns us against adopting Relling's reductive view that the life 'tolerable enough' (instead of the life 'worth living') should be the criterion of existence. A character who may come closer than we at first realise to embodying Ibsen's moral recommendations is the much-maligned Gina, who is charitable without fostering life-lies, who is unsentimental but sympathetic to others, who works tirelessly to keep the home and family together, and who has a distinct talent for salvage-operations: she even tries to make something constructive (Hjalmar's reconciliation) out of the horror of Hedvig's death. If the play's philosophers had followed her example by being more reticent and more attentive to the needs and claims of other people, they might have saved Ekdal.

One objection to my interpretation might be technical: that a suicide-attempt by means of a sabre (that sabre on Ekdal's belt which Ibsen's directions so carefully specify) requires a long arm and is likely to be frustratingly awkward. The answer is that sabres come in various sizes (a blade-length of only forty-five centimetres is quite possible), that suicides by sword 'in the high Roman fashion' are a well-known theatrical convention (as *Julius Caesar* and *Antony and Cleopatra* remind us), and that Ekdal might die by severing an artery in throat or wrist rather than by a stabbing thrust. A stronger objection might be this one: that if the covert plot culminating in Ekdal's suicide contributes so importantly to the thematic pattern, it is implausible that the event should be hinted at rather than dramatised overtly. Here the answer is that an overtly-dramatised death would not only make the play seem too melodramatic but would also, above all, fail to bring home eventually to us the play's major theme of 'tardy recognition of painful truth'. Ibsen found a variety of ways to reconcile his mature powers as a meticulous designer of a hortatory fictional world with the need to give an immediate impression of everyday experience in its loose variety. He extended the distance between initial and retrospective understanding, and rewarded those of us who by a process of inference and triangulation seek the patterns which unite the seemingly-disconnected events.[10] In *The Wild Duck* he has indeed, as he told Frederik Hegel, left critics of this play 'something to construe'.[11]

My heterodox case rests, finally, on a number of quite orthodox judgements: that in *The Wild Duck* Ibsen is at the height of his powers as a sophisticated, concise and adroitly ironical dramatist; that from the days of *Brand* and *Peer Gynt*, he was as attentive to the dangers of cynicism as to those of idealism; and that Ibsen emphasises far more systematically than most previous dramatists the significance within the apparently trivial, the design behind the seemingly accidental, and the tragic consequences that ensue when what is out of sight is also out of mind.

## (ii) THE PROTEAN DIONYSUS IN *DEATH IN VENICE*

Thomas Mann's *Der Tod in Venedig* (*Death in Venice*, 1912) has an important covert plot which derives predominantly from Euripides' play *The Bacchae*. In that ancient drama, a noble and haughty Theban ruler, Pentheus, sceptically scorns the worshippers of Dionysus, god of intoxication and ecstasy. From the east, in mortal guise as a priest at the head of bacchic revellers, Dionysus travels far to Thebes, in order to punish those who have denied his divinity. Pentheus attempts to imprison this long-haired, effeminately beautiful 'priest'; but Dionysus escapes and, almost like a hypnotist, asserts his power over his former captor by evoking Pentheus' prurient desires. Pentheus permits himself to be dressed as a woman and to don long flowing hair, is led out to spy on the Dionysiac revellers, is detected by them and torn apart. The play powerfully shows the dangers both of ascetic repression and of irrational ecstasy; and it suggests that lustful and homosexual desires may lurk within even the most ascetic and athletically spartan natures.[12]

The *overt* plot of *Death in Venice* concerns a famous and distinguished Bavarian author, August von Aschenbach, whose literary works have emphasised the value of austerity and restraint. After glimpsing a strange traveller at a cemetery, he feels impelled to travel on holiday to Venice, where he falls in love with a beautiful, long-haired boy, Tadzio. Although he tardily discovers that Venice is stricken by cholera, he remains there in order to be close to the boy; eventually he dies of the disease. The *covert* plot depicts Aschenbach as a great man who has wilfully denied the Dionysiac and thus incurred the wrath of Dionysus. The god appears in various guises, with the effect of luring Aschenbach into the very situations and emotions that he would once have opposed. Ensnared in Venice, Aschenbach dies of the cholera which, it is indicated, the vengeful god has brought from the east; and he dies while gazing enraptured on the boy who is one of the incarnations of Dionysus. (Subsequently, the crafty god has sometimes eluded identification by the tale's critics.)[13]

In *The Bacchae*, Pentheus had poured scorn on the spectacle of aged Teiresias and Cadmus mimicking youngsters in their service of the god; then he had scorned the 'scented silky hair' of the priest who is the deity's mortal guise. Later, subjected to the god's hypnotic power, Pentheus had revealed his prurience in a scene whose macabre horror lay in the spectacle of an unwitting victim becoming an eager, vain, effeminate accomplice in his own degradation. When Mann explores the Euripidean theme of the Dionysiac impulse which operates to destroy ascetic repression, he offers a close parallel to Euripides' ironies. On the ship to Venice, Aschenbach had looked with disgust on an old man in the midst of a group of eager young clerks: an old man disguised as a youth, in dandified suit, rouged cheeks and dyed moustache. Later, infatuated by Tadzio, the ageing Aschenbach lets the hotel's barber persuade him to 'rejuvenate' himself by means of rouge, mascara and dye; and even by his red tie and straw hat with gay striped band, Aschenbach increasingly resembles in appearance that man he had scorned — the man who was one of the mocking incarnations of the avenging deity.

Pentheus' hope, shortly before going forth to his death, of witnessing and participating in the wild Bacchanalian orgies on the hillside has its feverish counterpart in Aschenbach's dream of Dionysiac revellers:

Foam dripped from their lips, they drove each other on with lewd gesturings and beckoning hands. They laughed, they howled, they thrust their pointed staves into each other's flesh and licked the blood as it ran down. But now the dreamer was in them and of them, the stranger god was his own. Yes, it was he who was flinging himself upon the animals, who bit and tore and swallowed smoking gobbets of flesh — while on the trampled moss there now began the rites in honour of the god, an orgy of promiscuous embraces — and in his very soul he tasted the bestial degradation of his fall.

The unhappy man awoke from this dream shattered, unhinged, powerless in the demon's grip.[14]

Euripides' Dionysus was protean, capable of manifesting himself in various forms, as radiant god, as beautiful young priest, as the vigour of wild animals and the joy of intoxication. In *Death in Venice,* Dionysus is similarly protean, though sardonically so, in his mortal guises. His main appearances are as the traveller at the cemetery (with iron-shod staff for thyrsus), as the rouged old man, as the unlicensed gondolier who ferries Aschenbach to the Lido, as the vulgar itinerant singer, and ultimately as young Tadzio. Each of the five is an itinerant figure, a stranger to the region in which he is observed, since Dionysus was 'the stranger god', the wandering immigrant from the east. All five are linked descriptively by a network of recurrent features which include these: (i) slight build, (ii) snub nose, (iii) prominent Adam's apple, (iv) a strong frown or perpendicular frown-marks on the forehead, (v) lips which curl back in a grimace to expose the gums or to reveal conspicuous teeth that sometimes resemble fangs, (vi) a sailor suit or straw hat, (vii) a staff or pole, and (viii) a cluster of companions. The stranger at the cemetery is charaterised by items i, ii, iii, iv, v, vi and vii; the old man by v, vi and viii; the gondolier by i, ii, v, vi and vii; the singer by i, ii, iii, iv, v and viii; and Tadzio by i, iv, v, vi and viii. The references to the frown-marks on the brow and to the teeth exposed in a grimace lend these figures a fleetingly tigerish quality.[15] Euripides' Dionysus had been invested by the Chorus with his legendary multiple connections with the animal kingdom, particularly the bull and the tiger; and the reason for Mann's selection of two tigerish attributes for his Dionysus is not simply to indicate the predatory aspects of his vengeful deity but also to emphasise that in the course of his vengeance, this Dionysus brings Asiatic cholera from the Ganges delta, which Aschenbach sees as tiger-haunted during his hallucination at the graveyard:

He beheld a landscape, a tropical marshland, beneath a reeking sky, steaming, monstrous, rank — a kind of primeval wilderness-world of islands, morasses, and alluvial channels.....Among the knotted joints of a bamboo thicket the eyes of a crouching tiger gleamed — and he felt his heart throb with terror, yet with a longing inexplicable.[16]

The location is identified and linked to the disease near the end of the tale:

> For the past several years Asiatic cholera had shown a strong tendency to spread. Its source was the hot, moist swamps of the delta of the Ganges, where it bred in the mephitic air of that primeval jungle-island, among whose bamboo thickets the tiger crouches.....[17]

As Mann describes it, the modern world is permeated by pagan forces; his narrative style frequently modulates towards the epically periphrastic; and many of his allusions, such as those to the legend of Apollo and Hyacinth and, of course, the numerous echoes of Plato's *Phaedrus*, help to preserve the prominence of the ancient debate about the boons and perils of love between an older mentor and a youth. Of the wealth of classical allusions, however, those to *The Bacchae* contribute most fully to the ironic thematic structure of *Death in Venice*, adding greatly to the novella's richness and resonance. From *The Bacchae* Mann has clearly derived the central ironic theme: that a powerful figure may be subverted by the very anarchic energies he had once so energetically sought to combat. Nevertheless, the comparison inevitably draws attention to certain limitations in Mann's work.

The first limitation is obvious. By his concentration on a writer, von Aschenbach, whose very unusual past career is given extremely full delineation, Mann has dimished the range of implication. The far less convoluted characterisations in Euripides' play gave the greater prominence to important general problems of human psychology and attitudes to religion; whereas the more Mann (drawing largely on his own prior achievements and ambitions) specifies the distinctive life-history of Aschenbach, the greater will be the danger that the problems will diminish to one about the perils of the artistic life — and almost to one about the problems of a particular artist's life. Mann has, of course, striven to resist this tendency, firstly by his stress on the way in which Aschenbach's work has struck a sympathetic chord in the minds of so many readers of his generation, and secondly by suggesting that the cholera which assails the people of Venice is symbolic of a general corruption instanced in the hypocrisy and callousness of the Venetian authorities who attempt to conceal knowledge of the plague lest there be a decline in the profits from tourism. Yet the reader's sense that, compared with Euripides, Mann is dealing with relatively special and limited cases may be reinforced by the recognition that whereas recent history (the rise of Nazism; the growth of anti-rationalistic movements in art, religion and politics; the popularisation of Freud; the continuing debate about 'permissiveness' and restraint) has given Euripides remarkable contemporaneity, the terms of Mann's related discussion — like the too-conspicuous virtuosities of his style — begin to seem dated, for they derive so clearly from the late-nineteenth-century discussions of decadence in art, of the relationship between the moods of *fin-de-siécle and fin-du-globe*, and particularly of the idea that modern works of art may be *fleurs du mal*, exotic blooms arising from the marsh of vice and corruption.

In an earlier tale by Mann, 'Tonio Kröger', Tonio had lamented that he stood between two worlds and was at home in neither: one being the world of art (associated with homosexual love), the other being the world of bourgeois decency (associated with familial procreation). Mann himself experienced Tonio's ambivalence of attitude, and this is reflected in a central confusion in *Death in Venice*. We may define the confusion by seeking answers to the following questions. Is Aschenbach punished or rewarded by Dionysus? To the extent that he is punished, for what, exactly, is he punished?

When Aschenbach, after receiving Tadzio's smile, whispers 'Ich liebe dich!' — 'I love you!' — the narrator describes this 'hackneyed phrase' as 'absurd, abject, ridiculous enough, yet sacred too, and not unworthy of honour even here'; and during the tale the narrator's attitude to von Aschenbach varies between sardonic contempt for a writer who has become transformed into a disgusting and grotesque figure, and compassionate empathy for an ageing, ailing genius captured by a doomed homosexual passion which makes him tragic rather than contemptible.[18] The sardonic note is most evident shortly before Aschenbach's death:

> There he sat, the master: this was he who had found a way to reconcile art and honours; who had written *The Abject*, and in a style of classic purity renounced bohemianism and all its works, all sympathy with the abyss and the troubled depths of the human soul. This was he who had put knowledge underfoot to climb so high; who had outgrown the ironic pose and adjusted himself to the burdens and obligations of fame; whose renown had been officially recognised and his name ennobled, whose style was set for a model in the schools. There he sat. His eyelids were closed, there was only a swift, sidelong glint of the eyeballs now and again, something between a question and a leer; while the rouged and flabby mouth uttered single words of the sentences shaped in his disordered brain by the fantastic logic that governs our dreams.[19]

The tone is not only that of 'How are the mighty fallen!' but also that of 'So much for that so-called might!'. Yet, at other points in the text, the sense that Aschenbach is overtaken by a Nemesis appropriate to his hubris, by an utter downfall into degradation, is strongly undercut by the sense that he is, after all, attaining an intensity of emotional experience, and even, ultimately, a felicity, that he would never have attained had he remained the resolute and respectable writer. The narrator who terms Tadzio 'that instrument of a mocking deity' also caresses Tadzio's beauty with phrases of lyrical tenderness. And as Aschenbach dies,

> the eyes looked out from beneath their lids, while his whole face took on the relaxed and brooding expression of deep slumber. It seemed to him the pale and lovely Summoner out there smiled at him and beckoned; as though with the hand he lifted from his hip, he pointed outward as he hovered on before into an immensity of richest expectation.[20]

Yes, 'It seemed to him' ('Ihm war aber, als ob'): the vision may be an illusion; but to Aschenbach it is a fact, and a supremely fulfilling one. To him, Nemesis comes as apotheosis or ultimate benediction (by the 'lovely Summoner') although, from an external viewpoint, it can be seen that the ubiquitous power of Dionysus has punished Aschenbach by leading him via moral and physical degradation to death.

And if we ask 'And for what, exactly, is Aschenbach punished?', the text offers self-contradictory answers, one being that Aschenbach was guilty of being a *bad* artist, and the other being that he was guilty of being a *good* artist. The evidence for the former is that Aschenbach had rejected the Dionysiac: he was a defeatist, a reactionary, pleasing the bourgeoisie and an enfeebled society; an ascetic, austere, preaching a stoicism of martyrdom rather than a life-affirming ethic. As he had thus rejected the Dionysiac, Dionysus punished him by immersing him in the very experiences that his art had condemned or rejected. However, the evidence for the second and contradictory answer (that Aschenbach was punished for being a *good* artist) is equally specific. It lies chiefly in Aschenbach's reverie of a Socratic address to Phaedrus (which relates to, but differs from, Socrates' arguments in Plato's *Phaedrus*) which occurs near the end of the tale. There the speaker says that some artists lead men to the abyss, but others react against the abyss by a concern with beauty only — ' "and by beauty we mean simplicity, largeness, and renewed severity of discipline; we mean a return to detachment and to form" '. Clearly Aschenbach belongs to this latter group of the better or higher artists. But, the Socratic speaker proceeds, even these better artists are inevitably, by their very aestheticism, heading towards that abyss:

'But detachment, Phaedrus, and preoccupation with form lead to intoxication and desire, they may lead the noblest among us to frightful emotional excesses, which his own stern cult of the beautiful would make him the first to condemn. So they too, they too, lead to the bottomless pit. Yes, they lead us thither, I say, us who are poets — who by our natures are prone not to excellence but to excess.'[21]

The resultant tension exists as an area of contradiction in Mann's novella. Where the theme of Nemesis is concerned, Aschenbach can be seen as a man punished for betraying art, yet also, on the other hand, he can be seen as a man punished since, by being an artist, he was inevitably playing with fire and would be burnt. The contradiction remains unresolved because, evidently, Mann had not made up his own mind: as he recognised, there was in himself both the aesthete's distrust of the 'respectable' artist (who subjects art to morality) and the respectable bourgeois's distrust of those who dedicate themselves uncompromisingly to artistic endeavour.

There is a related moral ambivalence, extending perhaps to self-contradiction, in Mann's conception of the moral justice of Aschenbach's particular Nemesis. For part of the time, Mann supports a compassionate and adventurously exploratory liberal morality, and consequently he condemns the Aschenbach who had rejected the world of outsiders and outcasts and who had scorned the maxim 'tout comprendre c'est tout pardonner'. This Aschenbach is punished by being made into precisely the sort of outsider (irresponsible, hedonistic, homosexual) that he in his works would have condemned. However, for part of the time Mann also seems to be criticising all liberal morality from a radically anti-rationalistic viewpoint. He does this by stressing the sheer recalcitrant and primeval power of the Dionysiac, which can, it seems, seize any mortal and make nonsense of all his long-maintained moral principles, of whatever rational kind they may be.

Some of the stylistic riches of *Death in Venice* are indicated by this memorable descriptive passage:

> Now daily the naked god with cheeks aflame drove his four fire-breathing steeds through heaven's spaces; and with him streamed the strong east wind that fluttered his yellow locks. A sheen, like white satin, lay over all the idly rolling sea's expanse.....[22]

This is resonant and ostentatiously 'literary' writing: the opening sentence combines the martial fanfare of epic diction with a lingeringly sensuous eloquence. Nobody will doubt the descriptive richness; but doubts arise with regard to the description's status. Is it ironic or non-ironic? It is an authorial statement or a form of reported thought, *erlebte Rede*, conveying the view of the scene that Aschenbach rather than the author takes? The grounds for reading it ironically are, obviously enough, that it is periphrastic in style and anachronistic in reference; yet those who read it non-ironically could say that it is no more anachronistic to refer to sun-charioteer Apollo than it is to portray the actions in twentieth-century Europe of a protean Dionysus. The grounds for reading the passage as an authorial statement are strong: there is no distancing direction, such as 'It seemed to Aschenbach that now daily the naked god' ('Es schien zu Aschenbach, dass nun Tag für Tag der Gott.....nackend.....'). On the other hand, the phrasing brings to mind what we have been told of Aschenbach's stylistic elegance, fastidousness and formal mastery, and the end of this paragraph has the status of a reportage of Aschenbach's, rather than the narrator's, judgement of the scene:

> But evening too was rarely lovely..... Such nights as these contained the joyful promise of a sunlit morrow, brim-full of sweetly ordered idleness, studded thick with countless precious possibilities.[23]

The basic reason for the ambiguous status of that resonant sentence about the sun-god (and of several passages of kindred descriptive virtuosity) is clear enough. Mann is half in love with the writer whom he is endeavouring to criticise; and, to escape from an impasse or self-contradiction of judgement, he has here found an aptly equivocal style — resolute in tone, irresolute in basis — a style which may be ironic or non-ironic, narratorially authoritative or merely reportage of a character's non-authoritative point of view. It is a sentence which demonstrates both the ostensible majestic power and the underlying ambivalence of the tale. To such periphrastic glories we may sometimes prefer the eloquent silence of Euripides: the silence when *The Bacchae* has ended: a silence of reflection in which, by inference, we may hear the co-ordinating logic of Euripides' impeccably dramatised paradox.

In conclusion: a reading of *The Bacchae*, the main literary source of *Death in Venice*, emphasises the paradoxical theme common to both works (man subverted from without and within by forces he sought to suppress) and clarifies the symbolism of the later work by facilitating the identification of the protean Dionysus and the associated covert plot; but it also reveals in Mann's novella a cultural limitation (a preoccupation with a dated debate about Aestheticism) and an unresolved ambivalence caused by the author's Janiform view of the artist.

CHAPTER 12

# Covert Plots in Ostensibly
# Non-Fictional Works

Our discussion (in Chapter 9) of Conrad's Decoud and the *Tremolino* episode suggested that just as a work of fiction may be covertly infiltrated by the confessional and compensatory demands of autobiography, so an ostensibly non-fictional autobiography may be infiltrated by the fictional requirement of a dramatic and conclusive narrative. Various works which purport to be 'scientific' may owe their appeal partly to a covert narrative structure which provides excitement and promises conclusiveness; the more a discursive text claims to be 'objective', the more its inevitable ethical tenor may resemble a subversionary covert plot; and a common cultural irony is that the very works which most appear to promise 'demystification' may be the unwitting smugglers of an old mystical story or a vestigial myth.

Imagine this plot. Once upon a time, there was a character called Purposeful History. At his birth, it was mystically decreed that in course of many years he would eventually reach Utopia, the happy land. Accordingly, History made a long and arduous journey in quest of that goal. He encountered friends: shrewd or energetic beings who knew the way forward, and aided his progress. He also encountered many enemies: perhaps beings who though ignorance or selfishness sought to impede him. His way has been difficult and bloody; but his Utopia is in sight, and at last many people will share the new happiness.

Not a very plausible story, admittedly; nor one that seems

particularly original. It's as old as the Bible and *The Odyssey,* older than *The Oresteia* and *The Aeneid.* In religious writings, this plot is overt: the story of Paradise Regained or of the New Jerusalem. In some non-religious writings, this plot is often covert; and the enemies of History may be those whom the given writer has reason to dislike, while the Utopia may supply what the writer personally deems to be desirable.

Charles Darwin's *Origin of Species* brought a wealth of empirical observation to bear against the traditional Christian view of life on the planet, and it particularly challenged Paley's *Natural Theology: or Evidences of the Existence and Attributes of the Deity.* 'It is so easy', said Darwin, 'to hide our ignorance under such expressions as the "plan of creation", "unity of design", &c., and to think that we give an explanation.....' Yet the resilience of a teleological story of triumph after long struggle is illustrated not only by the patriotic, imperialistic mutations of popularised Darwinism, but also by the very tone and phrasing, conclusively affirmative, of Darwin's own peroration. It is as though an older, more consolatory story had risen into the relatively bleak exposition:

[W]e may look with some confidence to a secure future of equally inappreciable length. And as natural selection works solely by and for the good of each being, all corporeal and mental endowments will tend to progress towards perfection.
.....Thus, from the war of nature, from famine and death, the most exalted object which we are capable of conceiving, namely, the production of the higher animals, directly follows. There is grandeur in this view of life.....[1]

Darwin's contemporary admirer, Karl Marx, claimed that what most people understood as history was merely (in effect) its overt plot, the short-term conflicts between rulers or nations. He proposed to reveal its covert plot: the long-term economic war of class against class. Religion and mythology were a means by which the ruling class sought to conceal and secure the real bases of its power. Yet the more Marx stressed the inevitability of a historic progression from feudalism to capitalism and to the eventual classless society (whose midwife was the self-abnegating dictatorship of the proletariat), the more his account of history implied a covert plot which recalls the myth of Prometheus. Marx profoundly admired Aeschylus's

*Prometheus Bound*, which had provided a defiant epigraph for his doctoral dissertation: 'In a word, I detest all the gods..... I would not change my evil plight for your servility';[2] and he was strongly influenced by that legend of the great benefactor of humanity, punished by an oppressive Zeus, chained and tortured for long ages, who yet retains the power to vanquish the oppressor and inaugurate a new era of hope. In the Paris Manuscripts and *Grundrisse*, Marx suggested that the Aeschylean vision of regenerate humanity provided inspiration for makers of the future society.[3]

Like Marx, Freud claimed that his own theories possessed scientific objectivity; and he, too, assailed religious systems, seeing them as mass-neuroses and delusions. According to him, the covert plot of history was the story of how civilisation advances by repressing and sublimating the anarchic desires of the id. Nevertheless, a teleological covert plot sometimes infiltrates his own arguments, as in his repeated analogies between the religious masses and children and between the enlightened sceptics and adults. There came a time when he acclaimed 'Our god, Logos':[4] a god who combined science, scepticism and an appreciation of psychoanalysis, and under whose aegis a new and better era would dawn for everybody.

By withdrawing their expectations from the other world and concentrating all their liberated energies into their life on earth, they will probably succeed in achieving a state of things in which life will become tolerable for everyone and civilisation no longer oppressive to anyone.[5]

Freud had studied Milton's *Paradise Lost*, and the Freudian view of the human ego as the site of conflict between the super-ego and the id (or, in his subsequent scheme, between Eros and Thanatos) bears schematic resemblances to the Miltonic view of Adam as the centre of conflict between God and Satan. Another literary influence is suggested by Freud's hope that he might one day be commemorated by a bust bearing the words from *Oedipus Rex*, 'Who solved the riddle of the Sphinx and was a man most mighty'.[6] There is brilliant heroism yet also a Sophoclean irony about Freud's determination to solve the riddles of human nature, his repeated discovery that one solution was a matter of incestuous sexuality, and his proud boast that psychoanalysis had humbled man's pride by proving that the ego 'is not even master in his own house'.[7]

If teleological history has been the story within one hugely influential body of myth, its complement has been equally influential. Its complement is the story of the decline from some ancient Golden Age. Once there was a time, this says, when human beings lived in harmony with each other and with nature, but, by some sin or taint or hypertrophy of consciousness, division and strife entered and increased. The early forms of the story (in Genesis, Hesiod and Ovid, for example) have been rendered conspicuous as myth by the long process of historical change; but its covert variants still haunt politics (in nostalgia for the communal or patriotic past), biography or autobiography (the harmonious childhood, the adolescent idyll), or cultural theory. Within D.H. Lawrence's non-fictional writing lives the manifold story of transition from a pristine state of instinctual vitality and wholeness to a fallen state in which 'mental consciousness' has ravaged humanity; T.S. Eliot influentially imagined an Elizabethan age of unified sensibility before the 'dissociation' in the seventeenth century; and F.R. Leavis claimed that a traditional, 'organic' cultural community was being increasingly stifled by 'technologico-Benthamite civilisation'. To challenge historical assumptions related to the Golden Age myth stands the equally ancient myth of a former 'Iron Age', eloquently exemplified by Thomas Hobbes's 'state of nature' in which life was 'solitary, poor, nasty, brutish, and short' and which entails a need for strong, controlling authority.

We might say, then, that a myth is characterised by a simple plot (established originally in an era of religion or superstition) which constantly strives to become covert, its chief resource being an immense capacity for explanatory co-ordination, conceptual interpretation and narrative elaboration. When its historic work is complete, its plot becomes overt and can be identified as myth; but when its work is still proceeding, its plot remains covert and may be identified as history.

Claude Lévi-Strauss once asserted: 'Myths think in men, unbeknown to them.'[8] If this rule be true, he himself — as he conceded — may exemplify it. The myth that thinks in Lévi-Strauss and in other potent exorcists of mystery may sometimes be the Oedipal myth of the man who believes that by his wisdom he transcends the illusions, ideologies, myths and plots in which the majority of people seem trapped. To be infiltrated by mythology is probably unavoidable and not necessarily undesirable; the better the story, the more truths it may reveal.

The great endeavour to liberate history from story, and story from history, promises to render the truths of both the more liberating for humanity. The outcome of that promise is, perhaps, another story.

# Conclusion

I once discussed an ambiguous poem with a group of students; and at the end one of them said: 'You've talked about the meanings, but you haven't said anything about the feelings, and surely that's what matters in a poem.' I attempted to make the following reply: 'I've tried to define a structure of meanings. Meanings imply and evoke feelings; those implied can differ greatly from those evoked. Clarify the structure of meanings and you may eventually be clarifying, extending and intensifying the structures of feelings.' In this book, I have endeavoured to clarify various plot-structures; and though I have said little about the fact that literary texts can move us to tears, make us laugh or arouse our indignations, my analyses implictly have a bearing on such matters. To the sophisticated reader, naturally, some of those analyses may seem to labour the obvious, while others of them may seem to overstate as a 'covert plot' some parts of a narrative better left as suggestions and enigmas. Elsewhere in the book, concision will have bred reduction. When claiming originality, I may through forget-fulness or ignorance have denied particular predecessors their due acknowledgement; in which case, I apologise now, and concede additionally the largeness of my general debt to many authors and teachers, past and present. Nevertheless if, here and there, my discussions increase the reader's ratio of pleasure to toil when encountering a difficult text, I will feel sufficiently condoned, if not vindicated. Judging a narrative without noticing that it contains a covert plot is like judging a poem without noticing that it is ambiguous: the judgement may be unjust. Curiosity and a notion of equity, rather than any zealous theory, led me to offer evidence for some defendants and perhaps injustice to some judges.

The search for covert plots can be extended in various directions. In literary works, the more interesting findings may occur when a text with a radical or innovatory surface proves to contain a relatively conservative or traditional covert plot, or alternatively when an apparently traditional text proves to contain unconventional recesses in its plotting. Some of the works cited very briefly here could have been treated in considerable detail (Conrad's *Under Western Eyes*, Nabokov's *Pale Fire* and Golding's *The Inheritors* are obvious candidates); and there are many other novels which my space excluded but which deserve close attention (Nabokov's *Lolita*, Golding's *The Spire* and Fowles's *The French Lieutenant's Woman* come to mind). Much more could have been said on the covert plots of ostensibly non-fictional works, historical, political and philosophical. However, art is long and life is short; structural criticism in general and narratology in particular are rapidly-expanding centres of industry; and the sophisticated procedures of Todorov, Barthes and Genette, among others, offer guidance at levels far more advanced than that of my book, whose aim is introductory. Peccancy and the desire for clarity of presentation will have tempted me into immodest phrasing and intemperate judgement; but the reader who makes allowance for this will be little harmed, while the authors will retain the invulnerability conferred by time and the multiplicity of their texts.

# Appendix:

# The Suspense-Principle as the Basis of All Narratives

There is a sense in which every story requires at least two plots. Every narrative sequence, however simple, invokes a potential alternative sequence, even though it is normally the case that that potential is dispelled at the dénouement; indeed, what enables us to recognise the dénouement as such is precisely our realisation that this is where the potential is dispelled and the ghost of the alternative sequence exorcised. Even a work which has only a simple and overt plot depends for its interest on our subdividing the story, as soon as we begin to identify it, into at least two alternative sequences, of which we expect one to be eventually confirmed and the other (or others) refuted.

This basis is obvious, but crucially important; and it deserves rather fuller formulation here, because it has sometimes been neglected by literary critics and commentators. Their hindsight — their knowledge of how the story ended — can blind them to tentative multiple foresight. They then tend to talk as though any intelligent reader of a narrative perceives only the fulfilled sequence, and they therefore neglect the essential tension and suspense generated by the presence of an alternative (if ultimately vanquished) sequence. Thus the critic commonly resembles a traveller who, having been conveyed down road A40 from Cheltenham to London, talks as though any able traveller down that road should have known that the ultimate destination was London, whereas the reader has paused at many signposts, crossroads and side-turnings, and has appropriately felt that the narrative's road could quite as easily lead to Portsmouth or Dover. The familiar critical endeavour to summarise and clarify tends to freeze the dynamics into a static body of textual information and implication. Youthful and amateurish readers, who worry about what may befall the hero or who express perplexity about how the mystery can be resolved, may be closer to registering the defining principle of narrative than are the summarising commentators who sometimes make one wonder why the story-teller has sought to impart such information in ways so devious and elaborate.

Any narrative (whether written, oral or visual) which engages our interest does so through employment of the suspense-principle. The suspense-principle operates as follows. From the information presented in the initial stages of the narrative we elicit a salient problem; and in the act of formulating the problem we are simultaneously (virtually as a matter of logical entailment) formulating our prediction of the solution which the narrative will eventually supply. As the subsequent information arrives, after that initial stage, we inspect it to see that it confirms our understanding of the problem and to see whether our prediction is being supported or needs to be revised. For us to sense that there is a problem and for us to have a partisan interest in our prediction, it is obviously necessary for us to be aware that some of the information may support an alternative prediction or predictions; without this, there would be no problem, no tension and no suspense. For example, our partisan interest in our prediction that Pamela (in Richardson's novel *Pamela*) will preserve her virtue and eventually have a happy marriage grows in proportion to our awareness of the information that increasingly appears to support an opposed prediction that she will be cruelly deflowered and forced into prostitution. When we say that a tale is 'tediously predictable' we mean that too much information has supported the major predictive sequence and not enough has supported the alternative sequence. Conversely, the more evenly matched they are, the more engrossing is the narrative.

It is the reader's inference of the predictive sequence (and not the mere conjunction of characters and incidents) which creates the sense of plot; it is his awareness of at least two alternative sequences (two potential plots) which generates interest; and, in some texts, it is his awareness of their virtual and plausible equipoise which generates intense interest. The word 'plausible' there is important, for plausibility includes the matter of compromise between the sense of what real life is like and the sense of standards of 'reality' postulated in the narrative; and it reminds us that the principle defined here can govern the most intricate and sophisticated novels as well as the simplest yarns. At the simplest level, a tale in which (for example) a hero apparently deserves to proceed towards his eventual success will attempt to engage our interest by increasing the data to support a prediction of his failure; while a tale in which a hero is deservedly heading for defeat will tantalise us by increasing the data to support a prediction of his success. In a complicated novel like *Middlemarch*, our anticipations that Dorothea will eventually prosper, marry and live happily ever after will be counterpoised by our sense not only of relatively external impediments but also of flaws within her nature — and, above all, of an imaginative environment which so plausibly evokes non-fictional reality as to make us doubt that the traditional predictive sequences of fiction really apply in this case (though ultimately, with much qualification, muting and disguise, they do).

Indeed, one characteristic of realist novels is that the author strives to reduce the sense of a clear victory for one predictive sequence over the other: thus George Eliot's Dorothea eventually enjoys a happy marriage but has to renounce some of her idealistic aspirations; Conrad's Gould succeeds in material terms but loses his emotional integrity; and James's Strether fails in material terms but retains a battered moral decency.

When a literary work contains a covert plot, that, too, attains definition as a plot (as differentiated from, say, a mere theme) by the implicit presence of a challenging alternative sequence. For example, in the sea journey of *The Shadow-Line*, just as the secular overt plot has a dominant predictive sequence portending success for the hero and also an alternative sequence portending disaster, so the supernatural covert plot has two sequences, one portending the hero's triumph over the curse and the other portending his defeat by it. The relationship of overt to covert will itself be the basis of generic suspense as we sense the challenge offered by the latter to the former. And all the sequences conspire to generate the suspense or enigma of signification, as we strive to anticipate and define the general significance of the unfolding text.

One way of regarding the evolution of sophisticated novels is to consider that while readers become increasingly experienced in scanning texts so as to select efficiently the most cogent bases and evidence for predictions, authors become increasingly adept at concealment-strategies designed to resist easy scansion by the reader. Covert plots both aid and manifest such strategies. If, however, a novelist radically opposes the basic principle of scanning and prediction (e.g., by deliberately introducing inconsistencies, contradictions and gross breaches of causal and temporal progression), his work either dies as narrative or survives only to the extent that the reader preserves a sense of a potential story which is being wilfully opposed.

# Notes

## GENERAL INTRODUCTION (pp. 1–6)

1. See Appendix.
2. Samuel Beckett and Georges Duthuit: 'Three Dialogues' in *Samuel Beckett: A Collection of Critical Essays*, ed. Martin Esslin (Englewood Cliffs, N.J.: Prentice-Hall, 1965), p.21.
3. Terence Hawkes says that Roland Barthes was able to 'reveal the signifier-signified connection as the un-innocent *convention* (however politically bolstered) it is, and offer a sense that reality remains genuinely ours to make and to remake as we please'. (*Structuralism and Semiotics*; London: Methuen, 1977; pp. 120-21.) Jacques Lacan remarks: 'It is the world of words that creates the world of things.' (*Ecrits*, translated by Alan Sheridan; London: Tavistock, 1977; p.65.)
4. 'Man is not just *homo sapiens* but *homo significans*: a creature who gives sense to things.' Jonathan Culler: *Structuralist Poetics* (London: Routledge and Kegan Paul, 1975), p.264. When we recall the conduct of dolphins, whales and Lord Rochester's monkey, this claim may resemble a hyperbole of anthropocentric imperialism.

## CHAPTER 1 (pp. 9–12)

1. Lawrence: *Studies in Classic American Literature* [1924] (London: Heinemann, 1965), p.2. The words 'Never trust the artist. Trust the tale.' are frequently misquoted (if clarified) as 'Never trust the teller, trust the tale'.
2. Empson: *Seven Types of Ambiguity* (London: Chatto and Windus, 1930; rpt. 1956), p. vi.
3. Claude Lévi-Strauss: *Structural Anthropology*, trans. Claire Jacobson and Brooke Grundfest Schoepf (Harmondsworth: Allen Lane, 1968),

Chapter 11; criticised in *Reconstructing Literature,* ed. Laurence Lerner (Oxford: Blackwell, 1983), Chapter 5.
4. Michael Riffaterre: *Semiotics of Poetry* (Bloomington and London: Indiana University Press, 1978); Jonathan Culler: *The Pursuit of Signs* (London: Routledge and Kegan Paul, 1981).
5. Catherine Belsey: *Critical Practice* (London and New York: Methuen, 1980), Chapter 5.
6. Critical imperialism, sometimes a compensatory activity by critics whose social power is far less than that of the literary texts, or who fear that literature and criticism lack their former influence, has been well discussed by Alan Sinfield in 'Against Appropriation' (*Essays in Criticism,* XXXI, July 1981, pp. 181-95) and Gerald Graff in 'Pseudo-Politics of Interpretation' (*Critical Inquiry,* March 1983, pp. 597-610).
7. Culler: *Structuralist Poetics* (London: Routledge and Kegan Paul, 1975), p.15.

# CHAPTER 2 (pp. 13–29)

1. Ian Watt: *The Rise of the Novel* [1957] (Harmondsworth: Penguin, 1963), p.84. Watt cites the sceptical comments by Charles Gildon and Karl Marx.
2. Defoe: *The Life and Strange Surprizing Adventures of Robinson Crusoe of York, Mariner,* Vol. I [1719]. (Oxford: Blackwell, 1927), pp. 234-5.
3. 'Professor' Stanley Unwin was a British comedian who, between the 1940s and the 1970s, became well known for his solemnly intense utterance of pedantic gibberish; a relative of Beckett's Lucky.
4. Arnold Kettle: *An Introduction to the English Novel,* Vol. 1 (London: Hutchinson, 1951; rpt. 1969), pp.115-29. Graham Greene: 'The Young Dickens' [1950] in *Collected Essays* (Harmondsworth: Penguin, 1970), pp. 79-86.
5. Lady Dedlock in *Bleak House* and Estella in *Great Expectations* have a kindred implausibility born of their inhabiting the world of active corruption while having compunction for the world of relatively passive virtue. One solution to Dickens's problem would be the use of a detective: a person who could be hired to be active on behalf of the passive. Hence Dickens's 'invention' of the detective story with the arrival of Inspector Bucket in *Bleak House,* and hence the oddity of that name, Bucket: for, as Chapter 1 reminds us, there is an old Ciceronian proverb, 'Truth lies at the bottom of a well'. This bucket can descend and rise between the conflicting levels of the plot and of Dickens's imagination.
6. James: 'Preface' to *The Portrait of a Lady.*
7. Douglas Brown: 'From *Heart of Darkness* to *Nostromo'* in *The Modern Age,* ed. B. Ford (Harmondsworth: Penguin, 1961), p. 132. Robert F. Haugh: *Joseph Conrad: Discovery in Design* (Norman: University of Oklahoma Press, 1957), p.55. I discuss this problem more fully in

*Conrad's 'Heart of Darkness': A Critical and Contextual Discussion* (Milan: Mursia, 1977).

8. Dante: *Inferno* III, lines 41-2.
9. T.S. Eliot: 'Baudelaire' [1930] in *Selected Essays* (London: Faber and Faber, 1961; rpt. 1963), p.427.
10. William Golding: *Pincher Martin* [1956] (London: Faber and Faber, 1960; rpt. 1962), p.201.

## CHAPTER 3 (pp. 30–39)

1. *Op. cit.,* p.67.
2. A.D. Nuttall: *A Common Sky* (London: Chatto and Windus, 1974).
3. *Op. cit.*, p. 47.
4. Relationships between Lombroso's theories and *The Secret Agent* are discussed by Norman Sherry: *Conrad's Western World* (London: Cambridge University Press, 1971), pp.275-8; Cedric Watts: *A Preface to Conrad* (Harlow: Longman, 1982), pp.94-5; and Allan Hunter: *Joseph Conrad and the Ethics of Darwinism* (London: Croom Helm, 1983), Chapter 5. Robert Hampson will soon publish his researches in this area.
5. W.K. Wimsatt and M.C. Beardsley: 'The Intentional Fallacy' [1946] in Wimsatt's *The Verbal Icon* (London: Methuen, 1970). Its confusions are discussed in A.D. Nuttall's 'Did Meursault Mean to Kill the Arab? — The Intentional Fallacy Fallacy': *Critical Quarterly* 10 (Spring and Summer 1968), pp.95-106.
6. In *The Return of Sherlock Holmes* [1905] (London: Murray, 1960).
7. This conclusion derives from my discussion in ' "A Bloody Racist": About Achebe's View of Conrad': *Yearbook of English Studies* 13 (1983), pp. 196-209.

## CHAPTER 4 (pp. 43–46)

1. Ian Watt: *Conrad in the Nineteenth Century* (London: Chatto and Windus, 1980), pp. 175-9, 270-76. My usage of the term departs from that of Professor Watt, who would retain 'delayed decoding' for relatively small-scale descriptive effects but employ the term 'symbolic deciphering' for larger-scale narrative effects. I believe that the application of the term 'delayed decoding' to both small and large sequences is justified insofar as the same basic principle (the creation of a marked delay between the problematic data and their explanation) is at work in them.
2. Viktor Shklovsky: 'Art as Technique' [1917] in *Russian Formalist Criticism*, ed. L.T. Lemon and M.J. Reis (Lincoln, Neb.: University of Nebraska Press, 1965). He says: 'And art exists that one may recover the sensation of life; it exists to make one feel things, to make the stone

*stony*.....The technique of art is to make objects "unfamiliar".....' (This traditional critical claim was established by Blake, Wordsworth and Shelley.)

## CHAPTER 6 (pp. 54–110)

1. Obvious examples of dynamic symbolism naturally abound in novels which are strongly influenced by the Romantic tradition, particularly those of Emily and Charlotte Brontë, Hawthorne, Melville and Dickens. In *Jane Eyre*, when Rochester resolves to marry Jane bigamously, claiming 'I know my Maker sanctions what I do', the night grows darker, the chestnut-tree writhes and groans and is soon struck by lightning; easily inviting the accurate inference that his Maker does not sanction what he does and will vigorously prevent the planned marriage.

    Subtler dynamic symbolism is offered by Jane Austen. In *Mansfield Park*, Chapter 10, when Rushworth goes to fetch the key, Henry persuades Maria to by-pass the locked iron gates which their flirtatious conversation has likened to the 'restraint and hardship' of her impending marriage to Rushworth; and Fanny warns Maria that she may harm herself. One of the predictions invited by the symbolism is that after her marriage, Maria will elope with Henry and be damaged as a result; and this prediction is fulfilled. Later in the novel, William's cross fits Edmund's chain (rather than the necklace from Henry), so that both can be worn together round Fanny's neck; which portends that virtue, altruism and affection will eventually unite William, Fanny and Edmund, and exclude Henry.

2. See, for example, *PR* 25, 108; *NLL*, 190-91.

3. Conrad had a very personal interest in the Faustian theme, for he sometimes felt that whether one wishes to be a great writer or 'a great magician', 'one must surrender oneself to occult and irresponsible powers, either outside or within one's breast'. (PR, xvi-xvii.) Thomas Mann shared the feeling and the preoccupation.

4. The reference to 'the dark River of the Nine Bends' on which drifts a ship manned by 'a crew of Shades' (*NN*, 173) recalls the 'ninefold' ('novies') River Styx across which the Shades of the dead are borne (*Aeneid* VI, line 439); and when Marlow refers to both Kurtz's black mistress and the Intended as 'Shades' who extend their arms across the river of darkness, he recalls the Virgilian shades who stretched out their hands ('tendebantque manus') in their yearning to be taken aboard the ferry of Acheron (*Aeneid* VI, line 314).

5. In the autobiographical *A Personal Record*, when referring to the real Almayer, Conrad repeatedly (half-whimsically, half-seriously) refers to him as a shade. ' "What's in a name, O Shade?..... In your earthly life you haunted me, Almayer.....O complaining Shade....." ' (87-9.)

Vladimir Nabokov, particularly in *Pale Fire,* inherited Conrad's interest in that term's ambiguities (ghost, shadow, memory).

6. *NN*, 138.

7. A critic who does note both connotations is Eugene B. Redmond in *The Nigger of the 'Narcissus'*, ed. R. Kimbrough (New York: Norton, 1979), pp. 358-68.

8. *LCG*, 117.

9. W.E. Henley: *Poems* [1898] (London: Nutt, 1906), pp. 253-5. According to Henley, the poem was written between 1889 and 1892; and the preface to this collection is dated 4 September 1897. *The Nigger* was written in 1896-7 and was serialised in the *New Review* between August and December 1897; the book was issued by Heinemann on 2 December.

10. The enthusiasm might not have been shared by his old friend, Mr H.B. Donkin.

11. Knowles opposes Donkin's mutinous arguments by referring to some seamen who were jailed for six weeks after refusing duty on the advice of a 'Plimsoll man' who 'couldn't see no further than the length of his umbreller' (107).

12. 'Racism, or Realism? Literary Apartheid, or Poetic License? Conrad's Burden in *The Nigger of the "Narcissus"*' in *The Nigger of the 'Narcissus'*, ed. R. Kimbrough (New York: Norton, 1979), pp. 358-68. The quotation is on p. 368.

13. In England, probably the earliest satiric attack on 'nigger' as a pejorative term was made by Conrad's friend, Cunninghame Graham, in his essay ' "Bloody Niggers" ' *(The Social-Democrat* I, April 1897, pp. 104-9). Conrad praised it in a letter to him: 'You are the perfection of scorn..... Scorn that is clear in the thought and lurks in the phrase' (*LCG*, 87).

14. As James Wait is markedly black, Donkin is markedly white (he has albino characteristics: white eyelashes and red eyelids): a symmetry with anti-racist implications.

15. As there are numerous great literary works, from Juvenal's *Satires* to *Waiting for Godot*, in which white people are treated harshly, we should not exclude the possibility of a masterpiece in which black people are treated harshly; such an exclusion would itself be racist. Chinua Achebe's works do not veil the injustices in pre-colonial African communities (e.g., the killing of twins and the subjugation of the women).

16. See Norman Sherry: *Conrad's Western World* (London: Cambridge University Press, 1971), pp. 72-8.

17. The narrator of 'Youth' is not sure how Marlow spelt his name (*Y*, 3).

18. Carl Jung: 'What makes Goethe's *Faust* so profoundly significant is that it formulates a problem that had been brewing for centuries, just as *Oedipus* did for Greek culture: how to extricate ourselves from between the Scylla of world-renunciation and the Charybdis of its acceptance.' *The Collected Works of C. G. Jung*, Vol. 5 (London: Routledge and Kegan Paul, 1956), p.83.

19. This passage, in a review by Conrad published in 1910, partly anticipates Heyst's 'recantation' in *Victory*.

20. *Christopher Marlowe: The Complete Plays*, ed. J. B. Steane (Harmondsworth: Penguin, 1969), p. 330.

21. *Y*, 134.

22. F.R. Leavis: *The Great Tradition* [1948] (Harmondsworth: Penguin, 1962), pp. 196-201. Terry Eagleton: *Criticism and Ideology* [1976] (London: Verso, 1978), pp.136-7. Cicely Havely: *Heart of Darkness* (Milton Keynes: Open University Press, 1973), pp. 30-31.

23. Conrad, letter to Elsie Hueffer cited in Jocelyn Baines's *Joseph Conrad: A Critical Biography* (London: Weidenfeld and Nicolson, 1960), p.227.

24. I.A. Richards: *The Philosophy of Rhetoric* [1936] (London and New York: Oxford University Press, 1965), p. 96.

25. Even the phosphorescent gleam in the waters around Leggatt constitutes, for superstitious seamen, a bad omen. The ex-sailor, Arthur Mason, records that one of his captains felt particularly apprehensive 'when the sea was afire with phosphorescent glow'. (*Wide Seas and Many Lands*; London: Cape, 1924, p. 151.)

26. Versions of the superstition that ghosts haunt the living until they have received due propitiation extend from ancient folk-tale to recent films. Importunate literary ghosts include those of Hamlet's father, of Clytemnestra (in Aeschylus's *The Eumenides*) and of Lorenzo (in Keats's 'Isabella'); Coleridge's Wedding Guest fears that the Ancient Mariner belongs to this family. In Conrad's *Under Western Eyes*, Razumov feels that he is being haunted by the ghost of the man he betrayed, and eventually exorcises that spirit by confession: another metaphysical 'covert plot'.

27. This principle is further explained in the Appendix.

28. Leggatt and the hero are both former *Conway* boys; and on that training-ship the Seamanship Instructor, Wallace Blair, taught boys that a white straw hat could be used 'to *mark the sea*'. (John Masefield: *So Long to Learn;* London: Heinemann, 1952; p.71.) The *Conway* encouraged pupils to be loyal to each other in later life: see Masefield's *The Conway* (London: Heinemann, 1933).

29. Letter of 29 November 1921, quoted in Lowes's *The Road to Xanadu* [1927] (Boston: Houghton Mifflin, 1955), pp. 517-18.

30. Wordsworth and Coleridge: *Lyrical Ballads*, ed. R.L. Brett and A.R. Jones (London: Methuen, 1963; rpt. 1971), pp.14-15. The subsequent quotation is from p.14. This edition preserves the 1798 text.

31. The crew of the *Marie* (or *Mary*) *Céleste* vanished without trace, and much speculation was caused by the fact that the vessel, when found, was quite seaworthy. (See *The Times*, 30 December 1873, p.9.) A similar incident, the discovery of the abandoned *Niade* drifting in the Atlantic in the 1840s, is recorded by E. Keble Chatterton, who remarks: 'Many a good sea yarn has contained such an incident, but this happens to be fact.' (*Windjammers and Shellbacks;* London: Rich and Cowan, 1926; rpt. 1935; p.5.)

32. Thomas Hobbes in *Leviathan* [1651] remarked: 'For one man calleth

*Wisdome*, what another calleth *fear*; and one *cruelty*, what another *justice*..... And therefore such names can never be true grounds of any ratiocination.' (London: Dent, 1914; rpt. 1959; p.18.) David Hume in *A Treatise of Human Nature* [1739-40] pointed out that one cannot in logic deduce an 'ought' from an 'is'; and Wittgentein's *Tractatus* [1922], 6.421, asserted: 'It is clear that ethics cannot be expressed. Ethics is transcendental.'

33. In 'Gentlemen and Gossip: Aspects of Evolution and Language in Conrad's *Victory*', Tony Tanner discusses at length the possible implications of the term 'gentleman', but overlooks its major proverbial significance. (*L'Epoque Conradienne*, May 1981, pp. 1-56.)

34. *NN*, p.245.

35. *White Nights and Other Stories*, trans. Constance Garnett (London: Heinemann, 1918; rpt. 1970), p.76.

36. *Castles in Spain* (London: Heinemann, 1927), p.91.

37. In *The Great Tradition*, 1948, Leavis concluded that *Victory* is 'among those of Conrad's works which deserve to be current as representing his claim to classical standing'. Four years later Douglas Hewitt argued in *Conrad: A Reassessment* (London: Bowes and Bowes, 1952) that the novel is extensively marred by sentimental simplifications and stylistic clichés. John A. Palmer's case that *Victory* is allegorically profound is offered in *Joseph Conrad's Fiction: A Study in Literary Growth* (Ithaca: Cornell University Press, 1968). The argument spirals on.

38. John Conrad remarks that during the period 1910 to 1914 his parents gave him at Christmas a bound volume of the previous twelve monthly issues of *Boy's Own Paper*. 'I am pretty sure that JC read it after I had gone to bed because I found little spills of cigarette ash between the pages. There were always one or two adventure stories.....' (*Joseph Conrad: Times Remembered*; Cambridge: Cambridge University Press, 1981; pp. 31-2.)

# CHAPTER 7 (pp. 111–118)

1. See Norman Sherry: *Conrad's Western World* (London: Cambridge University Press, 1971), pp. 228-47.

2. The letter was published by Mario Curreli in *Conradiana* VIII (1976), p.214. The comparison of *The Secret Agent* with *The Premier and the Painter* was first made by Mario Curreli and myself in 'Conrad and Zangwill': *Kwartalnik Neofilologiczny* [Warsaw] XXII (1975), pp.240-42.

# CHAPTER 8 (pp. 119–132)

1. The first novelist to develop strongly the potential of this procedure was Samuel Richardson, who in *Pamela* and particularly in *Clarissa* combined a traditional suspense (will the heroine elude the machina-

tions?) with a new suspense (what are the nature and the extent of the machinations?).

2. For example, in Conrad's 'Heart of Darkness': A Critical and Contextual Discussion (Milan: Mursia, 1977), pp.82-92. Though challengeable (see T.G. Willy's 'The "Shamefully Abandoned" Kurtz': Conradiana X, Summer 1978, pp.99-112), my claim has gained adoption: e.g. by Allan Hunter in Conrad and the Ethics of Darwinism (London: Croom Helm, 1983), pp.15-17.

3. Albert Guerard, in Conrad the Novelist (Cambridge, Mass.: Harvard University Press, 1965; pp.30-33), claimed that 'the first two chapters are seriously defective' because of their narrative uncertainty, whereas the voyage-chapters are powerful.

4. The tale vindicates the belief of experienced sailors during the nineteenth century that 'Mauritius was too full of land sharks to make it a convenient calling place'. (E.Keble Chatterton: Windjammers and Shellbacks; London: Rich and Cowan, 1926; rpt. 1935; p. 186.)

5. Jocelyn Baines: Joseph Conrad: A Critical Biography (London: Weidenfeld and Nicolson, 1960), p.98.

6. Conrad often derived wry amusement from his sense of such mundane metamorphoses. When recalling the Bessborough Gardens lodging-house in which he began Almayer's Folly, he wrote: 'The girls in that Bessborough Gardens house were often changed, but whether short or long, fair or dark, they were always untidy and particularly bedraggled, as if in a sordid version of the fairy tale the ashbin cat had been changed into a maid.' (PR, 70.)

# CHAPTER 9 (pp. 133–150)

1. Since it is a matter of a coherent narrative (generally given coherence by continuity of characterisation), transtextuality is much more specific and localised in function than 'intertextuality', which Julia Kristeva has defined as the vast sum of linguistic and cultural knowledge that makes it possible for texts to have meaning: 'tout texte se construit comme mosaïque de citations'. (Semiotiké; Paris: du Seuil, 1969; p.146.)

2. Hans van Marle recently solved the mystery of Lingard's end by locating his death certificate at the General Register Office, London.

3. Hans van Marle located the petition in the Indonesian National Archives at Jakarta. Conrad spelt Berau phonetically as 'Brow' on the occasion when he forgot to change it to the fictional 'Sambir': AF, 42.

4. Conrad adapts the phrasing of the question in Henri-Frédéric Amiel's Grains de Mil (1854).

5. Recurrent characters in 'popular' fiction are less likely to age than those in more realistic works. Thus Leslie Charteris's Simon Templar remains young, energetic and debonair while more than half a century of adventures accrues to him.

6. *Johnson on Shakespeare*, ed. Walter Raleigh (London: Oxford University Press, 1908; rpt. 1957), p.28. The assumption that to discuss biographically a character's nature virtually entails mistaking a fictional construct for a real person can be found in L.C. Knights's 'How Many Children Had Lady Macbeth?' [1933] in *Explorations* (London: Chatto and Windus, 1946) and in Catherine Belsey's *Critical Practice* (London and New York: Methuen, 1980), pp.49-51.

7. The self-contradictory notion of linguistic and literary solipsism was variously and inconsistently propagated by Barthes, Lacan and their popularisers, often citing Saussure.

8. See Norman Sherry: *Conrad's Western World* (London: Cambridge University Press, 1971), pp. 163-8, 420. Sherry discusses from a relatively biographical angle the linkages which I here consider mainly as a problem of narratology.

9. Terence Hawkes, following Barthes, says that the text colours and shapes 'what (if anything)' can be seen through it. (*Structuralism and Semiotics*; London: Methuen, 1977; p. 119.) The 'if anything' genially embraces the texts, readers and world to which his own text refers.

10. *Within the Tides* (London: Dent, 1950), p.vi.


## CHAPTER 10 (pp. 153–160)

1. Just as Joyce's commentators have often accepted too solemnly Stephen's notion of 'epiphanies' (forgetting that the notion is vigorously mocked by Cranly in *Stephen Hero*), so they have sometimes accepted too readily the impression that *A Portrait* is non-ironic autobiography. Yet there Stephen is repeatedly invested by irony: not the malign type which condemns its object but the benign irony of an older author who can see his own younger self as immaturely egoistic. The surname 'Dedalus' is appropriately Janiform. It portends success for Stephen if we assume that he is a counterpart of the original Dedalus, the artificer who successfully flew from Crete to Greece; but when Stephen says, 'Old father, old artificer, stand me now and ever in good stead', he becomes the counterpart of the son, Icarus, who was heedlessly ambitious and plunged to extinction in the waves. (During *Ulysses*, Stephen has not a single novel to his credit.)

2. Writing was a therapy for Sartre, helping to exorcise the hallucinations (e.g. the crayfish that pursued him through Venice) which troubled his younger years.

3. *Words* [*Les Mots*, 1964] (Harmondsworth: Penguin, 1967), p. 156.

4. Camus reviewed *La Nausée* in 1938, complaining that Sartre over-emphasised the repugnant and offered a bathetic faith in salvation through writing. Sartre reviewed *L'Etranger* in 1943, complaining that its seemingly transparent style was strongly biased, being 'transparent to things and opaque to meanings': thus Camus 'slyly eliminates all the significant links which are also part of the experience', for

'meanings are also part of the immediate data'. (*Literary and Philosophical Essays*; London: Hutchinson, 1968; pp. 36-7.) Sartre's criticism could be applied to *La Nausée*, which makes an epistemological melodrama out of the Conradian technique of delayed decoding.

5. *Waiting for Godot* [1956] (London: Faber and Faber, 1965), p.91. The inquisitorial spotlight in *Play* and the invisible tormentor in *Act Without Words* [I] both imply a hostile seer-creator.

6. Such a credulous reading was warmly encouraged by Robbe-Grillet in *Pour un Nouveau Roman* (Paris: Minuit, 1963), esp. pp. 18-23.

7. For example, 'Flotsam and Jetsam', of which the setting is a shabby house (its verandah, like that of *La Jalousie*, is in need of fresh paint) amid a tropical rubber-plantation. A European couple lives there; a well-educated man from the neighbouring plantation visits them regularly, and has an affair with the wife. Eventually he is surprised and shot by the jealously vigilant husband, whose wife is then afflicted by compulsive repetitive mannerisms.

8. See, for example, Lucien Goldmann's *Towards a Sociology of the Novel* [1964] (London: Tavistock, 1975), Chapter 5.

# CHAPTER 11 (pp. 161–175)

1. Raymond Williams: *Drama from Ibsen to Eliot* (Harmondsworth: Penguin, 1964), p.87.

2. Hjalmar: 'Grosserer Werles vingeskudte jagtbytte, ja.' (p. 287.) (English quotations are from the translation by Una Ellis-Fermor: *Henrik Ibsen: Three Plays*; Harmondsworth: Penguin, 1950. Norwegian quotations are from Ibsen's *Samlede Værker*, Vol. IV; Kristiania: Gyldendal, 1907.)

3. Gregers:    'Jeg havde ventet så visst, at når jeg kom ind ad døren, så skulde der slå mig imøde et forklarelsens lys både fra mand og fra hustru. Og så ser jeg ikke andet for mig end dette dumpe, tunge, triste —'
   Gina:       'Nå så.' [tar lampeskærmen af.] (P. 286.)

4. He had previously, in Act II, said'The forest avenges itself '. The significant addition is 'But I'm not afraid, all the same'.

5. Raymond Williams, after referring to 'the old caricature Ekdal, with his uniform cap and his secret drinking', claims that 'we are evidently intended to accept the sentimental self-interpretation of *all* the characters in the play'. (*Drama from Ibsen to Eliot*, p. 88.) Yet Ibsen attacks 'sentimental self-interpretation', notably through the satiric presentation of Hjalmar's self-pity.

6. In *Hedda Gabler*, the portents of Hedda's off-stage suicide go unnoticed by the other characters; and the discovery of her body provokes the exclamation: 'One doesn't *do* that kind of thing!'

7. Gregers:    'Jeg skulde ha trådt op imod dig dengang, der blev stillet snarer for løjtnant Ekdal. Jeg skulde ha advaret ham; for jeg aned nok, hvor det vilde bære hen.'

Werle:    'Ja, da burde du samdelig ha talt.'
Gregers:  'Jeg voved mig ikke till det; så fejg og forskræmt var jeg.'
           (P.278.)

8. Koht: *Life of Ibsen* (New York: Blom, 1971), p. 356.

9. *Ibid.,* p.331.

10. It was during the later stages of composition that Ibsen apparently conceived the covert plot concerning Ekdal's suicide. In the early draft of the play (published in *The Collected Works of Henrik Ibsen,* Vol. XII: *From Ibsen's Workshops*; London: Henemann, 1912) all the details which imply this plot are conspicuous by their absence: there is no suggestion that at the time of his disgrace he had contemplated suicide; the disgrace is not linked to the felling of timber (and thus to the trees in the attic); his last words do not contain the ominous pronouncement, 'But I'm not afraid, all the same'; and the directions do not specify that he wears uniform or bears a sabre. Thus these details, when introduced, were conceived by Ibsen as a coherent sequence.

11. Michael Meyer: *Henrik Ibsen: The Top of a Cold Mountain: 1883-1906* (London: Hart-Davis, 1971), p.38.

12. It does not suggest that homosexuality and lust are synonymous; rather it suggests that repression can make any desire destructive.

13. Erich Heller's influential study of Thomas Mann rightly notes that in the tale a supernatural force appears in various human guises; but he identifies this force as 'Death itself' and therefore fails to explain the Dionysiac aspects of the manifestations, notably the tigerish traits and particularly the association with homosexuality. (*Thomas Mann: The Ironic German: A Study*; New York: Appel, 1973; pp. 103-13.)

14. English quotations are from the volume *'Death in Venice'; 'Tristan'; 'Tonio Kröger'*, translated by H.T. Lowe-Porter (Harmondsworth: Penguin, 1955, reprinting the translation published by Secker and Warburg in 1928); this passage is on p.76. German quotations are from *Der Tod in Venedig und andere Erzählungen* (Frankfurt am Main and Hamburg: Fischer, 1954). The original of this passage, on p.60, is:

Schaum vor den Lippen tobten sie, reizten einander mit geilen Gabärden und buhlenden Händen, lachend und ächzend, stiessen die Stachelstäbe einander ins Fleisch und leckten das Blut von den Gliedern. Aber mit ihnen, in ihnen war der Träumende nun und dem fremden Gotte gehörig. Ja, sie waren er selbst, als sie reissend und mordend sich auf die Tiere hinwarfen und dampfende Fetzen verschlangen, als auf zerwühltem Moosgrund grenzenlose Vermischlung begann, dem Gotte zum Opfer. Und seine Seele kostete Unzucht und Raserei des Unterganges.

15. Dionysus had assumed the form of a tiger or leopard when fleeing from the Titans. His traditionally effeminate appearance links him with Tadzio; his association with drunken revelry and Bacchic followers links him with the old man and the street-musicians, and his lethal vengefulness links him with the man at the cemetery and the

Charonesque gondolier. Mann's Dionysus variously mimics Hermes, Silenus, Charon and Eros.

16. *Death in Venice*, pp. 9-10; *Der Tod in Venedig*, p. 9:

> [E]r sah, sah eine Landschaft, ein tropisches Sumpfgebiet unter dickdunstigem Himmel, feucht, üppig und ungeheuer, eine Art Urweltwildnis aus Inseln, Morästen und Schlamm führenden Wasserarmen...sah zwischen den knotigen Rohrstämmen des Bambusdickichts die Lichter eines kauernden Tigers funkeln — und fühlte sein Herz pochen vor Entsetzen und rätselhaftem Verlangen.

17. *Death in Venice*, p. 71; *Der Tod*, pp. 56-7:

> Seit mehreren Jahren schon hatte die indische Cholera eine verstärkte Neigung zur Ausbreitung und Wanderung an den Tag gelegt. Erzeugt aus den warmen Morästen des Ganges-Deltas, aufgestiegen mit dem mephitischen Odem jener üppig-untauglichen, von Menschen gemiedenen Urwelt- und Inselwildnis, in deren Bambusdickichten der Tiger kauert.....

18. The tale fleetingly brings to mind the downfall of Wilde through homosexuality, and the notoriety of Baron Corvo at Venice. The ambivalence of Mann's attitude to homosexuality is understandable, given that in his journal Mann noted that he felt erotically attracted to various men and even to his own son Klaus (nicknamed 'Eissi'). 'Am enraptured with Eissi, terribly handsome in his swimming trunks. Find it quite natural that I should fall in love with my son.' (See Thomas Mann: *Diaries 1918-1939*, ed. H. Kesten, trans. R. and C. Winston; London: Deutsch, 1983; pp.42, 118, 119, 207; 100-103. This quotation is from p.101.)

19. *Death in Venice*, p. 80; *Der Tod*, p. 63:

> Er sass dort, der Meister, der würdig gewordene Künstler, der Autor des *Elenden*, der in so vorbildlich reiner Form dem Zigeunertum und der trüben Tiefe abgesagt, dem Abgrunde die Sympathie gekündigt und das Verworfene verworfen hatte, der Hochgestiegene, der, Überwinder seines Wissens und aller Ironie entwachsen, in die Verbindlichkeiten des Massenzutrauens sich gewöhnt hatte, er, dessen Ruhm amtlich, dessen Name geadelt war und an dessen Stil die Knaben sich zu bilden angehalten wurden, — er sass dort, seine Lider waren geschlossen, nur zuweilen glitt, rasch sich wieder verbergend, ein spöttischer und betretener Blick seitlich darunter hervor, und seine schlaffen Lippen, kosmetisch aufgehöht, bildeten einzelne Worte aus von dem, was sein halb schlummerndes Hirn an seltsamer Traumlogik hervorbrachte.

20. *Death in Venice*, p. 83; *Der Tod*, p. 66:

> seine Augen von unten sahen, indes sein Antlitz den schlaffen, innig

versunkenen Ausdruck tiefen Schlummers zeigte. Ihm war aber, als ob der bleiche und liebliche Psychagog dort draussen ihm lächle, ihm winke; als ob er, die Hand aus Hüfte lösend, hinausdeute, voranschwebe ins Verheissungsvoll-Ungeheure.

21. *Death in Venice*, p. 81; *Der Tod*, p. 64:

> 'Aber Form and Unbefangenheit, Phaidros, führen zum Rausch und zur Begierde, führen den Edlen vielleicht zu grauenhaftem Gefühlsfrevel, den seine eigene schöne Strenge als infam verwirft, führen zum Abgrund, zum Abgrund auch sie. Uns Dichter, sage ich, führen sie dahin, denn wir vermögen nicht, uns aufzuschwingen, wir vermögen nur auszuschweifen.'

22. *Death in Venice*, pp. 46-7; *Der Tod*, p. 38:

> Nun lenkte Tag für Tag der Gott mit den hitzingen Wangen nackend sein gluthauchendes Viergespann durch di e Räume des Himmels, und sein gelbes Gelock flatterte in zugleich ausstürmenden Ostwind. Weisslich seidiger Glanz lag auf den Weiten des träge wallenden Pontos.....

23. *Death in Venice*, p. 47; *Der Tod*, p. 38:

> Aber köstlich war auch der Abend.....Solch ein Abend trug in sich die freudige Gewähr eines neuen Sonnentags von leicht geordneter Musse und geschmückt mit zahllosen, dicht beieinander liegenden Möglichkeiten lieblichen Zufalls.

# CHAPTER 12 (pp. 176–180)

1. *The Origin of Species* [1859] (Harmondsworth: Penguin, 1968), p.459.
2. Marx added: 'Prometheus is the foremost saint and martyr in the philosopher's calendar.' (S.S. Prawer: *Karl Marx and World Literature*; London: Oxford University Press, 1976; p.23.)
3. *Ibid.,* pp.76, 286-8.
4. *The Future of an Illusion* [1927] (London: Hogarth Press, 1962), p.50.
5. *Ibid.,* p.46.
6. Ernest Jones: *The Life and Works of Sigmund Freud* (Harmondsworth: Penguin, 1964): p.14 of Lionel Trilling's Introduction.
7. Freud: *Introductory Lectures on Psycho-Analysis* (London: Allen and Unwin, 1929; rpt. 1968), p.241.
8. '.....les mythes se pensent dans les hommes, et à leur insu.' *Le Cru et le cuit* (Paris: Librairie Plon, 1964), p.20.

# Index